FOR DARE

DARE WRIGHT MEDIA, LLC

MMXIX

Publisher's Cataloging-in-Publication Data:

Names: Ashley, Brook, author.
Title: Dare Wright and The Lonely Doll / by Brook Ashley.
Description: Santa Barbara, CA: Dare Wright Media, LLC, 2019.
Identifiers: LCCN xxxxxxxxx | ISBN 978-1-7334312-0-0
Subjects: LCSH Wright, Dare. | Wright, Dare. Lonely doll. | Children's stories--Authorship. | Authors, American--20th century--Biography. Photographers--Biography. | Children's stories--Authorship. | BISAC BIOGRAPHY & AUTOBIOGRAPHY / Artists, Architects, Photographers | BIOGRAPHY & AUTOBIOGRAPHY / Personal Memoirs
Classification: LCC PS3573.R53244 D37 2019 | DDC 813/.54--dc23

ISBN: 978-1-7334312-0-0

info@darewright.com   www.darewright.com

DARE WRIGHT
AND
THE LONELY DOLL

A BIOGRAPHY

BROOK ASHLEY

Dare's father Ivan Wright was a Canadian actor and newspaperman. He left Edie and Dare before his daughter had turned three, taking Dare's older brother Blaine with him.

Dare's mother Edith Stevenson Wright, "Edie," was an internationally acclaimed portrait artist whose subjects included Sir Winston Churchill and President Calvin Coolidge.

THE CAST

Dare's brother Blaine was a WW II fighter pilot, writer and wildlife whisperer.

Dare Wright – actress, artist, fashion model, photographer and author – was Brook Ashley's beloved godmother.

Brook Ashley's mother Eugenia Rawls acted with Dare in *Pride and Prejudice*.

Dare's British fiancé Philip Sandeman was a WW II pilot and friend of Blaine's.

Brook Ashley's father Donald Seawell was Dare's confidant and protector.

The Lonely Doll family. Little Bear, Mr. Bear and Dare's childhood doll "Edith" starred in Dare's classic book series.

The stage and film actress Tallulah Bankhead was Dare's good friend and Brook Ashley's other godmother.

PROLOGUE

I lay red-faced and furiously annoyed in a bassinet in room 830 of the Hotel Bristol on West 48th Street. It was the summer of 1947. In two years, the New York tabloids would describe the hotel setting to their readers in lurid detail, but for that moment it only belonged to me and my godmother Dare Wright.

My parents had dropped me off with a bag of second-hand utilitarian baby garments, as well as the extensive paraphernalia required to render cow's milk into baby formula.

Dare was thirty-two and had never been solely in charge of an infant. I was a few months old and had never been cared for by an adult who actually focused on more than my tightly scheduled nutritional requirements.

Four days later, we were bonded for life.

When my parents reclaimed me, they were astounded to see their firstborn perfumed, cooing with happiness and wearing a handmade gown.

Decades on, I asked Dare how she had managed the transformation.

"Well, you seemed awfully lonely in that bassinet, and the formula was horrid," she answered "...so I made us both some oatmeal and took you into bed with me."

Wright was my fairy godmother. As lovely as any princess in a story book, she anchored my chaotic New York childhood with invisible filaments of security. The scent of Dare's *L'Heure Bleue* perfume, named for the evanescent hour between daylight and darkness, would signal my transition into her gentle world where the stars were waiting to appear.

Brook Ashley

Brook in the Hotel Bristol.

1

Dare Wright and Tallulah Bankhead were named my godmothers when I was born in the spring of 1947. It was an abundance of good fortune to bestow upon a baby the size of a stewing chicken.

Love and loss were the metronome beats in their childhoods. Tallulah was christened beside her mother's casket six weeks after her birth, and Dare's father left with her brother before she could even write their names.

We are all composed of bits of stardust, but Dare Wright seemed to radiate hers with an intriguing luminosity.

"She walked out of the sea," a friend once suggested, "...leaving the island of Atlantis behind her."

If Dare's beauty and innocence often suggested a mythical origin, her artistic work was grounded in the practical world of earning a living. She was a professional actress, artist, model, fashion photographer, and author of a best-selling series of children's books beginning with 1957's *The Lonely Doll*. The books, illustrated with Dare's haunting black and white photographs rather than conventional drawings, launched a new genre of children's literature.

Dare created the world of "Edith and The Bears" featuring her favorite childhood doll who was befriended by two teddy bears. Edith's character wasn't just an expression of Dare's own sometimes lonely childhood; she was the voice of every child's universal fear of abandonment.

Dare's Lonely Doll books showed Edith and The Bears as a family. An unconventional, cross-species one, to be sure, but perfectly relatable to a four-year-old reader. The trio was bound together with the love and loyalty that Dare wished for her own fractured heritage, although an irretrievable fragment had already been crushed into historical detritus.

Edith, Mr. Bear and Little Bear became a family in Dare Wright's 1957 children's book *The Lonely Doll.*

3

2

Dare Wright was born in Toronto on December 3, 1914 to Ivan and Edith Stevenson Wright. Early photographs of Dare show an enchanting baby with the slim, tapered fingers of a future artist. Her full name was Alice Dare, but she was always called Dare. Family lore told of her great-grandmother's birth in a log cabin somewhere in the Canadian wilderness as a banshee-wailing blizzard raged outside. The cabin door was flung open, and a distant relative stood in the threshold.

"Name the baby Dare!" the relative intoned, before announcing he was off to seek his fortune in the California gold rush. Dare's great-great grandparents, hoping that their baby might inherit some of the as yet undiscovered bounty, complied with the unusual request. No one heard from the treasure hunter again, but the name Dare stayed in the family.

Dare's parents made a beautiful and outwardly happy couple at their home in the Toronto suburb of Thornhill. Dare's brother, Blaine, two years older than his sister, was a mischievous counterpoint to Dare's obedient serenity. Should anyone have inquired, Ivan's loss of his job managing the theatre pages at the *Toronto Star* could be explained as the desire for a career change towards writing and theatrical producing. Fortunately for the young family's finances, Edie had already established herself as portrait artist both in Toronto and her birthplace of Youngstown, Ohio. The *Toronto Globe* described an idyllic version of Edie's marital life:

> *Mrs. Wright is an artist not only on canvas. The image of her haunts like a variable picture – sunny-headed, delicately molded, feminine in every look and gesture…Her paint creations are never more artistic than their author in the flesh, with her rare beauty, her studied simplicity of dress and attitude, and the subtle radiation of her spirit. With her boy or her wee girl-baby in her arms she represents a vision which could fitly bear the title, Italy Madonna é Bambino.*

Engagement photos of Ivan Wright and Edith Stevenson.

Edith Stevenson Wright as a new bride.

Dare's brother Blaine Wright at age three and a wistful baby Dare.

Edie's portrait of Dare at the beginning of 1917.

Dare as a little snow baby ready to take on Toronto's winter.

Ivan, Dare and Blaine in the last summer they would spend together.

Dare in Thornhill, Canada.

Dare and her brother Blaine. They both loved being on the water in unpretentious, and sometimes rickety, rowboats.

Dare and Blaine on one of their last childhood
adventures together.

Blaine's grandmother wrote on this photo "He brings this old hen to the house every day."

Blaine, Dare and Edie in 1917 shortly before Ivan departed for good taking Blaine with him.

Blaine at Thornhill with one of his beloved animals.

Edie's 1916 self-portrait shows the accomplished artistic technique and personal determination that she would need to extricate herself from an abusive marriage.

Edie painted her enchanting daughter at the age of fifteen months in March, 1916.

Edie didn't disclose the secrets of her marriage for over thirty years. In 1949, over a shared pitcher of martinis, she told my father of Ivan's violence towards her, his rages over his sexual failings and how it had taken two weeks for her new husband to consummate their marriage. Edie had feared that Ivan might turn his brutality towards their daughter, and she knew Dare had to be protected. In 1917, Edie and Ivan separated permanently. Ivan took Blaine to New York, and almost three-year-old Dare stayed with her mother. The children did not meet again until they were in their twenties.

It was the last time that Dare would ever see her father.

Edie's painting kept the newly reduced family of two afloat. When there were no portrait commissions, she painted for magazine covers. Sounding quite plucky under the difficult circumstances, Edie chirped, "I love to do children, and often do magazine covers of children I have known. There is no difficulty in getting a good price for that kind of commercial art in one's spare time."

Edie had always painted portraits as special gifts to her family and benefactors, and her painting of Youngstown attorney David Fitch Anderson was with special gratitude for facilitating a discreet divorce from Ivan Leonard Wright. With Ivan out of her life, the most felicitous way to skirt the social and professional carnage befalling a divorcée was for Edie to begin calling herself a widow.

She and Dare would make it alone.

Edie's portrait of her attorney David Fitch Anderson.

Dare in three thoughtful moments.

Dare had just turned five in December 1919 when seven-year-old Blaine sent her a storybook for Christmas titled *Tales From The Secret Kingdom*. He wrote "To Dare From Blaine" as an inscription.

The fairy tale describes the search for a lost father and son through a bleak and cursed land. When the evil spell is broken, and the family finally reunited, "… they went away…to the land where they regained their youth, and there they are to this day." From brother to sister, the book's refrain sealed a promise:

And when we part at our journey's end
And the giant is safely slain,
We'll make a vow at the wishing well
That we will meet again.

3

Dare was a perfect portrait subject for her mother. The child shimmered with a beauty and self-possession far beyond her years. Edie always spoke to children as her peers, and Dare's precocious qualities most likely began in conversations with her. While Edie worked at her easel, Dare painted tiny renditions of a bunny and swan on scraps of canvas, and absorbed her mother's lessons in line drawing and watercolor.

Rather than scribbling her mother a heart for Valentine's Day, Dare drew Edie a cherub and finished it off with a satin bow. The 1920 census lists them as lodgers in Youngstown, but it was a temporary setback while Edie finished her commissions there.

In 1921, Edie painted a portrait of six-year-old Dare gazing downward at her book with her hair styled in a sweet, blonde bob. Although Dare's hair color had actually turned light brown, her mother's artistic license always painted it golden. By the time she reached her twenties, Dare was coloring her hair to match Edie's idealized image.

Dare's early oil paintings.

Dare's Valentine for Edie.

Edie's portrait of Dare at age six. Dare's hair had turned brown by then, but Edie preferred to paint it as golden.

Dare's unsettled status – the childhood travels from Youngstown to Toronto and lodging with relatives, friends or as boarders – paralleled the mythical journeys of her fairy tale characters. Dare would have to be stalwart and resolute as she searched for a way to reunite with her father and brother.

They moved from Youngstown, Ohio to their own apartment in Cleveland where a 1923 article "Cleveland's Pioneering Woman" described the domestic scene. "We were talking of art in general in her pleasant little apartment on Hampshire Road, which is as unlike a studio as could well be imagined…Her little girl with a white cloth about her head upon which her mother had pinned a cross cut from red paper was playing Red Cross nurse to some decrepit dolls."

"Decrepit" seems an awfully harsh adjective for well-loved dolls, but perhaps the writer had forgotten her own childhood.

A 1923 *Cleveland News* article featured Edie's musings on what qualities she would desire in a husband. There was no mention of her former marriage to Ivan or his inability to consummate it for a fortnight, but Edie spoke candidly about sexual intimacy:

> *I would want him so to be so much a part of me that it would be difficult to distinguish between us.…He must be intense, this lover of mine who is to be my husband. And when he has become that, our minds must be merged in a companionship that knows no interruptions. He must have a spirit of domestic unselfishness so that the intimate things of marriage will take on the harmony of music. He must be ardent in his love-making, considerate of his sensitiveness to the physical and a gentleman in all his attentions and courtesies to me.…Through this communion of the mind and soul and body we might desire the companionship to go on even into eternity.*

Edie described the poetic and sensitive man she had believed she was marrying, and not the violent and impotent person in her wedding bed. The brutality Ivan inflicted upon Edie fueled her protectiveness of their daughter. Edie would see that Dare held off for the perfect man who would show a "sensitiveness to the physical" even if it meant waiting forever.

Edie painted a contemplative Dare in 1923.

A 1920's self-portrait by Edie. With her chin up, Edie was making her way in the competitive art world.

Dare and Edie on their own in Cleveland.

11

Edie in her Cleveland studio 1923. Dare's portrait is reflected in the mirror.

While Edie painted, Dare curled up with her books about brave little girls and enchanted princesses and absorbed the myths and magic in their words. Edie bought Dare the classic tale of *Undine*, a water sprite who marries a knight to gain a soul. For six days of the week, Undine is able to assume a human form, but returns to her mermaid shape on the seventh day. When the knight discovers Undine's secret, he rejects her cruelly, saying, "In the name of all the witches, abide with them…and leave us mortals in peace, sorceress."

The knight's rejection devastates the beautiful sea creature. "Poor Undine looked at him with fixed and tearful eyes. Then she wept, ever more and more bitterly, like an innocent child who feels that it has been sorely misused."

Dare was transfixed by Arthur Rackham's illustrations. Decades later, she created a photographic homage to Rackham's work in a series of self-portraits depicting herself as the cast-off nymph who could never be completely real.

Another favorite of Dare's was *A Faerie Romance*, where the hero is only able to enter the magical kingdom because he is not completely human.

Was being partially enchanted a blessing? For Dare, who would often be referred to as "other-worldly," it bestowed imagination and insight for writing her children's books. She could write for children from their point of view, because she never lost a child's capacity for wonderment.

Dare's trade-off, because fairy tales always exact a price, would be the relinquishing of a portion of her adult self. She would never have a physical relationship with a man.

Arthur Rackham's illustration of the water nymph Undine in Dare's childhood edition of the book. The drawings and story had a profound influence on Dare. Like Undine, Dare was rejected by her suitor as not being fully real.

Dare returned to the mythical Undine in the 1950s when she took a series of self-portraits as the tragic sea nymph.

4

Edie was now being called "…unquestionably among the very foremost women artists of America." That success gave her and Dare the financial stability they needed, but it came with the burden of a heavy workload. The little child who could be amused with books and dolls and snippets of canvas to color while her mother worked now needed peer companionship.

In the summer of 1924, Edie took Dare on a vacation to Cedar Point on Lake Erie and painted her at the water's edge. Ankle deep in the waves, nine-year-old Dare looks to the distance in the same pose she would place her doll, Edith, when she wrote and photographed *Holiday For Edith And The Bears* thirty-four years later.

Edie's 1924 painting of Dare wading on the shore of Lake Erie.

Dare photographed her childhood doll Edith in a similar pose three decades later.

Dare enrolled in Cleveland's Laurel School Fourth Grade in the fall of 1924. She would spend nine happy and productive years excelling in the all-girls environment. In her first year there, Dare wrote a story called "The Little Green Door."

Once, long ago, there lived two children, a boy and a girl who were nine years old, and twins. Their father was the king. In one of the highest towers of the palace there was a little green door. These two children had been forbidden to enter this door.

One day, they were wandering through the castle and they came upon the green door. The boy said, "Come, let us go through this door." But the girl said, "No, we must not. Father told us not to." At last, however, the boy coaxed

the girl to go with him. So they went in and shut the door. They found themselves in a very large room. Suddenly an old woman appeared who asked, "Who are you who dare enter my room? But as you have, you shall hear my story." And she led them into another room.

The king was worried when his children did not appear, and he started to search for them. In his search he came upon the door, and entered. The old woman came hobbling out. The king said, "Old woman, who are you?"

Just then the king heard voices. He asked the old woman whose they were, and she said. "Oh those are only my children." The king said, "Will you not let me see them?" The old woman called the children rather unwillingly.

When they appeared she suddenly ordered them

to go back. Then the king called out, "Give me my children, old woman." But the old woman said, "Not until you have covered this floor with something that is the color of gold."

So the king had everything that was the color of gold brought to the room. When everything was there, a very small place was still uncovered.

Then the girl cut off a lock of her golden hair and covered the vacant space and immediately the old woman and all the gold vanished. The king and his children went downstairs and lived together happily.

What magic would it take for Dare to reunite her family? Was there an equivalent of a lock of golden hair (for Dare's own tresses were now dark brown) that she could sacrifice to break the spell? For now, all she could do was mind her only available parent and not open that forbidden door.

After she and Blaine reconnected as adults, Dare incorporated "The Little Green Door" theme in her first children's book, *The Lonely Doll*. In the story, Little Bear cajoles the doll, Edith, into exploring a newly-discovered room in defiance of their paternal figure, Mr. Bear. Mr. Bear's subsequent displeasure terrifies Edith into believing he will take Little Bear away and abandon her forever.

Blaine was then living in New York City with Ivan and his stepmother Florence. Blaine always spoke fondly of the woman who willingly assumed the maternal role in his life.

Their apartment building at the corner of 75th Street and Broadway was named The Majestic and had

been built to accommodate the prevailing vices of the '20s with hidden staircases for prostitutes, gamblers and mobsters to make quick exits to the roof or basement. While his sister's imagination was being nurtured by fairy tales and fantasy, Blaine could explore the true-life underworld right in his apartment tower.

Entering the secret room in Dare's early mock-up of her 1957 book *The Lonely Doll*.

As headstrong as his sister was obedient, Blaine's stint at the prestigious Collegiate School in Manhattan lasted only until his contempt for the institution's inflexible authoritarianism got him booted into the New York public school system. Blaine would go on to find a measure of equilibrium when he boarded at Toronto's private Upper Canada College during his high school years.

Although Ivan was now working as an insurance agent, the prosaic day job would never be emotionally fulfilling, and he still dabbled in theatrical production. If Ivan drank to blot out mortality tables and annuity quotations, at least Blaine would remember the poetry it released, and use it in his own writing.

Blaine — Collegiate School

15

Edie and Dare spent the summer of 1925 in Maine where Edie painted several small landscape studies in oils which would be shown that fall at Cleveland's Gage Gallery. Both Dare and Edie delighted in creating diminutive-scale landscapes, and some of their later watercolors from the 1950s and '60s were smaller than a matchbox.

Miniature watercolors by Edie and Dare.

When Dare was not working on her own paintings, she read the story of *Keineth,* a little girl who also possessed a unique name and, like Dare, had lost a parent when she was three. Golden-haired Keineth has no memory of her dead mother. She lives with her father in New York's Washington Square, and is tutored at home instead of attending school. Keineth's life is very circumscribed, but she is always dutiful to her only parent, who asks her never to go alone outside of the square nor out of sight of the windows of their own home.

Keineth's world is turned upside down when her father tells her he is going away for a year on a secret mission. It is so secret that he cannot even tell his little girl where he is going, and she is sent to the countryside to live with a marvelous family called the Lees.

Mrs. Lee, a friend of Keineth's late mother, listens to the girl play her piano and remarks, "If that child had not lived that funny, lonely life in that big house… that gift of hers might never have developed. I wonder what the future may have in store for her."

Uncertain of her father's location, Keineth writes to him in care of President Wilson, who not only takes the time to forward it to her father but writes back that he hopes to someday make her acquaintance.

The story ends with Keineth and her father reunited in Washington, a song she has written being played by the Marine Corps Band, and President Wilson calling her a brave little soldier while her father was on his secret mission.

In a remarkable coincidence, Edith Stevenson Wright would soon receive her own Presidential invitation and be installed as U.S. President Calvin Coolidge's portrait artist.

KEINETH

JANE ABBOTT

Dare at summer camp looking very much like Keineth, the
heroine of her childhood book.

5

Edie bought an expensive doll at Halle's department store in Cleveland to celebrate Dare's eleventh birthday in December 1925. The twenty-two-inch felt little girl was made by Italy's Lenci Company, which advertised their dolls with the slogan, "Develop Artistic Tendencies in Your Children."

Dare named the doll Edith after her mother. With her short organdy skirt, Edith looked about the age of a five-year-old and had auburn curls very much like Edie's. Three decades later, Edith became the star of Dare's first book, *The Lonely Doll*.

Dare's childhood doll named Edith in her original outfit and wig.

Edie's Cleveland contacts now included the prominent Hanna family, and she moved her studio to the Hanna Building. She painted a posthumous portrait of Senator Marcus Hanna and the Senator's father, Dr. Leonard Hanna using an older portrait, photographs,

and ancient daguerreotype images as her guides.

Both Edie and Dare captivated Ohio's Lieutenant Governor, Charles Lewis, when he sat for his portrait in the Spring of 1926. This bald and bespectacled gentleman must have seen Dare's own portraits in Edie's studio when he replied to a letter eleven-year-old Dare had written him,

> *My dear little Dare,*
>
> *A letter from you seems a word from a little fairy girl, her name is so familiar and her sweetness so perfectly portrayed by a devoted artist mother. Sometime, soon we must meet, and I'm wondering, all to myself, so that we may be good friends right from the very first. I know you will charm me 'cause the Fairy Queen of little girls like you has told me, oh, so many beautiful things about all of you. And, yes, you are nicer than just a fairy. You are real in a real wonderful and, should I say it, world; so many heart aches, so many tears, along with sunshine and flowers; and where being good, like you are dear is the greatest task of all. Listen to mother. She's your best and truest friend, all the time, everywhere.*

Clearly Dare could entrance her own politician just as well as the fictional Keineth.

Edie was well aware of her own effect on men. Mary Rennels, Edie's champion at *Cleveland Topics* throughout the 1920s, wrote of the artist's charms:

> *She is a dainty young woman with blond curls hugging tightly to her shapely head. Her eyes are brown, deep and interesting, but her general make-up is a complete surprise in this day of emancipated women. She looks fragile and as though she needed to be protected.*

Edie maintained a precarious professional balance. She had to be feminine, yet not too coquettish or she would have been blacklisted by the wives of her famous subjects. It was best to bond with those women as a mother herself, and gently coax their offspring to remain still for their own portraits. Rather than lowering her large brown eyes demurely, Edie seemed to gaze straight into the soul of everyone she met. Edie's mother had scolded her for staring at people's faces when she was a child, but what had seemed impertinent in a small girl would prove to be an invaluable attribute for a portrait artist.

By 1926, Edie was firmly established as Cleveland society's preeminent portrait artist. No one questioned her implied widowhood and, soon after Dare turned twelve, there was no longer a possibility of her former husband showing up to complicate the matter.

Ivan Wright died in his New York City apartment at 215 West 75 Street on January 5, 1927. He was forty-three years old, and the official cause of death was given as epidemic encephalitis with contributory chronic nephritis. Ivan's production of *New York Exchange* had opened six days earlier at New York's Klaw Theatre to mediocre reviews.

Some thirty years after Ivan's death, Blaine told friends that his father had killed himself, and that it was he who had discovered Ivan's hanging body.

The *Toronto Star* gave Ivan's departure a good deal of coverage, considering how long it had been since he lived in Canada. Only Blaine was mentioned as a surviving child.

Edie pasted his obituary into her scrapbook next to their engagement announcement. She thought it best for Ivan's new widow, Florence Wright, to continue caring for the almost fifteen-year-old Blaine in New York. Edie's life revolved around Dare and her Cleveland portrait work. There was no way to integrate Blaine's male energies into their mother-daughter bond or explain the sudden appearance of a teenage son to her patrons. Blaine himself was old enough to speak up about his living arrangements and wanted no part of the mother he felt had abandoned him. Twelve-year-old Dare's aching desire to bring her brother back into her and Edie's life was not a part of the decision.

> *It sighs within me with the misting skies;*
> *Oh, all the day within my heart it cries,*
> *Old as your absence, yet each moment new –*
> *This want of you.*

> Ivan Leonard Wright's poem,
> "The Want of You."

FORMER TORONTO THEATRICAL PRODUCER DIES

Ivan L. Wright, formerly theatrical producer in Canada, and long a resident of Toronto, died in New York city yesterday, where he was producing "New York Exchange" at the Klaw Theatre. The late Mr. Wright was at one time a printer in Toronto, going to New York to enter the insurance business. Three months ago he re-entered the theatrical business, in which he had previously been successful in Canada. ABOVE are two recent photographs of Mr. Wright.

OVERWORK IS BLAMED IN PLAYWRIGHT'S DEATH

Ivan L. Wright, Former Toronto Man, Dies in New York Home

Ivan L. Wright, son of Mr. and Mrs. A. M. Wright of 278 Jarvis street, died yesterday at his home, 215 West 7th street, New York. Mr. Wright had been a resident of New York for some five years and the illness that occasioned his death followed a nervous collapse due to overwork in connection with his production of the play "New York Exchange" which opened at the Klaw theatre in New York on Christmas night. The deceased was about 43 years of age and was very well known in Toronto. He was educated at the Toronto model school and Dufferin street school and was a member of the Dufferin Old Boys Association.

His first business experience was as a linotype operator under the direction of W. J. Hambly on the Mail and Empire. While at work there he was taken ill one night and for nearly two years was an invalid, walking with a slight limp after his recovery. Mr. Wright was of studious habit and had been for years interested in dramatic production. Following his illness, he took over the Russell Theatre in Ottawa and converted it from a burlesque house to the production of legitimate plays. He later organized and managed a theatrical company which toured Canada.

On going to New York he became associated with the firm of Klaw and Erlanger for a time, and was later in the real estate and insurance business. Several months ago he returned to theatrical productions. He had not been a resident of Toronto for the last nineteen years.

Mr. L. A. Wright, of 43 Blantyre avenue, a brother of the deceased, was in Montreal when the news of Mr. Ivan Wright's death reached him. He left immediately for New York, where he will attend his brother's funeral. In addition to his parents and one brother, Mr. Wright is survived by his widow and one son, Blaine Wright, a student at Upper Canada College. The funeral service and interment will take place in New York.

19

6

C.S. Britton, the President of *Cleveland Topics*, thought it would be a splendid notion for Edie to paint President Calvin Coolidge. The magazine would reap the publicity from the portrait, and then donate it to the City of Cleveland.

Edie spent two weeks in Washington during the winter of 1928, painting President Coolidge at The White House and finding him far more accessible than his reputation had implied. The President asked Edie to paint him as a plain man, rather than a president. The portrait was presented to the City of Cleveland on May 7, 1928.

Edie's fetching 1927 photo in the *Pittsburgh Press.*

Edie (second from right) is looking uncharacteristically dowdy during the 1928 presentation of her portrait of President Coolidge. The other woman in the photo appears to have accessorized her outfit with a dead cat.

Artist Paints Him As Mr. Coolidge, Not President

Above, self-portrait of Edith Stevenson Wright, Cleveland artist; lower right, photographic study of the artist, and, left, President Coolidge.

CLEVELAND, O., Feb. 17 — A slight, golden-haired young woman, who looks more like a Dresden doll than a successful portrait artist, is to "do" President Coolidge in February.

She is Edith Stevenson Wright, painter of scores of the country's industrial and professional leaders.

Commissioned by a Cleveland magazine to do a portrait of the president, to be hung in the Public Auditorium of Cleveland, where he was nominated, this young woman, whose hair is most unbelievably curly, secured an audience at the White House through Representative Theodore E. Burton of Ohio.

Granted Sitting

"Would the president sit for her?"

Indeed he would, and gladly, for the artist told him she wanted to paint the kind of a portrait he wanted—not the kind she thought he ought to have.

"Does the president wish to be painted in formal or informal manner?"

And the answer came—"As Mr. Coolidge, please, not as Mr. President."

And the audience, set at ten minutes, stretched itself out to forty-five, while the daughter of the president of Mexico, Alicia Calles, waited in the anteroom to pay her respects to President Coolidge.

Mrs. Wright describes the president as an individual type and therefore fairly easy to paint. She was surprised to find him heavier than his photos indicate, and "pink and white" rather than sallow.

To Be White House Guest

An invitation has been extended to her to live at the White House during the time the president is posing for her. He probably will give her two sittings daily for about two weeks.

She works rapidly, often completing canvases in less than a week, and a large self-portrait was done in three days when Mrs. Wright was "resting" between commissions.

Ever since childhood, when she used to amuse her elders with sketches, Mrs. Wright has painted. She studied for three years in Toronto, then went to New York. One day, while she was copying Rembrandts in the Metropolitan Art Museum, an art dealer, delighted with her work, promised her a "show". She was the youngest woman ever to be given an exhibition in New York.

Since then, there never has been a time for more than six months when she hasn't been painting, and Mrs. Wright laughingly confesses she can't remember how many financiers, jurists and other prominent persons she has set down on canvas. Among her works are five generations of the late Senator Mark Hanna's family.

She prefers to paint men.

When the portrait of the president is finished it will be unveiled by Representative Burton at a dinner in Cleveland.

The honored guest will be a little golden-haired blond, first woman ever to paint an official portrait of a living president.

The *Cleveland Press*
February 17, 1928.

7

Dare was flourishing as a Laurel School boarder. Not only was she known as the "brains" of her class, she also excelled in sports and dramatics.

She spent weekends at home, but Edie wanted them to have a more prolonged period of time together. Dare was thirteen in the summer of 1928, when Edie took her on an extensive tour of Europe. Dare spent the two months filling a sketchbook with watercolor studies of France, Switzerland and Italy.

They sailed back to New York on the *Patria*, and stopped at Sand Lake, Ontario before returning to Cleveland.

Dare returned to the Laurel school, and Edie went back to painting the titans of Cleveland's industries, including three portraits for the Sherwin Williams Paint Company.

Dare loved her time at Cleveland's Laurel School.

Thirteen-year-old Dare kept a travel sketchbook from her 1928 trip to Europe.

Sam Katz, President of New York's Publix Theatres Corporation was another of Edie's subjects, and he became one of her greatest champions when he moved to Hollywood to run MGM Pictures.

She was commissioned to paint a portrait of the late Ambassador to France, Myron Herrick as a gift to the new Herrick War Memorial Building in Paris. In spite of The Great Depression, the citizens of Cleveland contributed $55,000 to the construction of Herrick Hall in the Memorial.

In June 1930, Dare and Edie sailed to Paris on the SS *France*, while the Herrick portrait traveled on the SS *Ile de France* with much Gallic fanfare. Edie was keeping her press service busy. A newspaper clipping shows the first officer of the ship looking at the painting with his cap over his heart, and is captioned, "A Silent Salute to His Precious Cargo."

In a photo taken aboard the SS *France*, fifteen-year-old Dare, in white socks and ankle-strapped low heels is already a head taller than her mother. The press caption stated that Dare might study in Cannes.

She certainly practiced painting technique that summer, but she learned it from Edie, and not a formal school.

Dare's talents had matured in the two years since her previous European trip. She sketched the rooftops of Paris from her hotel room with the assurance of a true artist.

They each painted watercolors of the Cannes harbor that look strikingly similar.

As Dare's technique improved, her watercolor studies became almost indistinguishable from her mother's.

Edie and Dare returned to Paris on the SS *France* in 1930.

Dare's drawings of Parisian rooftops in 1930.

23

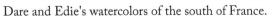

Dare and Edie's watercolors of the south of France.

During this trip to Paris, Edie bought Dare another Lenci doll. Unlike Dare's 1925 Lenci named "Edith" who had the body of a five-year-old child, this new doll represented the seductive Madame Pompadour, and was designed to be admired and displayed by adults. Thirty years later, Dare brought the doll she called "Lona" back to France and photographed her for a fairy tale about an enchanted princess.

They returned to the States in September 1930 on board the RMS *Caronia*, just in time for Dare to begin her sophomore year at Laurel School and for Edie to paint another portrait for France's War Memorial. This time, the subject was the late WW I hero Marshal Foch.

An international newsreel that played in movie theaters before the featured film showed Edie and the completed portrait early in 1931. The narration triumphed her achievements, adding, "Mrs. Wright combines her art activities successfully with those of motherhood. She being the mother of a 16-year-old daughter."

Edie, who did her best to obfuscate the fact that she was old enough to have a teenager, would have been less than pleased by the world-wide revelation.

The portrait was sent to Paris in February 1931. Edie sailed to Paris alone in mid- September and was present at the dedication on October 1.

The Lenci doll that Dare named "Lona" became an enchanted princess in Dare's 1963 book titled *Lona, A Fairy Tale*.

Edie and her portrait of World War I hero Marshal Foch

At almost seventeen, Dare was considered competent to care for herself while Edie was in Europe. She spent the week at Laurel, where she won both the 50-yard dash and the school track meet, and often took her friends Mary and Julia home with her on the weekends and during school breaks. Dare was also taking riding lessons at a private stable. She wrote to her mother in Paris:

Sept 21, 1931

To Mrs. E. S. Wright, Hotel Continental, Paris

Dearest Mummy,

I can't tell you how much I miss you 'cause it's so awfully much. Even with Mary here. Mary and I had a nice evening after you left and went to bed about eleven thirty.

I stayed home Friday and finished my nice striped underwear and in the evening Julia and I went to see Skippy at 105th. I connected with Mary at night Saturday and we took a cab up

to Halle's and checked her suit cases, went to a movie and took a taxi home. Mary likes our house, and our beds, and our couch and my books among other things. Every once in a while she sits up, clasps her hands, and says, "I'm so glad I'm here." Mary just said I was to thank you and tell you she was having a wonderful time.

Sunday we went to a movie in the afternoon. Mary to Keith's and I to the Circle because we'd both seen different ones. I saw Son of India and loved it. We had a nice dinner and fooled and read, and talked until about 1:30. At twelve o'clock we went out and ran twice up and down the hall. Every morning we have a fencing lesson and match in the hall. Today we got downtown about 1:30 and shopped until 5:30 just stopping for lunch.

I was afraid to count what I spent and don't think I'll tell you until I can kiss you at the same time. I got my two lamps for $2.50 for both and a rug about a yard long like the one in our *dressing room for $3.50. The hairbrush cost $1.50. So far so good, but the worst is coming. We found the kind of underwear we've been looking for so desperately in Higbee's. We each got one and ordered another cause they didn't have the size. I probably couldn't get them again. They're crepe de chine bound all the way around and with no pleats or gathers and a little flare at the bottom and very short. We'll forget how much they cost. A bra to go with them was a dollar or $1.25.*

The terrible thing was the hat. It matched my dress exactly and I love it. Mary really urged me to buy it and we took it on approval but I'm going to keep it. It cost ten whole dollars so I thought maybe I'd better not get any shoes. It was hotter today than it's been since I got home. We were dead when we got through and had to take a taxi home. You couldn't get on the streetcars. I did part of my packing tonight and everything is ready. We're going out to the Sunshine Pony Farm tomorrow afternoon and ride an hour there and go straight to school. We don't know what will happen when we arrive for the opening of school in riding breeches but it'll be funny... I'm all ready for bed and writing in bed while Mary reads and the fan blows.

It's awful long until the twelfth of October and I do miss you so. Have a wonderful time and be a good girl, behave as well as possible, and don't make too many mistakes. Mary says don't do anything she wouldn't do. I hope you miss me (you'd better) and hurry the 12th of October as much as possible.

Love, and love, + more love, Dare

In February 1932, Edie began painting Dare in her riding habit. She wrote on the back of the portrait, "To my good and precious child." *The Clevelander* described the painting in March 1932:

Edith Stevenson Wright, Cleveland portrait painter, is painting her daughter Dare, a young girl, in riding habit with cinnamon brown coat and boots, beige breeches, lemon yellow ascot tie. 'To me the most interesting portrait I have ever done,' says Mrs. Wright.

That September, Edie told the *Cleveland News* that her only hobbies were her daughter and her work.

Dare graduated from The Laurel School in 1933. She was a member of the Cum Laude Society, president of the Athletic Association and vice president of student government.

Her classmates chose a quotation from Sir Walter Scott's *The Lady Of The Lake* to accompany Dare's photograph in the *Laurel Leaves* school yearbook. It celebrated both Dare's rare beauty and her other-worldly quality of nymphs and naiads – those creatures that could venture into the world of mortals but would never become fully real. The little girl who had poured over Arthur Rackham's illustrations of the sea nymph, Undine, was beginning to resemble her heroine.

And ne'er did Grecian chisel trace
A Nymph, a Naiad, or a Grace
Of finer form or lovelier face.

8

Dare moved to New York City in the fall of 1933. As Edie had done in the early years of the century, she enrolled at The Art Students League to study painting, and she also took classes at The American Academy of Dramatic Art.

Dare's artistic talent was evident, but her aptitude for acting had yet to be tested except in productions of The Laurel School's Dramatic Club. It was Laurel's drama teacher Jane Douglass – an over-bearing woman besotted with Dare – who encouraged her to study for an acting career. Although Dare left both the American Academy of Dramatic Art and The Art Students League within a few months of enrollment, she continued to paint and look for professional theatrical work.

A newspaper article about Edie's painting techniques mentioned, "Her daughter, Dare, is employed in New York, awaiting an opportunity on the Broadway stage."

The opportunity would soon present itself, but there was nothing happening in the long hot New York summer of 1935. Dare and Edie went to Los Angeles where Edie could complete the commissions brought by her friendship with Sam Katz, and Dare would see if she had the acting potential or looks for a film career.

They returned to New York on September 2, 1935 aboard the SS *Virginia*. Hollywood had ignored Dare's camera-ready face and figure, but it was not a life that she wanted anyway.

She and Edie spent the voyage painting watercolors of Baja, Mexico and Havana, Cuba while working on their tans. Unlike the formal European ships, the *Virginia*'s dress code acknowledged the steaming weather they would encounter as they made their way through the Panama Canal. Poolside frolics that would have been banned on the *France* were indulged during this sultry passage.

Dare at nineteen when she was looking for acting work in New York.

Edie's 1935 watercolor of the Havana harbor.

That fall, Dare began rehearsals for her only Broadway role as a maid in an adaptation of Jane Austen's *Pride and Prejudice*. The production starring Colin Keith-Johnston as Mr. Darcy and Helen Chandler as Jane Bennet opened at The Plymouth Theatre on November 5, 1935 and ran until May 1936. It went on tour afterwards, affording Dare almost a year of continual employment, and the small role meant she had long stretches of time to sketch her fellow players backstage.

The script gave Mr. Darcy a larger role than Jane Austen's book, and London born Colin Keith-Johnston created the character of an impossibly handsome, languorously-lidded Regency hero that became a standard for any future casting. Eighteen years Dare's senior, Colin chose to be Dare's protector rather than, as he had originally planned, a suitor. "She was as delicate as a butterfly," he told my father, "and the theatre has no place for delicacy."

Dare also drew movie stars from magazine photographs. Twenty years later, Greta Garbo would pose for an oil portrait that Dare and Edie collaborated on, but for now Garbo was just a pencil drawing on scrap paper.

Dare sketched the dashing Colin Keith-Johnston as Mr. Darcy in *Pride and Prejudice*.

Dare and Colin during the run of *Pride and Prejudice*.

Jeanette Chinley — Ben Boyar — Mary Alice Rice — Dare

Dare with the play's general manager and cast members.

Dare's 1936 sketch of the actress Greta Garbo.

My mother, Eugenia Rawls, replaced Helen Chandler as Jane Bennet at the end of the Broadway run and continued on for the tour. She was a year older than Dare and had made her Broadway debut as a schoolgirl in Lillian Hellman's *The Children's Hour* in 1934. Born in Macon, Georgia, Eugenia slipped off the tulle-wrapped shackles and restrictive expectations of Southern womanhood to head to New York, while retaining a birthright of dramatic, magnolia-scented excesses.

Unlike Dare, who confessed to my father that acting embarrassed her, Eugenia had always possessed an ardent desire to be center stage and would spend her life elbowing into the spotlight. Outraged at the family's diverted attention when her first sibling arrived in 1917, four-year-old Eugenia devised an escape plan. There would be no playing mother's helper to her new sister or fawning over the baby's dimpled gurgles. Scraping a dining room chair across the heart pine flooring, Eugenia stood on the caned seat to reach a wall-crank telephone and called her grandmother fifty miles away. "I will be coming to live with you," she announced, and went upstairs to pack her suitcase. Since there seems to have been no dissent, Eugenia's family must have considered her fully capable of launching a raft into the nearby Ocmulgee River. Or, just perhaps, it was an answered parental prayer.

It was the same year that Dare and Blaine were unwillingly separated by their parents.

My uncle Malcolm, a judge who always chose his words carefully, waited until I was an adult to deliver his verdict on Eugenia's absence of nurturing, "Your mother should not have had children."

My mother became close friends with Dare during their 1936 tour. Eugenia had not yet married my father, Don Seawell, who described his initial encounter with Dare: "I first met Dare backstage after a performance of *Pride and Prejudice*. Eugenia had the lead role, and Dare had a non-speaking walk on as a maid. Eugenia and I were leaving the theatre when we saw Dare beautifully poised, or posed, on the stairway. I thought at the time that it was a deliberate though attractive posture, but I later learned it was usually unconscious."

Dare took a train to Cleveland when the tour ended, and the portrait Edie painted there shows a newly mature and mysterious side of her daughter.

Eugenia Rawls as sketched by Dare.

Dare in 1936 at the age of twenty-one when she played a small role on Broadway in *Pride and Prejudice*.

Edie's portrait of Dare at
twenty-four.

There were more Hollywood commissions for Edie, including a portrait of Sam Katz's wife, Sari Maritza. While Dare still failed to ignite any sparks of interest in Los Angeles, Edie continued to be celebrated by the media.

The July 12, 1937 Los Angeles *Evening Herald And Express* was as enthusiastic about the artist as her paintings, saying, "Edith Stevenson Wright…looks more like a movie star than a famous woman painter, to say nothing of being the mother of Dare Wright, Broadway actress."

Whenever she could, Edie saw that Dare was mentioned in her interviews. As soon as Edie returned to Cleveland, the Polly Parsons Society column gushed, "And so, who should come back to town this week but Edith Stevenson Wright. And with enough movie intimacies to fill a book…After looking over Hollywood in general…and M-G-M in particular…Myrna Loy and Carol Lombard drag out Edith's healthiest handshake as far as [film] stars go…After the 'summering' season is over on the west coast, she'll go back to Hollywood to finish some of the paintings she has already started. That means she'll be away from Dare (her daughter) who is scheduled to appear on Broadway again this year."

The Broadway role was imaginary. Dare, who had been much more comfortable sketching her fellow *Pride and Prejudice* cast members than appearing on stage with them, returned to New York to work primarily as a fashion model. The shyness, which prevented Dare from projecting herself on stage, could be read as cool and alluring in a still photograph.

In 1940, Dare moved into the Hotel Bristol at 129 West 48 Street. It was a respectably secure location for a New York career woman, and featured a fairly elegant restaurant off the lobby, although Dare was too frugal to eat there. Her room contained a small kitchenette, which was fine for heating soup and keeping milk cold, and the eighth-floor windows looked out on the skyscraper at 30 Rockefeller Center.

Edie brought Dare several small paintings from Cleveland along with a ceramic cherub lamp, and they sewed a burgundy and cream striped cover for the daybed and bolster, using the extra fabric as a dressing table skirt. The bureaus were given a buttercream yellow background and Edie painted ivy vines trailing across them. A small bookcase was repurposed to hold floral china, stemware and a selection of liquor for visitors. Through Dare and Edie's artistry, it became an elegant,

tiny jewel box set in an anonymous twelve-story hotel. Dare would have nine secure years in room #830 before a venomous lawsuit made it intolerable to live in.

Edie phoned almost daily and visited Dare as often as she could. Dare told my father that she was happy keeping a geographical distance between herself and Edie, although she was always loving and welcoming when they were together. It was my father's belief that Edie never wanted Dare completely out of her control, and Dare told him that her mother became upset if she was not welcome to go along on her dates. Don saw this more as a quirk than a character flaw and was very fond of Edie.

Eugenia's acting career was at its peak with a year and a half of continuous employment. In the fall of 1939 she stepped into the role of Tallulah Bankhead's daughter Alexandra in the Broadway production of

Tallulah and Eugenia as mother and daughter in *The Little Foxes*. Tallulah signed it, "To my Baby, With love from Mama."

Lillian Hellman's *The Little Foxes* and continued with the hundred and four city tour that finished in the spring of 1941. Tallulah, who had fled her native Alabama as a teenager, was only eleven years older than the ambitious twenty-six-year old playing her daughter and firmly established as a theatrical star. Her excesses of liquor, lovers of all persuasions and liberal sampling of controlled substances made her the darling of gossip columnists and scandal sheets, but she never missed a performance. Both Tallulah and Eugenia thrived on the standing ovations delivered nightly in venues as small as Butte, Montana. Eugenia wrote in her journal as the train portaged the cast toward the West Coast then looped down through Santa Barbara and Los Angeles before heading back eastward. Tallulah, who discovered old lovers and new conquests scattered along the itinerary, said only good girls kept diaries; bad girls never had the time.

Tallulah and Eugenia joined Colin Keith-Johnston in a touring company of summer theatres scattered along the East Coast like ice cream sprinkles. If *The Little Foxes* was an intense portrayal of familial evil and avarice where Tallulah's character watched her husband die onstage with icy indifference, *The Second Mrs. Tanqueray*'s fifty-year-old British script scampered up the theatrical scale to reach a level of melodrama that bordered on farce.

Tallulah played Colin's second wife, a woman with a shameful sexual history. Eugenia was Colin's innocent daughter whose engagement is shattered by Tallulah's revelation that Eugenia's fiancé is the very man who had wronged her. No one takes that disclosure very well. Tallulah slaps Colin, Eugenia taunts Tallulah with her sordid reputation, and Tallulah storms off to kill herself. The cast fled to the closest bar as soon as the curtain thumped down. Tallulah, who hated being alone and couldn't fall asleep until dawn, conscripted actors, stagehands and janitors to play poker through the muggy summer nights.

Summer theatre audiences came to see the stars, regardless of the plays, and Tallulah's name on the posters meant the seats were always filled. The bus took them from Maplewood, New Jersey, where *Time* magazine's review called Tallulah "as buxom as a milkmaid and in fine vocal trim," to Westport, Connecticut and along the straw hat circuit up to Ogunquit, Maine. Tallulah, stretched across any convenient lap with her feet out the window, frequently requested a poetry recitation to pass the time between stops.

Colin, who had rekindled an old affair with Tallulah for the duration of the tour, was delighted to comply, and stanzas of Swinburne, Yeats and Houseman hung in the fog of diesel exhaust and smoke from Tallulah's lung-searing British cigarettes. At the summer's end, they parted with poetic grace as Tallulah and Eugenia resumed the final seven-month tour in *The Little Foxes*.

The Second Mrs. Tanqueray featured screaming, slapping and a suicide.

Tallulah was the matron of honor at Don and Eugenia's small Philadelphia wedding on April 5, 1941 just before the last performance of *The Little Foxes*. The cast returned to New York – Tallulah to a suite at the Hotel Elysée at 60 East 54th Street with a newly-acquired monkey, and Don and Eugenia to their first apartment at 169 East 69th Street. Don, Eugenia and Dare began a tradition of inviting friends to drop by for drinks every Sunday, and Tallulah brought champagne for the mimosas. The monkey stayed behind at the Elysée, sulkily shredding the hotel draperies.

Dare's New York family was almost complete. Now it was time to find her brother, Blaine.

Donald Seawell and Eugenia Rawls at their wedding. After the reception, Eugenia and Tallulah got back in costume for the final performance of *The Little Foxes*.

Dare and her brother Blaine were about to reconnect.

9

Dare discovered Blaine's stepmother, Florence, listed in the New York phone directory. Florence was delighted by the surprising call from the young woman she had never met and told Dare that Blaine had joined the Royal Canadian Air Force a year earlier. He went back and forth between New York and Canada and would be, Florence assured Dare, eager to reconnect with his sister.

It was 1941. Twenty-four years had passed since the siblings had last seen each other, and Dare had little memory of the brief time they had spent together as children. She asked my father, Don, how she should plan the meeting. They agreed that Central Park would provide both privacy and a perfect backdrop for the initial reunion. If all went well, Dare would walk her brother over to Don and Eugenia's apartment afterwards.

Central Park's Bethesda Terrace and Fountain were two of Dare's favorite spots, and the most easily recognizable locations for a rendezvous.

My father said Dare was very nervous about the meeting, but she would not have shown it as she left The Bristol and walked northward through the park.

Blaine was impossible to miss in his RCAF uniform. As handsome as his sister was beautiful, even jaded New Yorkers stared when they saw them together.

They had the same sense of ridiculous wit, spoke in a similar clipped cadence, finished each other's sentences and unconsciously mirrored each other's gestures and facial expressions.

Dare at Central Park's Angel of The Waters Fountain.

Dare at Central Park's Bethesda Terrace.

Dare and her brother Blaine in 1942.

Dare was radiant when she brought Blaine back to my parents' apartment. She was twenty-six years old. Blaine was twenty-nine, the same age as my father. "Dashing" was the word my father used to describe him.

Blaine fit right in with Dare and my parents' friends. He was a raconteur with a gentle voice and an economy of gesture. And, like his mother and sister, Blaine always looked unblinkingly into your eyes.

Dare made a pencil sketch of Blaine in his uniform. With all of the artwork that surrounded her childhood, there was no evidence that Edie had ever painted Dare's brother. This was the first artistic record that Blaine really existed.

Dare's pencil sketch of her brother Blaine.

The United States entered WW II four days after Dare's twenty-seventh birthday. She spent that Christmas of 1941 in Cleveland with Edie. Edie's old friend Sam Katz from M-G-M Pictures wrote from Los Angeles wishing them both a good holiday season and expressing hope that there would soon be peace. No one really believed that would happen quickly.

One of Blaine's RCAF instructors was a British pilot named Philip Sandeman. Philip's family had founded Sandeman Port & Sherry and lived on the English Channel Island of Jersey.

In 1942, Blaine invited Philip to accompany him to drinks at my parents' apartment with the intention of introducing his friend to Dare. Philip and Dare seemed immediately comfortable with each other. Blaine thought their pairing so successful, that he left the party with the actress Erin O'Brien-Moore and was not heard from for two days.

Sandeman continued his attentions towards Dare in a quiet, gentlemanly fashion. Although younger than Dare, his British reserve made him seem mature for his years.

Philip Sandeman was Blaine's British friend and Dare's suitor.

Dare's sketch of Philip Sandeman.

Dare and Philip before he returned to England for the war years.

Blaine had transferred to the US Army Air Forces and was awaiting imminent deployment. Dare, Blaine and Philip made the most of the brief time together. They posed for photos of each other in Dare's hotel room, and Dare sketched a solemn Philip in pencil before he left for Europe.

Blaine sailed from New York to Scotland as an officer with the 56th Fighter Group on January 6, 1943. That spring, the squadron moved to a base at RAF Horsham St. Faith. Both Philip and Blaine would spend the war based in England.

Blaine's 56th squadron flew the P-47 Thunderbolt on support missions for ground troops and totaled more aerial victories than any other fighter group.

My father, Don, described a trip with Dare before he too headed for England to serve as a special counter intelligence agent on General Eisenhower's staff:

Before I went overseas, I had a great deal of rugged training. A seventy-mile hike or a ten-mile run was the easy part… When my training was over, I was given some time off. I donned my civvies, loaded Eugenia and Dare into our brand-new Buick convertible, and headed for [the country]. It was a lovely, but very hot summer day. Along the way, we stopped at a beautiful shady spot for our picnic lunch. Dare, dressed in short shorts of course, was pouring me ice cold lemonade when along the road marched the tiredest, dustiest, hottest, thirstiest group of soldiers I had ever seen… Wow were they mad. I could hear, '4-F bastard' and much worse. When I left for the war, Dare drew a picture of me carrying a club – off to do battle.

Dare's sketch of Donald Seawell.

Don Seawell in uniform at Versailles.

Virginia Cherrill was a lovely American actress whose greatest fame was her role as the blind flower girl in Charlie Chaplin's 1931 film *City Lights*. She hadn't liked Chaplin either personally or professionally and was equally disparaging of her ex-husband Cary Grant whom she accused of choking and beating her. After several international flings that included the Maharaja of Jaipur, Virginia married a rather weedy, but very titled British Earl and became the Countess of Jersey. She met my father when she hosted a party for American officers, and their affair lasted for the duration of the war. Virginia, along with her often-ab-sent Earl, was living in "The Old Palace" built over the ruins of Henry VIII's palace on the curling ribbon of the Thames. At her invitation, my father moved into a little cottage on the property with a companionable British bulldog. Four decades later, in a twist out of a soap opera, Virginia and I became neighbors in a small California seaside town. "I loved your father," she told me while describing their affair, and perhaps she had. I went to her funeral at Santa Barbara's Old Mission, wondering if the cassocked priest had any inkling of Virginia's libertine lifestyle.

While the men were engaged with bombings and the titled aristocracy, Eugenia went on tour in a 1943 wartime drama titled *Cry Havoc*. The play was set in a woman's barrack at a Bataan field hospital in the Philippines, and Eugenia played a cute, vacuous Southern nurse who surprised everyone by revealing herself as a cold-blooded Fascist spy. Scarlett O'Hara became Mata Hari when Eugenia brandished her pistol and dispatched her fellow caregivers. Had she known of the situation that was going on in England, Eugenia might also have turned her gun on the Countess of Jersey.

The American actress, Virginia Cherrill, had divorced Cary Grant before marrying into British aristocracy. She was living in London as the Countess of Jersey during WW II when she and Don began their affair.

Eugenia holding the *Cry Havoc* cast at gunpoint.

10

It was 1943 and Dare was almost thirty. It seemed pragmatic to consider Philip as her future husband even though they really did not know each other well and had made no formal commitment. There were the war years in which to sort out the details, and for now she could write affectionately to him while her daily life was unchanged.

She took an enigmatic photo of herself to send Philip, arranging a tableau on her dressing table with a bottle of his family's Sandeman sherry, a vase of roses and her pencil sketch of him in uniform. Looking into the camera, Dare's expression seems almost world-weary. This isn't a classic wartime pinup picture or a snapshot of a girl back home. There's a mystery and seductiveness—the satin shoulder strap stitched to a cotton undergarment--that belongs in a Raymond Chandler story.

Dare sent this mysterious and seductive photograph to Philip. He never really knew the woman he would ask to marry him.

Dare's self-portraits taken in Central Park during WW II.

Dare lightened her hair during Philip's absence. Edie had been painting her daughter as a blonde since her childhood, and now she would match the portraits. More significantly, light refracted more favorably off fair hair, and it would be a better look for her modeling and stage work. Dare used a timer on the camera to create a series of evocative self-portraits in Central Park. The Park looks almost deserted in the photos – just Dare, a picnicking family, a baby buggy and two soldiers on leave in the glorious summer weather.

Dare made her own outfits – dresses, suits, and even coats – on a child's toy sewing machine. Her sense of design was as distinctive and refined as her other artistic talents, and she was always her own best model.

Philip wrote Blaine in 1943, describing a letter he had just received from Dare, who was in rehearsal for a part in a touring company: "She is very happy and working most hard, and she says learning how to act every day….It's a big strain on her, but by golly she can do it, and she will be a star when we get back….It's not too late Blaine, everything is going to be alright."

The play Dare was rehearsing was *Death Takes a Holiday* starring Julie Haydon. Dare did not end up touring with the show. She wrote Blaine that the producers decided her look was too close to Haydon's. It was a big disappointment, and Dare said all she wanted was another chance to prove she could act. Dare drew a little cherub on the letter. Blaine had written about the fleas in the barracks, and Dare added a little butterfly net in the cherub's hands: "This cherub is an expert exterminator and guaranteed to rid you of every bug."

Thanks to Dare, Edie and Blaine were now in contact with each other and also exchanging letters and cables. Edie asked her son if he would go on a fishing holiday to Canada with her when the war was over. She also wanted to know if he would sit for a full-length portrait wearing his uniform. "I can see it," Edie wrote from Cleveland, "A full length to go with Dare's long one with a great dark sky back of you." That opportunity for Edie and Blaine to reconnect was never realized.

Edie shared her apprehensions about Dare's theatrical auditions, telling Blaine, "I am holding my breath for Dare. There are several things in the fire for her and I can't bear to think she might get let down for them all. Poor kid!"

Dare was as concerned as Edie about her career. She had been so nervous during a 1944 audition for producer Max Gordon that she had gone home and thrown up. Dare quite literally did not have the stomach for the theatre.

Edie's portrait of Dare when she was an aspiring actress. She was far happier as a photographer and author.

Dare and Edie used photographs to collaborate on a 1940s portrait of Philip Sandeman.

If the acting roles were not materializing, Dare busied herself with modeling and visits to Edie in Cleveland. She painted in watercolors, oils, and pencil and collaborated with Edie on a brooding portrait of Philip.

With her Rolleiflex camera around her neck, Dare explored the city and began developing her own photographic prints. She was too sensitive of strangers' feelings to become a "street photographer" and capture their candid moments. That intimacy between subject and photographer was reserved for her own nude sessions with the camera.

The bathroom at The Bristol became a tiny, but efficient, darkroom where Dare strung cord over the tub to hang the wet photos. She was, as she had always been, comfortable and resourceful in her own company.

11

The end of the war in 1945 meant Blaine, Philip and Don would soon be coming back into Dare's life. Edie and Dare spent that summer at our Maryland farm called "Mayport" on the Eastern Shore of the Chesapeake Bay.

The farm had belonged to my mother's family since the 1920s. An uncle of Eugenia's bought it after retiring as a riverboat captain, and he and his wife eked a precarious living farming wheat and tomatoes. They left the property to my parents in the early 1940s.

The small wooden farmhouse pre-dated the Civil War and had a secret stairway that might have been used by fugitive slaves on their journey along the Underground Railway. It was unpretentious, but sweet. My great-aunt was a schoolteacher, and she had papered the hallway with scenes from Regency England, which gave a refined contrast to the mice that skittered along the baseboards.

Every few years, the dining room ceiling collapsed in a cloud of white plaster. It was an impressive event for which no one had an explanation. Perhaps the raccoon population scampering on the joists reached a critical mass.

Mayport had been uninhabited during the war years. Unchecked vegetation surrounded the house and a varied assortment of wildlife had taken over the interior. The property had no electricity or telephone. The single toilet might flush if water could be pumped into the tank, but it was more reliable to use the outhouse located fifty yards away at the edge of the pear orchard. The pears had survived the seasons of drought and neglect by sacrificing sensual beauty for dense functionality. They no longer enticed with soft, rounded rumps which, after all, meant nothing to the deer and worms that ate them. Speckled with the holes of wasp larvae, they fell on the dry crabgrass as graceless as dirt clods.

For Dare and Edie, the absolute privacy outweighed the lack of amenities. Dare was never fearful of any animal, and the snakes, while alarming, were not poisonous. Mayport was at the end of a creek with no through water traffic. Dare and her mother could sunbathe nude on the dock or in the rowboat without being seen.

The eighty-acre property was close to returning to a primal state with five-foot black snakes draped from the trees in a Garden of Eden tableau. It was the perfect retreat for Dare – the original innocent. Edie and Dare were almost a mile from the nearest neighbor, an elderly black woman called Miss Georgie who walked through a wooded lane to help with the laundry. She used a heavy coal iron – unchanged since the Civil War – on cotton shirts and linens.

Edie exploring the overgrown thickets at Don & Eugenia's Maryland farm. The creekside solitude made up for the abundance of snakes.

The farmhouse was surrounded by vegetation that had been left unchecked throughout WW II, offering a fairy tale privacy.

Dare took a series of nude self-portraits in the isolated cove.

An ancient icebox on the back porch kept provisions from spoiling. There was an ice house seven miles away in the village of St. Michaels and Dare and Edie hitched a ride into town to bring back a large square of ice with their provisions.

Nights were difficult. Kerosene lanterns provided the only illumination, and the free-standing metal windmill that powered the well emitted high-pitched horror movie shrieks if there was any breeze. The whine of circling mosquitoes, along with the whoosh of snakes and scrabbling of mice in the walls, was not conducive to sleep. Edie said that every night she and Dare decided they would have to go back to the city as soon as it was light, and then could not bear to leave when dawn broke over the creek.

By the end of the summer, Dare and Edie were rested, tanned and as ready as possible for the postwar world ahead of them.

My father bought Dare a sterling charm bracelet to remember her Mayport summer. It was centered with a silver writing pad inscribed "Mayport 1945" and the forty-one other charms were all themed to her Chesapeake Bay sojourn – a martini shaker, flashlight,

sailboat, jalopy, coal iron, sandal, icebox, can of "Flit" bug spray, water pump, an outhouse with a person seated inside, and a book inscribed "I Love You."

Dare adored the bracelet, and often wore it wrapped around her ankle at the beach. Of the many declarations of love tossed her way, both casually and sincerely, Don's was most enduring.

Don, having distinguished himself in a cadre of wartime espionage agents dedicated to the success of D-Day, joined a small New York law firm when he returned from overseas. His partner, Nahum Bernstein, was a former OSS intelligence officer and they combined their formidable undercover skills to support the formation of the State of Israel. David Ben-Gurion, who would become the State's first Prime Minister, flew in for secret meetings at Don and Nahum's office. While conducting their usual legal business, Don and Nahum bought a dummy company named "Yardley Fabrics" which served as a front for their covert Zionist operations and never produced a single bolt of chintz. Part of an underground network of like-minded New Yorkers, Don wrote the charter for the new State of Israel with David Ben-Gurion's blessing.

Don at Mayport in 1946.

Dare wore Don's "I Love You" charm bracelet around her ankle when she took this self-portrait on Ocracoke Island, North Carolina in the 1950s.

12

Blaine had spent six years in the military where he witnessed unspeakable horrors and flew heroic missions of mercy. The bright spot was his love affair with a British girl, which ended tragically with her death in a German bombing raid.

At the end of the war, Blaine found a refuge near the village of Walton in Delaware County, New York. Butternut Island was a tiny dot down-river from the town and could only be reached by wading across a shallow stream on one side of the island. The Delaware River flowed swiftly alongside the other. The small cabin had only the most rudimentary of amenities, but it was the perfect place for Blaine to write and renew.

Blaine christened his new domain the Isle of Pot so that he, and any visitors, would be able to say they were going to pot.

There was still snow on the ground when Dare first visited Blaine on his island for the opening of trout season. Although she never embraced her brother's love of fishing, Dare was always a great sport about sharing rustic living arrangements with a few mice and the bats that flew through her bedroom.

Blaine and Dare in 1946 at Blaine's home on Butternut Island near Walton, New York. Dare was quite sanguine about the mice and bats that shared the small cabin.

Philip Sandeman joined Dare that summer of 1946, and Dare accepted his proposal of marriage. Blaine used Dare's camera to capture the couple in what were sometimes joyous, but more often emotionless, tableaux. Even given Philip's reserve, the lovers seem curiously distant. Perhaps it was due to their lack of physical intimacy – Dare would give him no more than a chaste kiss – but the pictures lack any hint of sensuality.

Philip and Dare became engaged in the summer of 1946. The photograph, taken on Blaine's Butternut Island, is reminiscent of Arthur Rackham's illustration in Dare's favorite childhood book *Undine* where the sea nymph is courted by a mortal man.

Dare brought Edie up to Butternut Island to visit Blaine. She might have been poised to become a married woman, but Dare's most fervent wish was to have her mother and brother love each other as much as she loved them individually. Three decades of estrangement would be hard to bridge, and perhaps a small island cabin was not the ideal place to achieve it, but Dare would devote their time together to that end.

Edie was not going to hover about the cabin waiting for the rapprochement. It would be too simple for Blaine to bounce angry words of recrimination off the old wooden walls. Any reconnection needed to take place in the meadows and streams her son loved. She set her easel in a field and painted the neighbor's Guernsey cows against the mountain backdrop. Blaine could walk over to comment if he wished, or they could remain in a companionable silence. Their past could not be altered, but perhaps there was hope for a future.

She and Dare explored the streams and woods where Dare photographed her mother in casual country skirts and sandals as well as more urban-appropriate suits and heels. It amused Blaine to see that Edie had traveled prepared for any sartorial contingency.

Edie's painting near Blaine's cabin.

Dare's fervent wish was to bring her mother and brother together. Edie's 1946 trip to Blaine's island near Walton, New York was their first rapprochement in three decades of separation.

Dare also found secluded spots at a distance from the cabin where she could continue the nude self-portraiture that she had begun the year before in Maryland. The unclothed photographs were taken only for herself. Neither Philip nor any other man would ever see her wearing anything less modest than a bathing suit.

13

Dare and Tallulah became my godmothers when I was born in the spring of 1947. The title didn't carry any religious significance, although they both belonged in my personal pantheon of secular goddesses. Dare was still engaged to Philip Sandeman although, or perhaps because, they had not seen each other since the previous summer.

Dare was quite familiar with the medieval concept of "courtly love" from her childhood books about knights and their fair maidens. It was an idealized perception of a noble and often sexless romance between a couple, where the independent woman was worshiped from afar as the knight labored to prove his worthiness.

Even if it happened to be a few centuries out of date, the concept provided a functional template for Dare to keep working in New York while Philip stayed in England.

Blaine's island gave Dare a respite from the un-air-conditioned Manhattan summer, but Edie was not enthusiastic about traveling there from Cleveland for a replay of their previous visit. She was sixty-four years old and still had a demanding artistic career. Edie wanted to spend her vacation with Dare on a beach in a remote but creatively inspiring location.

Edie and Dare would have returned to our Maryland farm, but it had been promised to my father's family that summer. And so it was that I spent my first August there with my grandparents, aunts and uncles experiencing the novelty of prickly heat rash and having large snakes dangle over my outside bassinet.

My mother, Eugenia, fled the crowd quickly. She was not particularly fond of her own relatives, and certainly did not want to spend her days wallowing with my father's. As always, she used the excuse of a potential audition to race back to the city.

I was watched over by a woman who had been hired as my temporary baby nurse, but who would spend the rest of her life as part of my family. "Nana" became an extra grandmother to me. She had left her native Germany after her fiancé was killed in the First World War. A registered nurse, she bounced around a roulette wheel of New York City families until stopping in our slot.

Nana had her quirks. She could not sit still for more than a few minutes, which meant she was unable to take me anywhere like a pediatrician's office where there was a possibility of waiting. To feed her constant restlessness, Nana embraced washing and ironing with a passion that exceeded any explanation of Teutonic housekeeping traditions. Happiest with the antique iron at Mayport that could be heated on the wood stove, she attacked electric models in the city by gouging out the spray mechanism with a kitchen fork.

My father suggested that Dare and Edie try the island of Ocracoke on North Carolina's Outer Banks. He knew it well, having grown up in the state, and thought its wild beauty would appeal to them. Reaching Ocracoke in 1947 meant taking a train to Raleigh, driving several hours to the coast and then catching the mail boat to the island. Dare wrote of the experience:

You got a quiet, friendly looking-over from the assembled islanders when you stepped off the boat after a four-hour trip from the town of Atlantic on the Carolina coast. The boat was not the ultimate in luxury. You might get a seat on a wood bench, or have to sit on some of the freight. You might be burned by the sun, or soaked by the rain, but it never seemed to spoil the trip.

Edie may have painted President Coolidge and hob-nobbed with international dignitaries, but there was nothing snobbish about her. She and Dare were immediately enchanted by the informality of this island where most people went barefoot, and wild ponies roamed the lanes and dunes. They settled in at The Wahab Village Hotel, of which Dare wrote:

There was plenty of plain food, a movie once a week, and no need to put on a pair of shoes from the moment you arrived until you reluctantly left.

Your host was C.F. Boyette, former Latin teacher, former physical education instructor, and an easy-going man with a delightful sense of humor. The hotel was on the beach but not on the sea. From an upstairs window, you could just glimpse the water like a ruler line on the horizon.

Newcomers might say, "We thought the hotel was up the beach."

"It is," said Mr. Boyette.

"But where's the ocean? We wanted a swim."

"Right over there about a mile and a quarter. You could walk."

"Walk?" you might ask.

"Or I could get Jake to carry you across."

A party of people just off a plane would ask, "What can we do for entertainment?"

"Might walk down and look at the docks. Don't know if it'd entertain you," Mr. Boyette would answer.

"What about night life?"

"Movie every Saturday," Mr. Boyette replied.

Ocracoke is not for people looking for entertainment.

C.F. Boyette, owner and raconteur at Ocracoke Island's Wahab Village Hotel.

Dare and Edie were perfectly happy to entertain themselves. The "Jake" whom Mr. Boyette had referred to was "Big Jake" Alligood, who provided the island's only taxi service. Dare wrote,

Big Jake…was his own man. I'm sure he would have been at home anywhere in the world, in his old cap with the broken visor shading his seamed, brown face, his eyes squinting and a pithy remark on his lips.

Dare's photo of Big Jake on Ocracoke Island, North Carolina. Her pictures and story of that unique community were published in *Ocracoke In The Fifties.*

Jake would drop Dare and Edie off on a secluded stretch of beach with a picnic lunch and large umbrella. As soon as he drove away, they dispensed with their bathing suits and spent the afternoon soaking up the sun in the nude. Their tans were always golden and seamless, and they never sunburned. As a pale, freckled child, I was mesmerized by their transformation.

Jake returned in his Jeep at five o'clock, as Edie gave him the all-clear sign by waving a white scarf.

14

Dare sailed to London in the fall of 1947. Her engagement to Philip Sandeman was announced in *The Times* of London on October 14. Philip's mother, Marie, gave Dare her own engagement ring and welcomed her into the family. If Marie Sandeman had any reservations about Philip's gorgeous American fiancée, they were dispelled the moment she met her.

Philip and Dare found a little home south of London on the Thames, and Dare measured the windows for curtains that she and Edie would sew back in the States. She also sketched a floor plan so that they could choose and ship furniture from the US. Edie ordered a refrigerator for the couple, which was a luxury in post-war England. A kitchen cabinet that vented to the outdoors was a more usual method of keeping food cool, and milk bottles were sniffed before consumption to see if the contents had "gone off."

Dare returned to New York to plan the wedding. My mother was to be matron of honor and my father would give her away. Edie intended to stay close to her only daughter. Between my father's and the Sandeman connections, there would be enough portrait commissions for her to relocate to London not far from Dare and Philip. She had just finished a portrait of Sir Winston Churchill for Bristol University, which was unveiled on November 28, 1947. Although Churchill and Edie never met – she had painted him from photographs – he wrote her that he was very pleased by her work.

When Dare went back to England in 1948, Philip was not at the airport to meet her. She checked into London's Savoy Hotel and waited four days before he finally showed up. As my father recalled it,

> *He appeared on the fourth day. He took her for meals for some three days and was, according to Dare, extremely polite. Finally it came out. He was sleeping with the wife of the man in whose house he was living…Her name, I swear, was Pussy. Pussy told Philip he could not marry Dare. Dare agreed.*
>
> *There was a short period of time when Philip couldn't make up his mind what to do. For some*

Edie, always elegant and with an artist's eye for detail, helped Dare plan her ill-fated wedding to Philip Sandeman.

reason, Blaine sided with Philip and made it clear to Dare that he felt she was to blame for the mess.

Blaine gave Dare the telegram Philip sent him explaining why he broke off the engagement. Philip had written that he could not go through with the marriage because, "I need a real woman." The illusion of their courtly love was shattered with Philip's words.

Dare, like the water sprite Undine in her childhood book, was rejected by her knight for not being a flesh and blood woman.

Philip could not live with Dare's pre-marital avoidance of a physical relationship, but why did he brand Dare as not being "real?" Dare kept the telegram in her desk until her death. Thirty years later, she wrote a children's book titled *Make Me Real.*

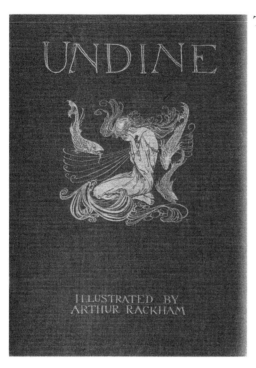

The rejected water sprite Undine.

Dare's self-portrait as a water nymph.

15

In 1949, *Town & Country* magazine hired Edie to take photographs of Dare modeling Spring fashions in an article titled "Silks Resurgent." The editors may have thought it an interesting twist to have a famous portraitist switch to photography, but it was an artistic medium that Edie could not master. For some reason, her shots were almost always out of focus.

Dare quickly learned that she had to set up the camera for her mother and then step back into frame as the model. They would work in tandem like that for the rest of Edie's life. When Edie was not around, Dare used the camera's timer to take her self-portraits.

Dare described her photographic technique in an interview. "I always could draw, and I knew about light and composition from watching mother. In a sense, photography used all the things I already knew."

SILKS RESURGENT

Rose Barrack's navy shantung afternoon dress symbolizes the new accent on silk. It has a gored skirt, an engaging roll collar, is worn with Viola Weinberger's pink shantung gloves. The Blum Store, Philadelphia; Wm. H. Block, Indianapolis; Boston Store, Milwaukee

→

Harvey Berin stresses back interest in a dress of Remond-Holland black-and-gray-striped tissue taffeta. At DePinna; Bonwit Teller, Philadelphia; B. Siegel, Detroit. Even cosmetics, as Rubinstein's Silk Tone Foundation and Silk Screen Powder prove, are in the silken swing

←

Ombré-striped silk taffeta in gray, black, and white makes Elfreda's V-necked, jewel-buttoned dress. At Jay Thorpe; Henry Harris, Cincinnati; Maison Mendessolle, San Francisco. Dull-white satin gloves by Viola Weinberger add a final filip to the all-silk, all-spring-of-49 picture

Edie's reflection can be seen in the mirror as she takes Dare's photograph in her Cleveland apartment.

Dare sewed elaborate costumes for her personal photographs. Her props came from Edie's collection of antiques – a quill pen, painted fan, glass decanter, Staffordshire pottery and…is it a menorah or candelabra? She often created moments of mystery that echoed classical paintings. Paused in her letter writing, Dare looks at the camera as if she were a subject of Vermeer.

Dare photographed me with my mother in the Spring of 1949. Eugenia did not like having her photo taken by Dare, and often looked annoyed and badly dressed in Dare's prints, but this was an uncharacteristically sanguine afternoon for her. Dare had made my mother a dress in sheer dotted Swiss fabric for the shoot, and Eugenia seemed at ease with herself and her child. The best photograph in the sequence has me in her arms, although Eugenia is leaning away from me and I am bending toward Dare. The photos Dare took of me with my father always seemed more natural.

Dare photographed her goddaughter Brook Ashley with her mother Eugenia and father Don.

Dorothy Tivis was a statuesque model who started her own agency called Figureheads. Dare joined the agency in 1949 and created her own modeling card.

Dare and Dorothy became close friends, and it was not long before Dorothy began dating Dare's brother.

Blaine and Dorothy made a gorgeous couple. Dorothy was almost six feet tall and had an icy-blonde beauty that could not photograph badly. She did not seem fond of children and didn't understand Blaine's intuitive rapport with them. There was an undercurrent of jealousy when she was with Dare and Blaine that I could not have articulated as a child. Now I can see that Dorothy resented Dare and Blaine's closeness. The siblings had their own manner of speaking to each other in clipped, almost British sentences that I thought was hilarious, but clearly left Dorothy unamused as did the humorously captioned photographs that Blaine and Dare exchanged.

Dorothy spent eight years hoping Blaine would marry her, although she must have known that he could never subscribe to that domestic convention.

The cigarette was a prop from a modeling shoot. Unlike her mother and brother, Dare never smoked.

Dare's friend Dorothy Tivis and Blaine were long-time lovers.

61

Dare posing on her brother Blaine's island in upstate New York. The dress, which Dare designed and sewed, seems as timeless as the setting although the self-portrait was taken in the 1940s.

Dare had become friends with a society couple, Fenimore Cooper Marsh and his wife, Mary. Cooper Marsh – often referred to as "The Castor Oil Heir" – had asked Dare to teach him photography techniques. Dare said she was happy to do so, and Marsh began spending time in her tiny darkroom at the Hotel Bristol.

Whatever Marsh's ulterior motives might have been – and it's difficult to imagine he did not have some – Dare truly believed he came to her hotel room to learn how to develop photographs.

Mary Amelia Marsh saw an opportunity to accuse her husband of adultery – one of the few grounds for divorce – and walk away with a good bit of Cooper Marsh's fortune. If she had to destroy Dare's reputation in the process, it would be an insignificant mote of collateral damage.

The saga unspooled like a 1949 film noir. Dare, the blameless victim, could have been cast by Hitchcock as the cool, blonde heroine. Mary Marsh, swathed in fur, played the duplicitous, outraged wife with an affected, clipped pattern of speech while her husband, Cooper, blustered his innocence behind his bow tie. Mary Marsh's private detective, a six-foot-three lug named Richard Shorten, had difficulty understanding multi-syllable words, and became tongue-tied when he struggled to spin his falsehoods before a judge. Shorten's assistant, Ruth Mason, had previously worked as a psychic researcher for the magician Harry Houdini and was well-versed in deception.

Cooper Marsh, the Castor Oil heir, whose wife Mary brought Dare into a 1949 courtroom scandal.

My father, Don, elegant in his three-piece suits, spoke with a precisely-enunciated and somewhat unplaceable accent that drew from both Southern and British sources. His law partner, Nahum Bernstein, a tall, handsome baritone who occasionally taught hand-to-hand combat, was both eloquent and intense in a courtroom. Kermit Jaediker, a hard-boiled reporter for the New York *Daily News*, wrote cheap crime novels – *Tall Dark and Dead* being one of his titles – when he wasn't coming up with snappy headlines like "Raiding Wife Seeks To Ditch Castor King" for his newspaper. There was even an off-camera role for Dr. Mortimer Rogers, a gynecologist to many of Broadway's actresses and the brother of composer Richard Rogers. As a bit of irony, Richard Rogers and Oscar Hammerstein's song "Some Enchanted Evening" from their recent Broadway hit *South Pacific* played as background music to Dare's humiliation.

On May 26, 1949, with the newly-released cast album of *South Pacific* on her record player, Dare opened the door to her room at the Bristol to find Mary Marsh, Mrs. Marsh's two brothers and private detective Shorten. Dare told my father, whom she called immediately to represent her, that they yelled at Cooper Marsh, who was standing behind her, "Now we've caught you!"

The tabloids went wild after Mary Marsh named Dare as correspondent in her affidavit against her husband. On July 7, 1949 the New York *Journal-American*'s headline read: "Wife Says Heir Wore Smile, Girl A Negligee." And the paper's article, based on Mary Marsh's affidavit, continued to paint the encounter at Dare's door:

> *Knock, knock.*
>
> *And the door opened at room 830 of the Hotel Bristol…and there inside, "In the process of getting dressed" and "wearing a sickly smile" was the Social Registerite Cooper Marsh.*
>
> *And with him in a "yellow negligee" and a "pair of bedroom slippers," the affidavit continued, was "a female person by the name of Dare Wright."*

An affidavit by her brother, Henri, says he heard "laughing and giggling" in the room prior to the raid, and on entering "my brother-in-law stood with a sickly smile and made no attempt to deny the obvious implication of the situation."

Another affidavit by [Private Detective] Shorten says he peeked through a crack in the transom and saw the lights go on and off several times during a couple of hours' wait before the raid.

The same paper followed up the next day with a story titled, "At Least They Agree She Wore Something!"

Just what was the lady wearing, gentlemen?

Was she wearing something you could see through, just dandy for the boudoir but scarcely suitable for the rush hour on the East Side IRT?

Or was she wearing something you could NOT see through, suitable for street, bistro, a stroll in the park?

This question became the crux today in the divorce battle between the socially prominent Fenimore Cooper Marsh, castor oil tycoon, and the Social Registerite wife, Mary Amelia Veit Marsh.

The lady in question, of course, is Miss Dare Wright, a professional photographer of the Hotel Bristol, 129 W. 48th St.

Yesterday, asking $1,000 a week alimony, Mrs. Marsh described a raid on Miss Wright's suite the night of May 26. Mrs. Marsh said she found her husband there "in the process of getting dressed" and Miss Wright in a yellow negligee

and bedroom slippers.

Today Marsh and Miss Wright entered vigorous denials.

"As a matter of fact," said Miss Wright, "I was dressed in a yellow silk shirtwaist and quilted cotton skirt of red and yellow of the kind customarily worn in the street, public places or at home."

"Mr. Marsh was fully clothed except that he had his jacket off, which as his wife and friends know, is a fetish with him."

Mrs. Marsh entered a counter affidavit.

"At the time we entered the room", she insisted, "Miss Wright was wearing a light-yellow negligee of diaphanous material and flowing cut not suitable or proper for the street or even as a hostess when receiving."

It was a miserable summer for Dare hiding out in her steamy hotel room. The outside temperatures reached over 100 degrees, as the New York *Daily News* and the *Daily Mirror* joined the *Journal-American* in following the juicy story.

The New York papers were filled with salacious headlines:

JURY TOLD OF MODEL AND DENTED BED

WIFE TO CHARGE HOCUS-FOCUS IN THE DARK-ROOM

WIFE SAYS HEIR WORE A SMILE, GIRL A NEGLIGEE

Dare in the Hotel Bristol hallway.

Blue Book Wife Tells of Raid On Heir and 'Other Woman'

When Mary-Amelie Veit was married Nov. 7, 1940, in St. James Episcopal Church to Fenimore Cooper Marsh, the whole Blue Book was out to witness the union of the daughter of Russell Charles Veit, now ECA attache at the U. S. Embassy in Paris, with the young heir of several proud American names and fortunes.

But a much smaller and less elegant company was present, the 1940 bride yesterday told Supreme Court, when she led a raid last May 26 on Room 830 of the Hotel Bristol, 129 W. 48th St., and allegedly found Fenimore with "a female person" identified as Dare Wright.

The former Junior Leaguer, who says she left her husband flat in the family duplex, 737 Park Ave., on the day of the raid, demands $1,000 weekly alimony and backs the demand with 7-figure estimates of Marsh's fortune, in hand and to come.

He is, she says, sole heir of Kendall Marsh of New York and Darien, Conn., who died in 1918, leaving an estate valued at $3,500,000 to $5,000,000, in addition to a $175,000 collection of family jewels.

She estimates her husband's current income at $250,000 a year

Dare Wright's self-portrait in the Hotel Bristol, August 1949.

Fenimore Cooper Marsh and Mary-Amelie Veit as they appeared following their marriage

from his inherited holdings and his job as president of the Baker Castor Oil Co., 120 Broadway.

Detailing the raid, Mrs. Marsh avers:

"In the company of my brothers, Henri Charles and Richard R. Veit, and private detective Charles Shorten, we knocked on the door and were admitted by this female person.

"The said Dare Wright was in a yellow negligee and bedroom slippers. My husband, who was hastily dressing, stood there with a sickly smile on his face and made no attempt to deny the obvious implications of the situation."

New York *Daily Mirror*, July 8, 1949

My father and his law partner, Nahum Bernstein, prepared Dare's affidavit to Supreme Court Justice James McNally. Dare referred to herself as a "children's photographer" to distance herself from the possibly sleazy implications of being a model, although I was the only child Dare was photographing at the time.

Dare's affidavit countered Mary Marsh's charges of impropriety both in action and dress. She was quoted in the New York *Daily Mirror* on July 9, 1949 that asked, "How Flimsy Is Organdie?"

> *Hurt by Mrs. Marsh's charges, Miss Wright declared: "They are false and vicious, as Mrs. Marsh must have observed that my garment was not a transparent yellow negligee, but a yellow silk shirtwaist with a quilted cotton skirt of red and yellow pattern—an ensemble I have often worn on the street."*

Cooper Marsh also took exception to his wife's testimony:

I deny misconduct with Miss Wright at any time, anywhere. Miss Wright and her mother, Mrs. Edith Stevenson Wright, are old friends of mine and we share an interest in photography. Miss Wright, being a professional specialist in child portraiture. I have been privileged to help Miss Wright at times in her dark room work.

My wife fails to mention that she knew Miss Wright socially, through me, having entertained her and been entertained in return.

That was true. Dare and Edie had welcomed both of the Marshes to their cocktail parties and Dare often played badminton with them. Mary Marsh's cruel perjury was baffling to Dare.

Judge McNally ruled that Mrs. Marsh had probable grounds for a divorce and awarded her $3,000 a month alimony until the case went to court in December. My father and Nahum Bernstein were ready to take on Mary Marsh when the case went to trial.

New York *Daily Mirror*

MRS. MARY VEIT MARSH
"Private eye" backs up her charges against socialite mate.
(Mirror Photo)

Dare waiting for the Cooper Marsh trial to begin.

Divorce Jury to Study What 'Developed' in Dark-Room

The question—What were wealthy socialite Fenimore Cooper Marsh and lady photographer Dare Wright doing in the dark-room when the light went out?—will be answered by the jury selected yesterday before Supreme Court Justice O'Brien to hear Mrs. Mary-Amelie Veit Marsh's suit for divorce.

SUING FOR DIVORCE

MRS. MARY MARSH

The 11 men and one woman will hear Mrs. Marsh's story of what she found when she raided Miss Wright's suite in the Hotel Bristol, 129 W. 48th St., on May 26.

Marsh, heir to millions as well as to the name of America's greatest weaver of Indian tales, denies all misconduct charges, and was present with lawyer to fight for custody of 7-year-old twin girls Mary and Laura, and against a demand for $52,000 annual alimony and a dower share of the fortune from which he derives an income of a quarter-million a year.

Miss Wright also was present, with lawyer, to fight for the fair name she has won as a photographer of children.

Marsh, whose 4-million-odd dollars are invested in the Baker Castor Oil Co., 120 Broadway, of which he is president, lives at 737 Park Ave. in the duplex his wife left following the alleged dark-room raid.

The New York *Daily Mirror*, December 8, 1949.

Dare in her room at the Hotel Bristol with Rockefeller Center in the background.

The NY *Daily Mirror* headlined its December 8, 1949 coverage, "Divorce Jury to Study What 'Developed' in Dark-Room."

> *The question – What were wealthy socialite Fenimore Cooper Marsh and lady photographer Dare Wright doing in the dark-room when the light went out – will be answered by the jury.*
>
> *Miss Wright…was present with lawyer[s] to fight for the fair name she has won as a photographer of children.*

The first witness was private detective Richard Shorten, who had been hired by Mary Marsh to lead the raid on Dare's hotel room. Shorten told the court he had taken room 829 at the Hotel Bristol to spy on Dare next door.

The *Journal-American* described his testimony as, "Peeping Sleuth Backs Mrs. Marsh."

> *Q. (by Stanley Sabel, attorney for Mrs. Marsh) How were the parties dressed?*
>
> *A. Miss Wright was wearing a yellow negligee and slippers. Mr. Marsh was dressed in his trousers, shoes, a white shirt, and was tying his bow tie.*
>
> *Q. How many beds were there in the room?*
>
> *A. A single bed.*
>
> *Q. How did the bed look?*
>
> *A. The covering on the bed was mussed up.*

Nahum Bernstein, an attorney hired by Miss Wright to defend her good name, asked if the model's negligee was diaphanous. The 6-foot 3-inch Shorten looked puzzled.

> *"Was it what?" he asked.*
>
> *"Diaphanous," Bernstein repeated.*
>
> *Shorten still hesitated.*
>
> *"Was it transparent then?" Bernstein inquired.*
>
> *"It could have been," the witness answered. "I didn't see through it though."*

The judge and jury struggled to suppress their laughter.

Nahum Bernstein turned to the judge, "Your honor, the plaintiff's case is so ridiculous that I must move for a dismissal, but you should know that we have medical proof that Miss Wright is a virgin."

The judge pronounced the trial over on December 9, awarding a yearly sum of $28,000 to Mary Marsh for alimony and child support. He noted that Mrs. Marsh should provide Dare with a written statement of apology and added, "I can tell you that the charges made here were without basis in fact. If [the Marshes] wish to secure a divorce or have any further proceedings, they will have to go elsewhere."

The NY *Daily Mirror* wrote on December 10, "A lady photographer yesterday got a clear negative after exposure to charges of misconduct with a castor oil tycoon." It also mentioned that two gynecologists (Dr. Mortimer Rogers being one of them) were prepared to verify Dare's virginity. Nahum Bernstein and my father had saved that shocking news for the maximum courtroom impact.

Tells of Candid Peep At Pair in Dark-Room

His story of how a private detective hung perilously out of a bathroom window of the Hotel Bristol, 129 W. 48th St., trying to spy on the intimate doings of petite Miss Dare Wright, in room 830 on the floor below, was related yesterday to Justice O'Brien and a Supreme Court jury by Richard Shorten, chief witness for Mrs. Mary Veit Marsh, ex-Junior Leaguer who is suing Fenimore Cooper Marsh, castor oil tycoon, for divorce.

What he said he saw leaves it up to the jury to decide what Marsh and Miss Wright were up to when the lights went out for an hour in the lady's bedroom about midnight May 13 last. Shorten said:

Fenimore Cooper Marsh

"Marsh entered Miss Wright's room at about 8:30. The lights went off at 11:30 p.m. and came on again an hour later. Ten minutes later, he left."

It was indicated the defense will contend the pair were engrossed in dark-room photographic experiments during that hour. Miss Wright is a professional photographer, and Marsh devotes a small part of his reputed $1,000,000 fortune to camera and flash-bulb as a hobby.

Shorten was more specific in further testimony about a raid staged by himself. Mrs. Marsh and her two brothers on May 26, when they crashed Miss Wright's boudoir and found her and Marsh in less than street attire. He said:

"Miss Wright was wearing a yellow negligee and slippers and Marsh was in trousers and shirt and was tying his bow tie. There was a single bed in the room and its coverlet was rumpled."

Attorneys for both Marsh and iss Wright, who is defending r good name, attempted, on oss-examination, to show that e attire of the pair was seasonnot wicked, May 26 being a rm day.

The battling Marshes, both of om seek custody of twin sev-·year-old daughters Mary and ura, are socially prominent. rsh is president of the Baker stor Oil Co. He lives at 737 rk Ave., apart from his suing

FIGHTS "RIVAL" LABEL.

Child-photographer Dare Wright in Supreme Court yesterday.

(Mirror Photo)

wife, who has taken quarters with the children in the Hotel Sulgrave, 60 E. 67th St.

The trial will continue today.

The New York *Daily Mirror,* December 9, 1949.

Peeper Says His Eyes Popped

L. to r., Mrs. Mary Amelie Marsh, Fenimore Cooper Marsh and Dare Wright at Supreme Court yesterday.

By DICK CORNISH

A patch of clear glass one-sixteenth of an inch wide is plenty big enough for a private eye to peep through, Richard Shorten, head of the Shorten Bureau of Investigation, testified yesterday in Supreme Court.

New York *Daily News*, December 9, 1949.

He was the principal witness in the divorce trial of Mrs. Mary Amelie Marsh, socialite wife of Fenimore Cooper Marsh, the castor oil heir, who alleges that her husband and Dare Wright, a pert, blonde model, committed adultery in Room 830 of the Hotel Bristol the evening of last May 16.

Shorten and Mrs. Marsh led a raid on the room that night and found the model in a yellow negligee and Marsh, in shirt and trousers, tying his bow tie.

He Climbed to Peep.

Just before they went in, Shorten told Justice Kenneth O'Brien and a jury of 11 men and one woman, he got on a table and peeped into the room. Blue paper covered the transom, he declared, except for that one-sixteenth of an inch. What he saw convinced him Mrs. Marsh had a case.

Nahum Bernstein, an attorney retained by Miss Wright to defend her good name, asked if the model's negligee was diaphanous.

The 6-foot-3-inch Shorten looked puzzled.

"Was it what?" he asked.

"Diaphanous" Bernstein repeated.

Shorten still hestitated. "Was it transparent then?" Bernstein inquired.

"It could have been," the witness answered. "I didn't see through it, though."

The trial will continue today, when Miss Wright may take the stand.

Marsh Divorce Triangle Squared

Quick as the bang of a judge's gavel, the very social Mrs. Mary Amelie Marsh suddenly withdrew her divorce suit against cast or oil heir Fenimore Cooper Marsh in Supreme Court yesterday.

Ater a brief huddle among counsel, it was announced that Marsh had settled for $28,000 a year alimony for the missus and their two children, and Mrs. Marsh expressed regrets she had ever started the suit.

Model Gets Apology

She was particularly apologetic to Dare Wright, blonde model with whom she had accused Marsh of committing adultery in the Hotel Bristol on a balmy night last May.

"I wish to withdraw all charges against Miss Dare Wright made in my divorce proceedings," Mrs. Marsh told the court. "I sincerely regret that Miss Wright has been involved in this suit."

Judge Tickled.

The sudden end of the suit, which a jury of 11 men and one woman had been hearing for a week, pleased Justice Kenneth O'Brien no end.

"I am happy," he told the jury, "to announce that this litigation has been settled. It has been most unfortunate that such a suit and its charges had to be brought by these very nice people. The proceedings are terminated chiefly for the sake of the children."

He said Mrs. Marsh would "sign a statement of apology to Miss Wright and Miss Wright in turn will accord her a release."

(NEWS foto by George Mattson)
Mrs. Mary Amelie Marsh as she arrived in court yesterday.

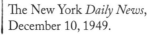

The New York *Daily News*, December 10, 1949.

(NEWS foto by George Mattson)
Dare Wright arrives in court to receive Mrs. Marsh's apology.

Clear Photographer As
Divorce Suit Is Settled

A lady photographer yesterday got a clear negative after exposure to charges of misconduct with a castor oil tycoon. This development came when Mrs. Mary Veit Marsh, suing Fenimore Cooper Marsh for divorce, reached a settlement with her husband and withdrew her charge that he and Miss Dare Wright had been intimate at Room 803 in the Hotel Bristol while supposedly engaged in photographic activities.

Supreme Court Justice O'Brien called counsel for both parties into his chambers after hearing testimony by Richard Shorter, a private detective, two investigators, and Mrs. Marsh's two brothers. Later, O'Brien announced the settlement.

The testimony centered on Miss Wright's attire at the time of the raid. Ruth Mason, one of the raiding party, one-time psychic researcher for the late Harry Houdini, hinted she had seen more spiritual manifestations than the scene in the hotel room when the party entered.

After O'Brien announced the settlement, Stanley Sabel, attorney for Mrs. Marsh, read a statement expressing regret by his client that Miss Wright had been involved.

As part of the agreement, Miss Wright was to be given a letter from Mrs. Marsh clearing her of any allegations of misconduct.

O'Brien told the jury the charges were without foundation in his opinion, and said the settlement includes $28,000 yearly as alimony for Mrs. Marsh and support of their twin daughters.

Miss Wright's attorney said after the settlement that he had subpoenaed two gynecologists who were prepared to testify his client was a virgin.

MRS. MARY V. MARSH
Offers her apologies and receives a $28,000 settlement.

... Wright

The New York *Daily Mirror,*
December 10, 1949.

Dare did not blame Cooper Marsh for the humiliation his wife had inflicted on her, and continued to have contact with him after the trial.

Cooper Marsh proposed to Dare when he finally divorced.

Her attorney, Nahum Bernstein, would also ask Dare to marry him after he became a widower. That infuriated another colleague of my father who confessed that he too, although married, was in love with Dare.

She declined the offers.

Dare took a series of ethereal self-portraits at the Bristol during the summer of 1950. Her room, where Mary Marsh had made the dark accusations a year earlier, seemed suffused in lightness. This time Dare really did wear a negligee.

16

Dare was ready to leave the sordid memories in the Hotel Bristol behind her. While Dare looked for her first apartment, Edie planned to paint my portrait as a thank you gift to my father for defending Dare in the trial. Dare made me a green plaid dress with a white apron and took my photograph in it so Edie could begin her preliminary sketches. I was only three, and although I tried to cooperate, it was impossible to stand still long enough for Edie to do her work. The dress was packed away for almost a year until I grew less fidgety.

Brook attempting to hold still so Edie could paint her portrait in 1950. It would take another year before she learned a modicum of self-control.

At the end of the summer of 1950, Dare and Blaine took a road trip through the Florida Keys along with family friend Susan Valliant. They caught fish in the Keys, camped on the beaches and stayed in small cottages where Blaine's dog would be welcomed.

EVERGLADES CITY

Both Dare and Edie found new homes in 1950. Dare left the Hotel Bristol for a studio apartment in a former private townhouse at 29 W. 58 Street. It was just off Fifth Avenue, right around the corner from the Plaza Hotel, and the perfect perch for a creative spirit in an era when artists and "career girls" could still afford to live a block away from Tiffany's. The five-story building was faced with white limestone block, and Dare's apartment at the back of the second floor had fourteen-foot ceilings and a tiny kitchen area with a miniscule refrigerator and stove top, but no actual stove. This had been the formal living room before the home was broken up into apartments and the ground floor leased to Madame Louise's Dry Cleaners. Quite astonishingly, Dare's large windows opened to a private terrace as large as the gardens in the neighboring town-homes.

The apartment was neglected and dirty but filled with potential. Dare set about scrubbing the floors and balancing on a ladder with a paint roller. She brought lumber home in taxis, with cigar-chomping cabbies more than willing to carry the boards up the stairs for her, and built bookcases in one corner with space for a daybed to roll half-way under them. Edie came from Cleveland to help sew quilted curtains, and they used the excess fabric to make themselves robes. Dare often used quilting for her dresses and skirts – just like the one she was wearing during the Cooper Marsh raid at The Bristol.

Edie's new flat was the penthouse of Cleveland's Hanna Building where she could combine her work studio with living quarters. She sent Dare her childhood books and the Lenci doll named Edith.

As soon as the apartment was presentable, Dare and Edie gave a cocktail party to unveil the transformation. I was always the only child in attendance and positioned myself on a floor pillow next to the coffee table and as close to the potato chips as possible.

Dare's Edith doll surveying her new home.

Dare moved to 29 West 58th Street in 1950 doing the painting and carpentry herself.

Dare's terrace at her new apartment was an oasis of privacy and a perfect spot for her to photograph a variety of subjects ranging from fashion models to stuffed teddy bears. Central Park was only a block away.

Dare and Edie preparing for company.

17

Dare agreed to Dorothy Tivis' suggestion that she pose for an article in the October 1950 issue of *Esquire* magazine. "Women in Advertising" showed the ways beautiful women were used to sell products. Dare photographed herself in her new apartment in a series of seductive, yet anonymous poses. No one else saw the front of her undraped torso or was likely to identify her from the back. The photo was deliberately uncredited.

Dorothy also convinced Dare to pose for a Maidenform bra ad. Wearing a skirt, hat and gloves, there was not all that much flesh on display. She had worn much less posing in an abandoned military bunker on Ocracoke.

A 1950 self-portrait shot for *Esquire* magazine.

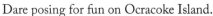

Dare posing for fun on Ocracoke Island.

Dare in a Maidenform bra fantasy ad campaign.

I was deemed mature enough to stand for my portrait in 1951, and the plaid wool dress was brought out again. It was now too tight and quite itchy, but I would never have distressed Dare or Edie by telling them that.

Edie was infinitely patient with a squirmy four-year-old. I adored that she spoke to me as if I were an adult. She bent down to my level with her face exceptionally close and her cigarette holder held high, whispered how she wanted me to hold a position and then returned to her easel.

Brook posing for her portrait in Dare's apartment as Edie adjusts her stance.

Edie's portrait of Brook was shown on a television interview. Both Brook and that entertainment medium were quite young.

Dare and Edie had become friends with the celebrity nutritionist Gayelord Hauser through my godmother Tallulah Bankhead. Tallulah was so fond of Hauser that she named her parakeet after him. It was not until the parakeet, Gayelord, laid an egg that anyone realized he was actually a she.

Edie's portrait of her close friend, Gayelord Hauser. Hauser, a celebrity nutritionist, was Greta Garbo's protector. He tried, without any success, to convince Brook's godmother Tallulah Bankhead to follow a diet of seeds and molasses. She named her parakeet in his honor.

Hauser was Greta Garbo's great friend and confident and wanted Edie to paint Garbo's portrait as she had done his. He brought Garbo to Dare's apartment when my portrait was almost finished, and Garbo fell in love with it. The woman who was famous for her silence declared, "I just want to pat that little bottom."

Garbo agreed to have Edie paint her portrait at Dare's apartment. The reclusive actress lived just around the corner and liked having Dare around to talk to while Edie worked. Dare collaborated with her mother for many of the brush strokes, and both of them signed the finished painting.

Greta Garbo as painted by both
Edie and Dare.

On June 18, 1951 Squadron Leader Philip Sandeman's plane collided with another RAF aircraft killing both pilots during an air show. Philip had told his mother a few weeks earlier that he had made a mess of his life and would try to put things right. Now he was gone in his mid-thirties. Dare's suitor would never grow old, never again disappoint, and never challenge her story that he had died in the war.

Philip Sandeman

Alas, how easily things go wrong!
A sigh too much, or a kiss too long,
And there follows a mist and a weeping rain,
And life is never the same again.

From Dare's childhood book, *A Faerie Romance.*

Dare continued to model for major fashion magazines, including a 1951 cover of *Cosmopolitan*, but she was getting close to the point where she could make her living as a photographer and not have to put herself on public display. Within a year after Philip's death, Dare was established as a regular photographer for *Good Housekeeping*'s columns and articles. The magazine even did a feature on Dare's own apartment renovations with the text, "If you simply like what you like, regardless of the country or period that inspired it, you can make your personal preferences your personal point of departure. Here, the one-room apartment of a young photographer who has done just that – completely ignored rules and, with her own very catholic taste as a guide, created a charming, individual home."

HEARST'S INTERNATIONAL COMBINED WITH

COSMOPOLITAN

May, 1951 · 35¢
CANADA · 40 CENTS

The fantastic story of Gayelord Hauser

2 Stunning Short Novels Complete

Dare posing in her living room next to Philip Sandeman's portrait. She painted the parquet floors in black and white squares.

You Like the Look of Old with New

If you simply like what you like, regardless of the country or period that inspired it, you can make your personal preferences your decorating point of departure. Here, the one-room apartment of a young photographer who has done just that—completely ignored rules and, with her own very catholic taste as a guide, created a charming, individual home.

Homemade draperies of quilted satin give a Victorian air to the tall bay window (see "after," above), which encloses a dining alcove. (See "before," right.) The little stools that slide under the trestle table are actually luggage racks with cushions, which match the rug. The radiators have been enclosed, and the jalousie blinds painted dark green to match the dark-green sateen that covers the little couch.

Left: The living area is a fascinating combination of Victorian woodwork, conventional couch, and very modern coffee table. The lamp tables were cut out with a jig saw. Behind the couch is a screen, illustrated by its photographer owner; it rolls up like a window shade to give various backgrounds for photographic sittings. The white satin is repeated in quilted wall hangings.

Accessories from colonial America and half a dozen European countries mingle harmoniously with a Victorian mantel (see "before," opposit, bottom) and many modern pieces. The sofa bed rolls under storage cupboard, becomes inconspicious owing to unorthodox furniture arrangement.

18

Life magazine commissioned Dare to photograph and write an article that featured me titled, "The Life of a New York Four-Year-Old." It was never published, but I was thrilled to have Dare follow me around nursery school and visit the doll houses in the Museum of The City of New York.

My report card mentioned that I had a difficult time when I realized other children were not like adults. The school had a point. The four years I'd spent learning the nuances of mature conversation with Dare and Tallulah had not prepared me to deal with a group of forty-inch-high peers.

I had an extracurricular agenda when Nana picked me up from nursery school on December 3, 1951. Waving a painting of a kangaroo I'd finished that morning, I told Nana that I needed help getting Dare a birthday cake to go with it. My parents had mentioned Dare was having a birthday, and I intended to have a celebration.

Neither of my parents was home when Nana and I stopped by to phone Dare. Nana didn't like telephones any more than steam irons, but she wasn't going to show up unannounced. She looked up Dare's number PLaza 3-9516 in the directory and began the slow process of dialing the rotary phone. New York City's telephone exchanges were divided geographically, and the PLaza territory covered the area around that exclusive hotel. Although I had learned to recite my own phone number RHinelander 4-7553 in case I got lost and had to give it to a policeman, I couldn't have dialed it myself and had no idea that it identified me as living in the German neighborhood called Yorkville.

Nana handed the receiver to me when Dare picked up, and she sounded delighted when I told her I was coming over with a cake and a kangaroo.

After swiping a washcloth over my dirty knees, Nana and I set off on the thirty-plus block journey to Dare's apartment. I held Nana's hand quite happily,

Dare's photos of Brook at her nursery school captured her annoyance at a child interrupting her favorite story of *Ambrose Kangaroo* as well as a little boy's refusal to be her dance partner.

even though it was always a bit sticky from the adhesive tape she wrapped around the fissures in her fingers. Nana used a strong powder made with lye to wash dishes, in spite of it ravaging her hands.

Rosenblatt's Candy store was only three doors down from my apartment building, and I asked Nana to make a quick stop there. The Rosenblatts spoke Yiddish rather than formal German, and Mrs. Rosenblatt wore fingerless, dark wool gloves to pick the perfect candy pieces from the case. She slipped wax milk bottles, little paper rolls stuck with colored sugar pellets and red licorice coins into my paper bag as extras while Mr. Rosenblatt raised a dubious eyebrow. I knew he was just pretending to be grumpy. Dare's birthday adventure was beginning on a promisingly sweet note.

Nana chose the next stop as we walked up York Avenue. Ihde's Honey store was the tiniest shop I'd ever seen. It was no wider than a hallway, which was what it probably had been before the building was partitioned. Mr. Ihde lived in New Jersey, where he kept a hive of bees that produced the honey for the store's products. At the back of his shop was an ancient lozenge machine which he poured heated honey into to make the healthful candies.

Each one came out with a sharp edge that could almost cut your tongue but made a nice contrast to the sweetness of the lozenge. Mr. Ihde's hands were very old, very thin and almost velvety from the honey balm cream he sold in his miniscule shop. Nana bought a jar of his clover honey, and I muttered a muffled *danke* when he slipped a knife-edged lozenge into my mouth.

Crossing York Avenue at a dangerous hill where both Nana and my mother would later be hit by cars, Nana and I made it to the cake shop on Lexington Avenue. Nana spoke German in our neighborhood Yorkville stores, and the older lady at Bauer's Bakery, whose braids were wrapped on top of her head, told Nana that I was a *liebchen* as she gave me a *heidesand* shortbread cookie.

I licked the pearl sugar off my fingers and curtseyed a "thank you" as Nana and I moved down to the cake display. Originally disappointed that they didn't have one with a cowgirl decoration, I noticed a cake in the back of the case topped with garlands of marzipan flowers and realized it was a much-tastier option. I loved marzipan, and with any luck Dare would offer me several of the pink roses.

The braided lady slipped the cake into a white box and tied it with thin twine from a large spool near the cash register. Nana asked her to fill another box with *schnecken* and *linzertorte* as we had one more neighborhood detour to make before heading downtown to Dare's.

Dare and Brook spent an afternoon at the Museum of the City of New York. The "Don't Touch!" rule was suspended for the photo session.

Nana often brought me over to her friends' apartments. Like Nana, each of these elderly German women had lost a fiancé in the First World War, where a generation of young men had been obliterated. Without any chance for a traditional *Küche, Kinder, Kirche* lifestyle, they found their way to New York City's German neighborhood and a comforting cohort of women in similar circumstances. Their elegantly soft hands would unbutton my coat and untie my wool hat before pouring raspberry syrup and seltzer into Bohemian glass tumblers for me.

Miss Siebler was the eldest of the group, and Nana led me up the three flights of stairs to her friend's tiny apartment as she balanced the bakery boxes from Bauer's, my rolled-up painting of the kangaroo and her purse containing Mr. Ihde's jar of honey. Nana was well under five feet tall, but Miss Siebler was even more elfin. I was fascinated by her arthritic knuckles and rubbed my thumb in circles over them as she squeezed my hands in welcome. After the cookies were shared and the sugared seltzer was buzzing up my brain stem, Nana and I bid Miss Siebler *auf wiedersehen* and we headed westward towards Central Park and caught the downtown Fifth Avenue bus.

The bus halted in front of Bergdorf Goodman's, and Nana grabbed my arm as I jumped off the back exit into a fog of idling exhaust. Half a block and a bit of jaywalking finally got us in front of 29

West 58th Street. A puff of chemical fumes wafted into Dare's lobby from Mme. Louise's French Dry Cleaning on the ground floor of her building. "It's me, it's me!" I shouted up to the intercom as Dare buzzed us in and I bounced up the stairs to the welcoming scent of perfume and polished wood.

Dare loved my kangaroo picture and pinned it to a folding screen in her entryway so we could stand back and admire the artwork with proper deference. Neither she or Nana mentioned that the kangaroo looked more like a beagle than a marsupial, and Dare complimented me for adding a jaunty beret to the creature's head.

Although Dare said that I could have as many of the cake roses as I wanted, I found that I couldn't eat more than two. The second flower might even have been pushing it. It was dark by then, and Dare most likely had a dinner date, but I couldn't tell time and would happily have segued into spending the night. Nana, aware of both time and distance, got me up and to the door before I started napping. She left the jar of Mr. Ihde's honey on a side table as a birthday gift. Dare bent down and cupped my face in her hands. "No one," she said quietly, "...has ever given me a kangaroo. You made this a perfect birthday." It seemed quite perfect to me as well, and I fell asleep against Nana as the bus headed uptown.

19

My other godmother, Tallulah Bankhead, owned a large country home called "Windows" in Bedford Village, New York, and Dare and I often spent weekends with her in the early 1950s.

Tallulah and my mother were bonded by their experience playing mother and daughter in *The Little Foxes*. They even looked somewhat alike, but there was a vulnerability to both Tallulah and Dare that Eugenia lacked.

Tallulah was a force of nature who blew, rather than stepped, into a room. You half-expected to see wet leaves plastered to the walls in her wake. She would shrug the mink coat off her shoulders without slowing her pace, confident that there would be someone there to catch it.

Dare always made a quiet entrance, but it had the same effect as Tallulah; everyone stopped to watch.

I arrived at Tallulah's after the departure of her lion cub and ill-tempered monkey. As I was house broken and showed no inclination to bite or shred furniture, my presence was welcomed by both Tallulah and her staff.

There were several dogs at "Windows," but a tiny Maltese called Dolores was my favorite. A devious Hungarian puli whom Tallulah had named "Donnie" in honor of my father, liked to nip me when no one was looking. The dreadlocked nemesis once ate my stuffed rabbit and threw it up on my new shoes.

Dolores was always in Tallulah's arms or by her side, even if it meant diving for cover when Tallulah was engaged in amorous bedroom activities. In a television interview with Edward R. Murrow, Tallulah batted Dolores against her bosom like a powder puff when Murrow made a slip and almost revealed their affair on camera.

Tallulah, Dare and I were family. I knew this at four, although it was not the kind of family that I had in my small, tin doll house – a mother, father, little girl and baby brother. They didn't make the appropriate dolls to fill my godmothers' homes. A Tallulah doll would have needed batteries to move around as much as she did. She could talk, smoke, drink and hug me all at the same time. Dare's figure would have had angel wings to fold around me. The plastic mother in my doll house stood at the kitchen sink in a yellow dress and her hair was hard, sculpted curls. Tallulah's hair poured onto her shoulders like honey from a jar. I couldn't imagine her in the kitchen. Most of the time she wore pants or, in the summer, shorts and a halter top. Tallulah went to bed around the time I woke up in the morning so I could kiss her goodnight before my breakfast. She only wore a tiny cashmere baby sweater to sleep in and nothing on the bottom. No one made a fuss in Tallulah's house if people didn't feel like wearing clothes.

The doll house family had their clothing stuck on to them. I had to give the father a bath in his business suit. Tallulah's and Dare's homes made more sense.

Dare took many photos of Brook with her other godmother, the actress Tallulah Bankhead. The small creature with a gumdrop nose was Dolores.

One gray afternoon, after Tallulah had her late breakfast of Planter's Punch – she considered the fruit quite healthful – she brought out an issue of *Time* magazine with Senator Joseph McCarthy on the cover.

She tucked Dolores under her arm for safety and put a container of straight pins on the bedspread. Explaining the basics of voodoo, Tallulah looked me in the eye,

"Brook, swear to me you will never, ever use this except in the service of goodness, virtue, and the cause of democracy. Swear it now!"

I swore.

"Joe McCarthy is a...hmm...bad man. If people don't stand up to him, he is going to continue this insane devastation, and I am not going to see it happen."

Tallulah told me to take a pin and stick it in the Senator's face. She punctured the magazine next, and we alternated until the box was used up and McCarthy rendered barely recognizable. Afterwards, I ran off to play with my dolls.

Gayelord, the resident parakeet Tallulah had named for Gayelord Hauser, flew freely about the house. Any momentarily-abandoned champagne glass was fair game to the bird, who would duck his head in for a swift sip.

Gayelord was fond of the pompom on my wool hat, where he liked to hitch a ride. Tallulah, who was given to shucking off her clothing to jump naked into the pool, believed I should be similarly unfettered, and no one commented when I wandered about in July, wearing only a wool hat with a parakeet attached to it.

Brook practiced posing at Dare's apartment before their photo shoot at Tallulah's country home. Dare drew a circle of tiny feet on the paper to show Brook where to stand.

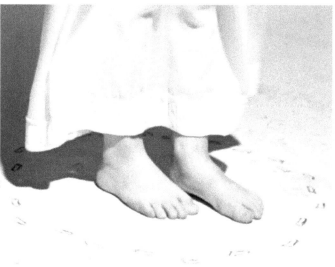

Dare captured Tallulah's maternal side in a series of photographs she took in 1951. She made an empire nightgown for me, and I practiced posing in Dare's apartment before we left for the country.

During the shooting, Dare managed to keep me from jumping about, but it was hard to keep my head still while listening to Tallulah's running monologue.

"Look, I have tiny feet too, Brook. Dear God, how do you get this doll's dress off?"

My time at Tallulah's meant a less conventional living arrangement than that of my peers. The nursery schoolteacher sent a note of concern: "Brook has spent the morning running around the schoolroom shouting 'champagne and cigarettes!'"

There was a simple explanation. Tallulah, Dare, my parents and I had been watching Milton Berle on our black and white television when the set died with a dispirited "Pfft." As we raced down the hallway to our neighbor's apartment, Tallulah realized we had left two important items behind. "Champagne and cigarettes!" she shouted over her shoulder and I appropriated the battle cry as my own.

Everyone smoked at Windows. Scorch marks cratered the carpets from dropped cigarettes. When I ran to her, Tallulah would drop to her knees, stretch one arm out to welcome me, and lift the other holding the cigarette protectively towards the sky.

It was the same technique Edie employed to keep her cigarettes from setting me aflame.

There were always other guests at Windows. Tallulah hated to be alone, and I was used to company wandering about the house on the weekends. The puppeteer Burr Tilstrom brought his Ollie The Dragon puppet from the popular *Kukla, Fran & Ollie* television show to visit, and we set Ollie a place at the table. With Ollie on his left hand, Burr and Tallulah discussed Willie Mays' chances for the upcoming baseball season while Ollie and I debated the culinary merits of spaghetti (Ollie thought he could twirl it up easily with his single tooth) versus macaroni (which got my vote because I could spear it with a fork). Ollie passed me a dinner roll in his dragon's mouth, and Dare offered him a celery stick. Tallulah's parakeet, Gayelord, flew in from the kitchen, circled the dining table and landed in the butter dish.

Windows eventually became too much for Tallulah to maintain. Guests arrived but did not always depart. The cook, Lucille, spent her time drinking with the guests, and often forgot to put dinner in the oven. One evening she staggered out of the

kitchen with a silver platter holding rolls of her stockings garnished with sprigs of parsley. When I squinted, they almost resembled roasted potatoes.

Tallulah bought a townhouse at 230 East 62nd Street within walking distance of Dare's apartment and gave up country living for good.

Smoke and dragons from Brook's childhood. Tallulah's lit cigarette appears perilously close to igniting her party dress and Edie inhales pensively. Ollie The Dragon of television fame was a frequent dinner guest.

Tallulah endured much of December 1951 in a New York courtroom, just as Dare had done two years earlier. My father once again became the gallant attorney, defending the honor of a beautiful friend and client. Tallulah's maid, a sour-faced woman with the impossible-to-spell name of Evyleen Cronin, had been altering her salary checks and faced thirty-two counts of grand larceny and forgery.

The fact that Tallulah was the accuser and not the defendant became obscured in the New York tabloids when Mrs. Cronin admitted to adding a few digits to the checks, but tearfully explained that she had done so to pay for Tallulah's drugs, liquor and sex partners.

"God damn it!" was Tallulah's outraged response. "No one has EVER accused me of paying for sex!"

The *New York Journal-American* called Tallulah "La Bankhead" and wrote of a moment when she asked my father to open the courtroom windows only to have an attendant promptly put them back down.

"I'll faint away," Tallulah said as she brought a dangling wrist to her forehead.

The etiolated Mrs. Cronin, her damp eyes enlarged by thick-lensed glasses, was described by her defense attorney as "frail and elderly" although she was only fifty-nine. When his earlier defense strategies seemed to falter, the attorney moved for a mistrial citing my father's on-camera comments that the defense charges concerning Miss Bankhead were "so despicable and absurd that they really need no answer." Mrs. Cronin's attorney added, in a final attempt to defame Tallulah, that she had been known to consort with "Negroes" including the late Harlem night club owner, Dickie Wells and Sidney Bechet, an elderly saxophonist.

Presiding Judge Harold Stevens, the first black judge elected to the New York General Sessions bench, delivered the jury's verdict of Evyleen Cronin's guilt to the crowded courtroom. Tallulah promptly asked the judge not to sentence Mrs. Cronin to serve any jail time. It was enough that she had won the case.

Although I was too young to read, I looked at the photos of my father and Tallulah in the five daily papers and could identify a romantic bond when I saw one. "Daddy and Tallulah are getting married," I announced to my family.

Brook was beginning to understand the complexities of human interaction. Love, friendship and casual couplings of various persuasions were often on display when she stayed with Tallulah. Her doll seems more easily shocked.

A news photographer caught Brook's father Don with Tallulah in an unguarded moment outside the courtroom. They were friends and lovers for three decades.

Don lifting Tallulah over a snowbank in front of the New York courthouse. The tabloid caption was "Legal Aid."

Tallulah and Don savor their courtroom victory. Tallulah, ever gracious, asked that the guilty party not be sentenced to jail.

20

My father and I often took Dare down to Maryland without my mother, Eugenia. There was a lightness around Dare that contrasted with the weight of Eugenia's self-absorption. Dare's energy lifted me into a magical place where I could see pirates burying their treasure in the little cove off the dock and naiads swimming underneath the swirls of seaweed.

Dare posing elegantly in the Maryland crabgrass.

Dare had read her childhood book *Undine* to me, and I was as captivated by Arthur Rackham's illustrations of the tragic water nymph as Dare had been at my age. My world at five was often mystifying. I would watch Tallulah perform a role on stage and then see her shape-shift into my godmother after the show. It wasn't a stretch for me to believe that Undine could live in both the real world and an enchanted one under the sea.

There was an afternoon in Maryland when the water sparkled with golden light. Dare and I took the rowboat out into the creek and I swam in the shallow water dazzled by the sun glinting off the surface and the promise of infinite possibilities.

Undine as a child in Arthur Rackham's illustration.

Brook as a young Undine.

Dare captured the innocence and joy of
Brook's childhood summers.

Brook and her father Don look into the distance from the barn. Dare's photo evokes a poster for a collective farm in the USSR or perhaps a kibbutz in Nir Yitzak.

Brook dressing up for a photo session with Dare.

What child could ask for anything more than a strawberry cone and Dare's company? Brook's strand of pearls and beaded purse might have been excessive accessorizing for a trip to the country store.

Each summer, Dare and Edie returned to Ocracoke Island. Sherry O'Neal and her mother worked at the Wahab Village Inn in the early 1950s and looked forward to their yearly visits. When Dare and Edie later switched to the Pony Island Motel, Sherry would drive them to the beach after breakfast.

Dare described Sherry as having "the face of an eighteenth-century sailing lad."

To Sherry, Dare and Edie were "just like us." She said that Ocracokers responded positively to them because there was never any bragging, even though Dare was a famous model and Edie had painted Winston Churchill. Ocracoke native, Alton Ballance, agreed. He said the exotic looking pair were welcomed because they never patronized the islanders.

Ocracoke Island native Sherry O'Neal.

Sherry thought Dare and Edie were more like sisters than mother and daughter, just the way she felt that she and her mother Katie O'Neal were.

Dare suggested Sherry get into modeling and arranged for her to travel to New York to meet Dorothy Tivis. Although she never became a model – the fresh-faced look would take another decade to supersede the mannered elegance of the Fifties – Sherry said that Dare had changed her life by opening it up to new possibilities away from Ocracoke Island.

If someone ever formed an erroneous impression about Dare, Sherry was quick to tell them, "You didn't know her, and I did!"

Dare with Ocracoke friends. The admiration was mutual.

Dare on the Ocracoke dunes.

Ocracoke was a quiet refuge in the 1950s and early '60s. Dare could sunbathe nude on the unpopulated beaches and explore the abandoned World War II military bunkers without encountering another soul.

In the Ocracoke Island Lighthouse.

On the steps of the Ocracoke Lighthouse.

The Ocracoke Post Office opened in time for the mail boat's arrival from the mainland.

Dare introduced her brother Blaine to North Carolina's Ocracoke Island.

Dare cutting bait. She wasn't at all squeamish.

Blaine with his girlfriend Dorothy Tivis.

Dare and Blaine on Ocracoke driftwood.

Dare took a trip to Ocracoke without Edie in 1953 and introduced Blaine and Dorothy Tivis to the island. They brought along Lee Wulff, who was pursuing Dare at the time. Wulff, ruggedly handsome and a decade older than Dare, was a pilot and expert fisherman who flew wealthy angler clients to his remote lodge in Newfoundland. Edie believed that Lee's two divorces (he would go on to have two more) disqualified him from having any future with Dare. My father Don, himself a master of the self-deprecating boast, declared Lee a braggart.

I rather liked him, especially after Lee included me in a dinner invitation with Dare. He could not have taken much pleasure in the company of a six-year-old chaperone, but was kind enough to occasionally direct the conversation my way as I lay siege to Ristorante Mercurio's bread basket.

Wulff, who was often featured in sporting magazines, arranged for Dare to appear with him on the May 1954 cover of *Flying* magazine posed against a pontoon plane. Dare is shown holding a fly rod and dressed in skimpy pink puffy shorts she had sewn herself, while Lee wears full fisherman's gear.

The caption reads, "A day in spring, a plane on floats, good fishing, a beautiful girl – what more could anyone ask?"

Perhaps a second pair of waders?

Wulff told my father and others in 1954 that he and Dare were engaged, even though Dare had not accepted his proposal, and had no intention of doing so. After waiting a few months for an answer, he finally drifted away and married someone else. When he crashed piloting a plane at the age of eighty-six, Lee Wulff was eulogized as "the Einstein of fly fishing."

Dare was nonjudgmental, but not apolitical. She, like my parents and Tallulah, supported liberal causes and championed civil rights. Dinner and cocktail topics frequently revolved around current politics. At the age of seven I decided to donate most of my allowance to the State of Israel and a home for battered donkeys in Cairo. My father had written the new country's charter, and his law partner, Nahum Bernstein, arranged to get ships and weapons around the British blockade. That explained my connection to Israel, but I cannot remember how I learned about the abused donkeys.

In the mid-Fifties, after Lee Wulff's departure, Dare tolerated the attentions of a man named Russell

Dare and Lee Wulff on the cover of *Flying* magazine.

Lee Wulff courting Dare.

Aitken. Russ often bellowed about his skills hunting big game in Africa, and I found his bombast and love of blood sport thoroughly loathsome. With the feral intuition of a child, I sensed that he was circling Dare for the kill.

There was a yellow melding to Russ' teeth – as if they were brushed with over-ripe Camembert – that blurred the lines of individual dentition. His Harris tweed jackets were as bristly as his nose hairs, and there wasn't a part of him I considered redeemable. It wasn't my nature to judge grownups harshly, but this was a deserving exception.

Russ phoned Dare late one wet afternoon as we were finishing a photo shoot. She invited him to come by for a drink, mentioning that I'd be there, and he arrived shortly afterwards. Before shaking out his raincoat – an elaborate British garment with epaulets, flaps and concealed pockets suitable for an espionage caper – Russ extracted a bottle of scotch and a small blue tin. He walked over to the coffee table, raised his mustache exposing his gums, and put the tin down in front of me.

"They're chocolate covered ants, Brook. I know you'll enjoy them."

I smiled charmingly – my theatrical training kicking in – and opened the tin. This was Russ' challenge, and I wasn't about to let him win. Opening the lid, I saw that the ants were packed as tightly as sardines. If I squinted, I could almost imagine them as chocolate sprinkles. Nope, they had heads and segmented bodies.

Dare looked into the tin, understood my discomfort and asked if she could share them with me. We ate half the tin before Dare suggested I wouldn't want to spoil my dinner, and I replaced the lid saying,

"Thank you, Russ. They were delicious."

Russ never wanted to let Dare go, even after his 1957 marriage. It wasn't enough for him to have wed a wealthy widow ten years his senior; Dare was on his life-list of big game conquests and he was astounded that she couldn't be bought, trapped or cajoled into submission. He phoned and wrote Dare frequently, trying to discover the wedge that would get him, married or not, back in her life. In the 1960s he began commissioning Edie to paint several small portraits of Dare in as provocative a state of dress as he could persuade her to deliver. A length of leg and a bit of cleavage was all that he got.

Russ got to spend a fair amount of time at Dare's when Edie painted his portrait in 1965. He dressed up, in full Scottish regalia with a kilt, sporran and dirk, and puffed his chin and chest out in a fine imitation of a seventeenth-century laird clasping the ornate hilt of an antique sword. The man loved his weaponry, and the Russell B. Aitken collection of swords, guns and armor filled several galleries at The Metropolitan Museum of Art.

Edie, who often dressed in a seemingly impractical elegance while she painted, wore a bouclé suit, pearls and heels as she worked on Russ' portrait. She thought of Russ as a good patron, but never as a contender for Dare's favors.

If Edie considered Russ something of a harmless, besotted, and quite married buffoon, she underestimated the extent of his frustrated lust for her daughter. Russ was used to bagging any creature in his rifle scope, but the closest he would ever get to owning Dare's body was on a painted piece of canvas.

In rage and desperation, he sketched a vile cartoon-like depiction of his engorged privates and mailed the bizarre billet doux to Dare. She put it in a desk folder I would later call the "File of Bewilderment" along with Philip's accusatory telegram.

Edie working on Russ Aitken's portrait, dressed in a bouclé suit and pearls.

Blaine was living on the proceeds of a fishing lure he had invented called the "Phoebe." He told one young friend that he had named it after his British girlfriend who had been killed in the London Blitz.

When the lure became successful, Blaine worried that it would catch too many fish and took an advertisement out asking people not to buy it for that reason. Naturally, it only increased sales.

Blaine once brought a vintage birdcage down from Butternut Island as a birthday present for me. Inside were two, fluffy chicks.

"Brook, you must take them out for a walk every day. When people ask what the birds are, answer 'Tasmanian quail!' They are really bantam hens, but no one will dispute you."

Blaine was correct. As I carried the cage through my New York neighborhood, everyone agreed they were fine examples of Tasmanian quail.

Blaine on the porch of his Butternut Island cabin near Walton, New York.

116

Dare's brother Blaine was handsome enough to have been an actor. Instead, he withdrew to a small cabin in upstate New York to lead a quiet life of writing and exploring the natural world surrounding his retreat. Like his sister, Blaine had an intuitive rapport with animals and charmed turtles, crows and a three-legged coyote.

21

I began attending the King-Coit children's acting school at the age of five. The school produced classic plays – Shakespeare's *A Midsummer's Night Dream*, Thackeray's *The Rose* and *The Ring*, and the ancient Sanskrit epic, *The Mahabharata*. There were no cute animal outfits or childish antics in the productions. Our costumes were designed by Mme. Karinska of The New York City Ballet who was so impressed by Dare that she allowed her to borrow them for my photographs.

Dare made a matador costume for me when I turned six. I liked the fact it was not too valuable to play in and ran around twirling the cape dramatically at Dare's ceramic Minoan bull.

Brook in the matador costume that Dare created for her.

My mother, misreading an invitation to the sixth birthday party for my classmate Aileen Robbins, told me to get into my matador outfit, put me in a cab by myself and sent me across town to Riverside Drive. Aileen's apartment was a saturnine penthouse with an elevator opening directly into her foyer. Eugenia had coached me to flourish my cape and say, "Ta, da!" when I arrived.

Brook posed in Dare's apartment and on her private terrace where they collaborated on *The Lonely Doll* books.

The elevator doors opened, and I had just gotten the "Ta…" part out when I saw the astonished faces of the other guests. All of the girls were wearing frilly party dresses with black patent shoes. Eugenia had not looked closely enough at the invitation to see that it was not a costume party.

Realizing my humiliation, Aileen put her arm around me and announced, "Girls, doesn't Brook look fabulous? Why didn't I think to have a costume party?" It's no wonder that she became my dearest friend.

My North Carolinian grandmother took a beach rental on Ocracoke for the summer of 1954. I spent a month with her and my cousins, never putting on shoes, managing to acquire a bit of color and perfecting a southern accent to keep my relatives from taunting me as a Yankee.

A New York casting agent remembered meeting me with my mother and asked if I could audition for a new Broadway play by Horton Foote called *The Traveling Lady*.

Nana brought me back to the city dressed in my summer outfit of a faded cotton dress and ratty Keds sneakers. We went straight from the train station to the audition where I was appalled to see a room full of little girls in party dresses and patent leather Mary Janes. It was Aileen's sixth birthday party repeating itself.

The other children, with their city pallor and elaborately curled hair stared in disbelief. By simple luck, the role called for a small-town Texas child, and I was the only one at the audition who both looked and sounded the part.

We toured several cities by train before opening in New York. Edie came to see me at the Hannah Theatre in Cleveland and brought me back to her penthouse studio. We spoke of travel and work, and she told me she was very proud of my professionalism. I was on stage for almost every scene and played the part of Margaret Rose for eight performances a week.

Dare was in the audience for the Broadway opening, seated with Tallulah. They both came back to my dressing room after the curtain, and I offered them drinks from a modest bar that had been stocked for the occasion. Tallulah's hugs buried me in her mink coat, and the prickly little animal hairs tickled my nose.

I relished my freedom on matinée days when I could walk around Times Square by myself between shows, intoxicated by the signature New York scent of urine and salt pretzels wafting up from the subway gates. The stagehands watched out for me and we played catch with a ball they made from crumpled newspaper wrapped in electrical tape. I bought a little corncob pipe at Woolworths and bummed cigarettes from them to crumble the tobacco into the pipe bowl. The pipe never stayed lit for more than a couple of puffs, but I loved how it made the crew laugh.

If, like Dare's childhood, mine had exceptional expectations of maturity, then the reward of independence seemed more than worth the burden. During one performance, Kim Stanley, who played my mother, pulled me off-balance and I fell onto a protruding nail head. It was shocking and quite gory as blood gushed from my knee while I blotted it with the hem of my dress. The ladies in the first row of the matinée audience formed their mouths into ovals of concern resembling baby birds waiting for worms to be dropped in, but I stayed in character and finished the act.

It *was* both physically and emotionally exhausting for a seven-year-old to play the part each night (with two matinées a week) and get up for school the next day. The Brearley School in New York City was a Dickensian institution for girls run by a terrifying Scottish woman who always dressed in her black academic robes. Most of my acting peers attended the Professional Children's School which catered to their theatrical schedules. Academic compromise was never a Brearley tradition, and they were not about to begin with me.

Dare's apartment was my refuge, where we invented pirate stories and played with her childhood Edith doll. I once asked Dare if she thought there might be a treasure map hidden inside Folly, her Victorian wooden horse. "Let's investigate!" she exclaimed. Dare grabbed a knife and we dug a small plug out of the antique steed.

There was no treasure map, but that didn't matter. Dare's willingness to enter my fantasy was reward enough.

THE TRAVELING LADY

Brook on Broadway in *The Traveling Lady* with Kim Stanley in 1954.

Dare with her Victorian wooden horse named Folly. She and Brook dug a plug out of Folly's flank to check for a treasure map.

120

I first held Dare's Edith doll when I was three years old. She had been Dare's favorite childhood plaything and wore a beautiful orange organdy dress. Her felt face and body were much more welcoming than my own plastic and china dolls, and my thumbs traced the places on Edith's arms where the felt had worn away three decades earlier.

Soon, I was spending most weekends with Dare and we began dressing Edith in a variety of outfits. Dare loved pink and white gingham, and in 1954 she made Edith a new cotton dress with a crisp, white apron. The colors clashed with Edith's original, curly auburn wig, so Dare fashioned a new one with straight, blonde hair and swept it into a ponytail. Edith's tiny ears were pierced for gold hoop earrings just like the ones Dare wore, and suddenly she looked very much like Dare herself.

Dare's childhood doll Edith became the star of Dare's first children's book *The Lonely Doll.*

Dare on her terrace wall.

22

Blaine came down from Butternut Island to visit Dare in January 1955. They took a walk along Fifth Avenue, stopping at FAO Schwarz to find a gift for a friend's child. It was the first time these two siblings had ever been in a toy store together and both were entranced by the display of stuffed animals. They returned to Dare's apartment with a small Steiff teddy and a much larger Schuco growler bear. Dare brought her Edith doll out to meet them, and she and Blaine immediately began a dialogue between the three toys. Dare decided she would keep the little bear and borrow the larger one - now named Mr. Bear - from the little boy she had bought it for.

Blaine affected outrage. He left Dare's studio and returned with another Mr. Bear for Dare to keep. "One does not borrow other people's bears," Blaine informed his sister.

An unpublished early version of Dare's first book *The Lonely Doll*.

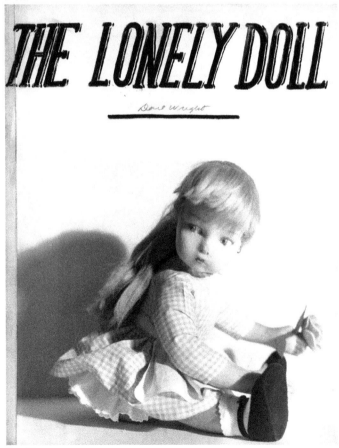

Dare and Mr. Bear.

Dare and I immediately began creating adventures and character traits for the trio. Mr. Bear would be a lovable, if slightly grumpy, father figure who puffed on his pipe while reading the newspaper. Little Bear was a pesky, but endearing, ursine brother. Edith's personality was both timid and impetuous. Like all children, she longed for a stable family and lasting friendships while expressing a universal fear of abandonment.

Dare quickly began photographing the story lines we were imagining for Edith and the two bears. Soon they turned into a mock-up for our very own children's storybook called *The Lonely Doll*.

Edith and The Bears hosted my eighth birthday party in March 1955 at Dare's apartment. Dare served my favorite chocolate cake on her antique china, and Edith presented me with a fine leather jewelry box. My Broadway play had closed, and I moved on to acting in television dramas. There were dark circles under my eyes in Dare's photographs, but the surprise celebration was incredibly joyous. For once, I felt dressed properly in an organdy outfit and Mary Janes.

Brook's 8th birthday party with Edith and The Bears.

In the summer of 1955, I played the murderous child Rhoda Penmark in *The Bad Seed*. We opened at the Bucks County Playhouse in Pennsylvania, and I gave eight performances a week as the child who killed a little boy, an old lady and the janitor of her apartment building. In one scene, I played "Clair de Lune" on the piano as the man I had set on fire screamed in agony offstage.

The director had cast me against type and told me to play the part "straight." There was nothing camp or comedic about my performance. I was a ruthless murderess behind the facade of an engaging strawberry-blond child with big blue eyes. In the movie version of *The Bad Seed*, little Rhoda didn't get away with her murders and was struck by lightning at the end. The play stayed true to the book, and it was clear that Rhoda would go on to murder again.

My mother stayed with me at a motel near the theatre, although I preferred spending the night with the actress Mary Sinclair who played my onstage mother. Mary, as Rhoda Penmark's desperate mother, gave us both an overdose of sleeping pills in the last act, but I survived to carry on my evil agenda. I had not yet learned how to swallow pills, so a stagehand rolled little pellets of bread for me instead. They were colored gray from his dirty hands, but that was the least of my concerns.

I had no way to convey the horror I was feeling. The play was so dark, and my character so un-redeemingly evil, that I awoke frequently with night terrors. At

123

each performance, it got harder to say lines like, "But I had to kill him, mother, he had my penmanship medal!" It felt as if my chest cavity had been packed with rough, starched tulle like a ballerina's tutu, and the raw edges scraped the inside of my ribs and scratched against my heart.

It was not possible to tell Eugenia, because I did not want to let her or Tallulah down. Actors went on no matter what the circumstances; Tallulah had played *The Little Foxes* as her father lay dying. My mother was already annoyed with me for asking to spend time with Mary Sinclair. She was jealous that Sinclair got the part instead of her, and I could not risk upsetting her further. When she puckered her chin into a pin-pricked circle resembling a smallpox vaccination scar, it meant a flood of tears was about to follow.

Almost unconsciously, I began speaking my lines very softly so that they became little puffs of voiceless air. At first the director just asked me to be sure to speak up, but when my whispering could not be heard past the first row, he had to fire me.

I was humiliated, but incredibly grateful to be freed from the play. I told Dare the story one night when I was staying over at her apartment, but I had to whisper it in her ear. She hugged me and said she was happy I was out of that horrid play.

Dare offered to pierce my ears that evening. She told me how Edie had pierced hers by sterilizing a needle and putting a cork behind each ear as a backstop. It was tempting, but I said I'd wait.

The next morning, we walked over to a little toy shop called "Brett" which carried handmade stuffed animals. I chose two large, sad felt mice. Each held a handkerchief in one paw and had a pearl tear sewn under an eye. I called them Marvin and Melvin – most of my toys had names appropriate for eighty-year old shuffleboard players – and walked up Fifth Avenue with the mice cradled proudly in my arms.

It was later in 1955, when my father and I took a trip to the Maryland farm with Dare to rebuild the listing dock. On the second afternoon, the weather turned unseasonably cold as Dare and Don stood in the murky water hammering boards. I found a recipe for hot buttered rum in an ancient cookbook, brushed the silverfish from the page, and made two steaming mugs of liquor to keep the adults going.

The intimacy between my father and Dare as they worked on the construction project – the fact that they seemed to enjoy every moment of each other's company – was an almost dizzying insight into adult relationships. I cleaned up the kitchen and left a gingersnap for the mouse that lived under the stove.

Somewhere before midnight I woke up to the sound of laughter under my bedroom window. Dare and Don were illuminated in moonlight as I watched my father hold a broken umbrella frame to the sky. The fabric was ripped away and only the bare metal ribs remained. As his father had taught him, Don was using the frame to reference and name the constellations above them.

They turned as Don shifted the umbrella to the different stars and, looking skyward, twirled together to a music that I could not hear.

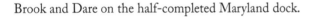
Brook and Dare on the half-completed Maryland dock.

Brook took this photo of Dare and her father, Don Seawell. Their chaste love story spanned sixty years while he remained married to Eugenia and indulged in an incalculable number of affairs. Dare's mother Edie considered him the only man truly worthy of her daughter. Don's gallantry towards Dare, and his acceptance of the fact that she did not want an intimate relationship, made him the perfect courtly knight who would overlook her inability to be a "real woman" as Philip Sandeman had demanded of her.

23

I appeared in many stage and television productions after *The Bad Seed*. Dramas in that Golden Age of Television had me witnessing my mother's ax murder, finding a preacher hanging from a barn rafter, almost dying of a childhood fever, and trapped in an orphanage fire. "Drama" was the operative word and the shows squeezed as much pathos as possible into the hour's time-slot. Fortunately, I wasn't asked to kill anyone on camera, and was able to act with the era's luminaries such as Helen Hayes, Trevor Howard, Judith Anderson, Eli Wallach, Patty Duke, Jack Lord and Kim Stanley. Tallulah even brought me on *The Jack Paar Show* with her.

Brook on Dare's terrace dressed in costume for an episode of *Kraft Television Theatre*.

Brook in costume for a stage production of *The Wisteria Trees* with Helen Hayes.

Tallulah seemed exhausted on the mid-Fifties afternoon when Dare and I held a photo session at her East 62nd Street townhouse. Although Tallulah often pasted paper wings called "Frownies" to her forehead before bedtime, her brow was furrowed as if scored by fork tines. Tallulah's familiar world had begun to shift. Always a renowned beauty, she would no longer be hired for her looks alone. Many of her great loves had died or otherwise departed. Some had been reclaimed by their wives. Politically, it was the era of post-war conservatism and the lingering stench of Senator Mc-Carthy. Liberal opinions were best left unvoiced – although Tallulah had no intention of doing so – and television could only show married couples sleeping in twin beds. At times Tallulah confided that she was turning into her own caricature, a cartoon figure with slash of crimson lipstick and a voice that seemed to resonate from the bottom of a molasses barrel.

As she embraced me on the bed, Tallulah's cigarette hovered over my organdy dress, but I never considered that the combustible fabric might flame up like Cherries Jubilee. Being with Tallulah or Dare, or better yet both of them, meant absolute security.

Tallulah phoned Dare the following day. Although she had already given me a copy of *Charlotte's Web* for my birthday, Tallulah had something else on her mind.

"Dare, Brook doesn't have a decent doll house. Can you help pick out one for her?"

Dare and I reassembled at Tallulah's home and began our pilgrimage across 62nd Street and down Fifth Avenue to FAO Schwarz toy store. Dare's blond ponytail bounced to the rhythm of our gait as we swung our hands together in anticipatory delight. Tallulah, her mink coat opened to catch a bit of the spring breeze, was recognized immediately and responded, "Bless you, darling!" to every "I love you, Miss Bankhead!" A taxi driver blew his horn and shouted, "Tallulah!" out his window as he drove past. We might have been in a sophisticated *Little Golden Book* with a very narrow niche-market.

Bracketed by Tallulah and Dare, I walked into the wonder that was the 1950s FAO Schwarz. No toys beeped or chattered to mar the serenity of its endless counters and cases of dolls and stuffed animals. Tallulah pointed to an enormous white doll house with wooden siding and green shutters. Two saleswomen brought it down from the shelf and placed it on the glass counter. "This one will work, don't you think?" Tallulah asked rhetorically as she tossed her mink to a man wearing a suit. He must have been a store manager or perhaps just a startled customer, because he stayed perfectly still until he returned the coat to her.

Unlike my first tin doll house with its plastic-furnished rooms, this one came with solid wooden furniture and real pillows and quilts for the beds. The refrigerator even had a tiny freezer with metal ice cube trays. The bedroom was papered with rosebuds and the kitchen had miniature ivy vines climbing the walls. It was, in every possible way, the most beautiful doll house I could ever have imagined.

The saleswoman asked me to choose a doll family and pointed to the options in the display case. There was a bendable cloth family from Germany – the little girl had braids and wore a dirndl – and a painted wooden set from Italy with jointed arms and legs. The American contribution was a molded plastic, immobile foursome with the mother permanently fused to her white apron.

Dare and Tallulah – two beautifully complicated angels – were waiting for my decision. Neither of my godmothers belonged in a conventional family, and I didn't want some toy company's concept of domestic perfection inhabiting my new doll house.

I glanced over at the next case and saw a row of wooden penguins. Mama, Papa and Baby penguin seemed the perfect family for my new doll house, but should I choose the black and white or brown and white trio?

"Take both, Brook," Tallulah decided. "They can sort out their own sleeping arrangements."

Dare and Tallulah were Brook's complicated angels.

24

Dare began photographing her first iteration of *The Lonely Doll* in 1955 while helping me set up my own book about Edith and The Bears. I called it The *Great Camera Mystery,* and the plot revolved around Mr. Bear's dismay at finding nose smudges on his camera lens. Adding a couple of my own tiny bears and a German troll, I arranged the shots while Dare did the photography.

Dare could switch seamlessly from her own projects to helping me with mine without any hint of annoyance or inconvenience.

Much of our original playful story, along with many of its photographs, would be folded into the final version of *The Lonely Doll* that Doubleday published in 1957. But Edith, while endearingly sweet and caring in the early part of 1955, was a bit boring without a rebellious side to balance those thoughtful qualities. That was about to change.

Dare photographed Brook's story *The Great Camera Mystery*.

Pausing book photography to take a birthday picture for Blaine.

128

Once there was a lonely little doll.
Her name was Edith. She lived in
a nice house and had everything she
needed except some one to play with.
She was very lonely.

Photos and Dare's handwritten text from the first unpublished
version of *The Lonely Doll.*

Then one day she looked out into the
garden ——— and there stood two bears,
looking tired but friendly.

"Are you Edith?" asked the bigger one,
"I'm Mr. Bear and this is Little Bear.
We heard that you are very lonely and
we've come to keep you company."

She could hardly wait to get acquainted.
She had never met any bears before
but she liked them at once.
"Where did you come from? And how
did you know I was lonely?" she asked,
"And what — ?"
"Now, now," Mr. Bear interrupted in a
kindly way. "Little girls mustn't ask
too many questions."
"Please, just one more question," she
pleaded, "Will you truly stay and be my
friends <u>forever</u>?"
"Indeed we will," promised both bears,
"Forever and ever!"

From then on her prayer was answered.
She had somebody to play with her all
day ———

— and someone with whom she could
plan adventures.
   Little Bear was always full of ideas
for adventures. He especially liked
to climb high places and sometimes
he got into trouble and Edith and
Mr. Bear had to scold him.

One day they heard him shouting, "Come
quick and see what I've found!"
He was standing at the foot of a great,
tall stepladder.
"Come on — let's climb it," he coaxed. He
would have liked to do it alone but the
steps were too big for him.
"It's awfully high," said Edith cautiously.
"Well, now, I think perhaps we can
manage it," said Mr. Bear.

"Now you take my hand, Edith," ordered Mr. Bear, leading the way.

"Come on, Little Bear," said Edith, and she looked back to make sure he was safe.

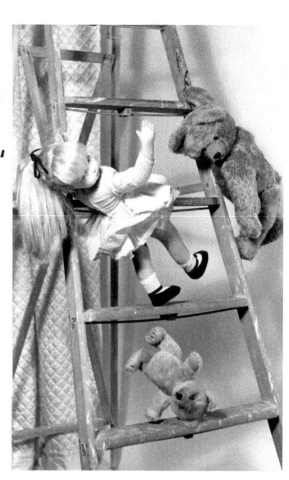

But he wasn't safe!

"He's fallen!" shrieked Edith, and, in her excitement she slipped too. "I'll save you," said Mr. Bear, but he only fell himself!

"Oh dear, there's a big bump on Mr. Bear's head," cried Edith, and she kissed it to comfort him.

"Come on— come on," said Little Bear impatiently, "Let's try again."

This time they were very, very careful.

Up and up they went!

And suddenly there they were — safely at the very top!

"What a view!" exclaimed Mr. Bear.

"Y-y-yes," said Little Bear, hanging onto Edith almost as though he were a little afraid— but of course he wasn't.

"And how do you like it, my dear?" Mr. Bear asked Edith.

But Edith didn't answer because she was saying to herself, "How wonderful it is to have friends at last!" and dreaming of all the other adventures they would have together.

131

Shortly before Christmas of 1955, I took a taxi over to Dare's apartment to pose for a little book she titled *The Angel And Her Doll*. Dare had created angel customs for me and Edith with gossamer wings and glittery halos, and I followed Dare's instructions on how to look appropriately beatific.

At the end of that formal session, when it was okay to break character, I pretended that Edith had been a very naughty cherub who had broken into a celestial dressing room to douse herself with forbidden glitter. Dare kept the shutter clicking as I decided to bend Edith over my knee for a spanking, and that was the genesis of the spanking scene in the final version of *The Lonely Doll*.

Dare wasn't manifesting any dark childhood traumas when she changed *The Lonely Doll* story to include Edith and Little Bear's dressing room naughtiness and their punishment for defying Mr. Bear. She only echoed the innocent impulses of a young child who knew what it was like to be spanked, and, like Edith, occasionally showed her petticoat.

Brook and Edith as 1955 Christmas angels.

Brook's angel breaks character in an unexpected manner.

Brook changed out of the angel costume and into the type of short dress that little girls wore in the 1950s. Their legs froze, the skirts blew up in the wind exposing their underwear, and the long sashes often dipped into toilet bowls.

Dare immediately incorporated my ideas into a story she called *Spring Fever* where Edith's misbehavior in dressing up and wearing forbidden lipstick warrants a spanking from Mr. Bear.

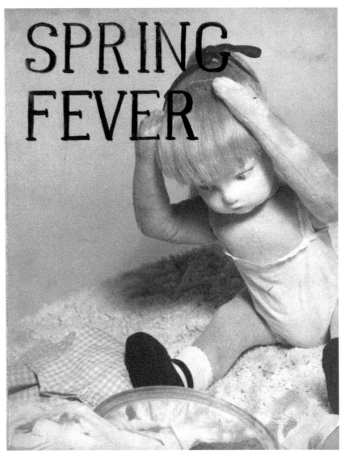

SPRING FEVER

It was spring time, and Edith was very discontented. "My hair looks dreadful," she said to herself, "and I haven't a thing to wear but these same old clothes."

She climbed up to the dressing table for a better look at herself, and was just wondering where to begin when along came Mr. Bear and Little Bear. They'd been walking in the garden and had picked her a daffodil. When she told them how much she wanted to look different Mr. Bear shook his head gravely. "You look very nice as you are", he said, "Just the way a little girl should."

But Little Bear encouraged her.

"Now lipstick", said Little Bear, holding out a bright red one. Mr. Bear was shocked. He knew Edith was far too young for lipstick.

Mr. Bear was at the end of his patience. He turned Edith over his knee. She couldn't believe it. "You wouldn't spank me!" she said in an astonished voice, "Oh, yes, I would", he replied, "You've been behaving like a very vain little girl and disobedient too." And he spanked her very firmly. Little Bear hid his face and was sorry he had helped lead her into trouble.

"There, there," said Mr. Bear, "I know you didn't mean to be naughty. It's just spring fever."
Edith was still inclined to feel hurt, but Mr. Bear told her to put on her own pretty dress and apron, and he'd take them all out for a treat.

As soon as she'd finished *Spring Fever*, Dare asked my father to come over to her apartment for cocktails and a literary critique. She wondered if there was a niche in the children's book market for stories that were illustrated with photographs instead of drawings. As always, she was hesitant about her talents and almost embarrassed to ask my father's opinion. He turned the pages of the mock-ups of *The Lonely Doll* and *Spring Fever*, marveling at the artistry of Dare's camera work and the simple eloquence of the story lines. With Dare's blessing, he took the books with him to show to several friends in the publishing industry. Two of them immediately offered to publish Dare's first book. She chose Doubleday to represent her.

Both Doubleday and my father felt that the two books should be combined and expanded into a single volume, and everyone agreed to keep the beguiling title as *The Lonely Doll*. It was the late spring of 1956, and Dare was more than ready to embrace a career change.

Brook's father Don Seawell found a publisher for Dare's book.

Dare on her apartment terrace during photography for *The Lonely Doll*.

The final version of *The Lonely Doll* took Edith, Mr. Bear and Little Bear outside the confines of Dare's apartment and into the larger world of Central Park, early dawn on the Brooklyn Bridge, and even the beaches and docks of Ocracoke Island.

Edith and The Bears befriending the Central Park fauna in the final version of *The Lonely Doll*.

Dare's iconic photograph of Edith and Little Bear on a deserted Brooklyn Bridge.

25

I was very fond of Dare's suitor, Vincent Youmans, Jr. The son of a famous song writer and a dancer in one of his musicals, Vincent never had a relationship with his father and had grown up just down the road from our Maryland farm. He often landed his small private plane in a plowed area of our tomato field. With his fuzzy saffron hair and rounded tummy, Vincent reminded me of Little Bear. He had a sweet and mischievous nature and was always agreeable to playing games with me. It took Vincent a while to realize that Dare regarded him as more of an affable companion than potential love interest, but he accepted that role if it meant being around her.

Vincent's only misstep was mailing Dare a live butterfly from Maryland. It had turned to powder by the time Dare opened the envelope. He redeemed himself by climbing on a rickety ladder to paint the wall of Dare's terrace and assisting on many of Dare's photo shoots in the 1950s and 60s.

Vincent Youmans painting Dare's terrace wall.

Dare, my father and I took a trip to Maryland early in the summer of 1956. Edith and The Bears naturally came along. Dare and I took them into the woods, along with a few other little animals I stuffed in my pockets, to photograph a story I had in mind. Dare let me pose them without any interference, and never suggested there might be a more artistic way to set up my scenes.

I dictated the text to Dare as I set up the story of Little Bear falling asleep in a tree and causing Mr. Bear great panic. Little Bear is finally found with the help of my own little Steiff bears, and all ends happily. Dare bound the finished book, *A Walk in The Woods*, as a gift to me.

As Eugenia did not come to Maryland that summer, I was allowed to adopt a neighbor's smoke-colored kitten. With either a precocious sense of humor or simply a New York child's experience of gray slush, I named her "Snowball." When I phoned my mother to say I'd be bringing the kitten back with me, she told me that it was a "summer kitten" and not meant as a permanent companion.

Brook photographing Edith.

Snowball was left with people who had no experience with animals and died soon afterwards.

Dare shot photos of Edith and The Bears at various places around our farm. The fields, woods, orchard, old farmhouse and dock were inspirational for many future scenes in *The Lonely Doll* series.

Brook's kitten Snowball with Edith and Little Bear.

• S they all sat down in a circle and were very happy.

"I like walks in the woods," said Edith, "You make such nice friends."

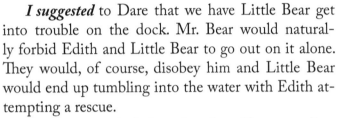

I suggested to Dare that we have Little Bear get into trouble on the dock. Mr. Bear would naturally forbid Edith and Little Bear to go out on it alone. They would, of course, disobey him and Little Bear would end up tumbling into the water with Edith attempting a rescue.

Dare never minded getting herself wet or dirty in the service of creativity and let me toss Little Bear into the creek for our story. She fell into the creek herself as she backed up the dock to take Mr. Bear's photo and emerged laughing with her camera held high.

Two years later, Dare would use many similar shots, including Mr. Bear's horrified dash down the dock, in *Holiday For Edith And The Bears*. We had learned that Little Bear floated, but someone would have to hold him from under the water if we only wanted his head and arms to show. Vincent Youmans gallantly held his breath while keeping Little Bear partially submerged in the later book photos.

26

In July 1956 Dare and Edie sailed to England with my parents on the *Ile de France*. They had only made it as far as the coast of Nantucket when a distress call came out that two ships, the *Stockholm* and the *Andria Doria*, had collided. The captain of the *Ile de France* changed his course to rescue passengers from the sinking *Andria Doria* throughout the night.

Dare watched with my father, who suggested she photograph the rescue effort and survivors who were being brought on board their ship. He knew that any major magazine would pay her a large sum for the pictures.

They were close enough to see the *Andria Doria* passengers clinging to the netting along the ship's side and hear them crying out for help.

"I can't photograph suffering," she said quietly. She went to her cabin and brought out clothing as the lifeboats disgorged the freezing survivors. My mother, Eugenia, kept her suitcase firmly shut.

They returned to New York with the refugees, and then set out again for London.

Edie, Dare, Eugenia and Don were assigned to the same table for each dinner during the crossing. One evening, Dare and Edie were late arriving and my father went to their cabin to see if one might be ill.

The cabin door was ajar, and he heard Edie speaking forcefully to Dare, "Don is the right man for you," she told her daughter.

My father slipped back to the table without their knowing they had been overheard.

I was aware by then that Edie preferred my father's company to my mother's. Most people did. Eugenia had a narcissistic requirement to have the focus on her no matter what the situation, and sharing was not her strong suit. Eugenia did not like to go to parties unless she was being honored or could make a dramatic entrance, which often resulted in last minute cancellations and a variety of fanciful medical excuses. A touch of phlebitis or a broken leg capillary were often invoked to escape social obligations. Eugenia once claimed to have had a mastectomy, going so far as to share the fictitious experience with a woman who had recently lost a breast and had no reason to doubt her veracity.

Dare and Edie left my parents in England to visit Gayelord Hauser at Villa Apomea, the home he shared with his partner Frey Brown in Taormina, Sicily. Greta Garbo often stayed there as his guest to soak up the strong Sicilian sun without being recognized.

Edie was called "the woman who looks through you" as she walked through town. Human faces had fascinated Edie since early childhood, and she had once walked into a tree while gazing intently at a playmate. I had been accustomed at an early age to having Edie peer closely at my features, and never minded our noses almost touching when she did so. Dare collected her photographs of the Taormina trip into a private volume called *Memory of Sicily*.

They returned to New York at the end of September for Dare to finish readying *The Lonely Doll* for its 1957 publication.

Gayelord Hauser at his Villa Apomea in Taormina, Sicily.

Frey Brown, Gayelord Hauser's partner, stands barefoot in the doorway of their villa.

Breakfast on the balcony in Taormina.

Dare in the gardens of Villa Apomea.

27

The Lonely Doll's combination of simple text and professional photographs was a revolutionary concept in children's literature. Dare described how the process worked:

> *I'm very careful never to use miniature sets. If you scale down objects you have a cute toy universe. A reverse comparison would be to have adults move in a child-like world.*
>
> *I have to be very careful about the relationship between eyes. Edith is only twenty-two inches tall, [Mr. Bear] about the same size, and Little Bear is only nine inches high. So when I photograph them, I have to be absolutely certain about how their eyes meet. If I'm off by one eighth of an inch, it will distort the entire illusion. If one of the dolls looks just beyond the other, the photo loses.*
>
> *Edith photographs beautifully because she's a little primitive. She is not like a plastic doll with perfectly formed hands and everything too perfect to photograph. She's proportioned like a real child. A pediatrician once said, "Do you know why she photographs well? It's because the size of her head in relation to her body and the bulk of her little tummy are proportionally right for a five-year-old. A child can associate."*

When Dare was not making Edith's wardrobe, she was sewing her own, often fanciful outfits. A bolt of charcoal wool fabric could serve for an elegantly tailored suit or a doll's dress and cap.

THE LONELY DOLL

STORY AND PHOTOGRAPHS BY
DARE WRIGHT

The cover of Dare's book *The Lonely Doll* first published in 1957.

Edith and Little Bear on the Brooklyn Bridge.

The *Cleveland Plain Dealer* featured both Dare and Edie's artistic triumphs in a July 1957 color spread called "Mother's Artful Influence." In one photograph, Dare wears a cocktail dress she's sewn from an 18th century church robe.

The article describes how Dare helped decorate Edie's Cleveland penthouse and transformed the bathroom into a spa by painting a Grecian mural on the wall and turning vertical water pipes into columns. "The scene is complete even to a pigeon perched on the foot of the tub."

MODERN MOTHER AND DAUGHTER—Mrs. Edith Stevenson Wright, portrait painter, and Dare Wright, professional model and photographer. Dare's self-designed cocktail dress is made from an 18th century church robe

The Cleveland *Plain Dealer*, July, 1957.

The Lonely Doll reviews were amazing. Dare had combined her creative talents of photography, design, painting, sewing and decoration with her ability to write from a child's point of view into an artistic medium of her own creation. Her text never condescended to her young readers. Part of Dare's "other-worldly" quality made her incapable of cruelty or being patronizing. Dare is the only person I have ever known who never spoke unkindly of anyone, and she was bewildered by those who did.

Not one of *The Lonely Doll* reviewers found any fault with the scene where Mr. Bear spanks Edith and Little Bear for disobeying him. It was simply not an issue in the 1950s. Of the fourteen books Dare wrote featuring dolls, three had Edith spanked.

If a reviewer mentioned it at all, it was as an amusing and expected conclusion to Edith and Little Bear's naughtiness.

A Massachusetts reviewer called *The Lonely Doll*, "One of the sweetest books for little girls from two to eight that I have ever seen." She went on to describe the illustrations giving equal weight to all of Edith's adventures with The Bears, "The photographs of their experiences are outstanding; having lessons, going to the park, going fishing, getting into mischief, being spanked."

The *Columbus Enquirer* simply wrote, "Like many mischievous children, Edith and her little bear friend get into trouble by playing with adult things, the makeup and jewelry box. To children who have done these things (and have any not?) a fine moral is told."

The review in the *Florida Times-Union* concluded, "[Edith] also manages to get into some little girl scrapes – trying on Mommy's clothes and getting a spanking for it – before all ends happily."

And, in example of how adjectives and parental discipline have evolved since 1957, the *New Haven Register* commented, "Edith's loneliness in her lovely house vanished when Mr. Bear and Little Bear came to visit. Playing at the beach, fishing, or doing homework, Edith loved her gay companion, even Mr. Bear's fatherly discipline. One day, Edith and Little Bear, left alone, romped into too much mischief in the dressing room closet with shoes, jewels and lipstick. Mr. Bear soundly spanked them, but, eventually, all was forgiven."

Not that there weren't other concerns. A woman with the astringent name of Myrtle Harlow warned that families might find the mingling of Edith and The Bears inappropriate, stating, "The substitution of toys as imaginative playmates rather than the use of real children may not meet with the approval of some parents," while a librarian for a Christian organization took umbrage at the photograph of a doll praying for friends.

The Lonely Doll made the *New York Times* Best Selling Children's Books list and readers begged for more Edith and The Bears stories.

Newspapers were as fascinated about Dare as they were about her book. Children's authors were not often photogenic, and Dare's beauty and back-story captivated the press.

The *New York World-Telegram* ran a feature story about Dare with a photograph of her holding Edith:

> *Edith the blond doll and her owner, the equally blond Dare Wright, have teamed up with two teddy bears to provide children in the 4-7 range with proof that their world of fantasy really exists.*
>
> *Miss Wright has accomplished this happy feat with a sensitive photo story titled "The Lonely Doll" brought out by Doubleday.*
>
> *A former New York actress and model turned professional photographer, she has combined the artistry of all three fields to produce in her first venture as a children's author a tale to delight Mom and Dad as well as the small fry.*
>
> *Miss Wright got into photography "by accident"*

> *four [sic] years ago and has stayed with it in preference to stage and modeling "because I had to make a living."*
>
> *Her mother, Mrs. Edith Stevenson Wright, a successful portrait artist was responsible for the transition. Mrs. Wright had been hired to do a fashion spread with Dare as the model.*
>
> *Mother told them she wasn't a photographer, but they had seen some shots she had taken and insisted she could do it. Mother had her doubts, so I did the focusing and then ran around in front of the camera.*
>
> *Why the preference for dolls?*
>
> *Well, they'll stand still for two to three hours for one photo – with never a complaint about wages. And all that bending over keeps a girl trim.*

Dare visited Blaine on Butternut Island in Walton after *The Lonely Doll*'s publication. The siblings goofed off for the camera and roasted marshmallows outdoors. It was like a summer camp for forty-year-olds.

Blaine and Dare having fun with Vincent Youmans.

28

Dare and Edie spent a month on Ocracoke in the summer of 1957. Dare had an idea for her next book, which would show Edith and The Bears vacationing on the island. She had used some earlier Ocracoke shots of them in *The Lonely Doll* and mixing the trio with the island's wild ponies and empty beaches would be a perfect contrast to the urbanized setting of her first book.

She and I spent an afternoon playing around with

Edith and The Bears before they left New York. We posed the trio on her terrace for a scene with Mr. Bear mopping his brow in the intolerable heat. Clearly, he had to get Edith and Little Bear out of the city for the summer.

Dare took fanciful self-portraits when she was not posing Edith with the wild ponies or Little Bear taking a rowboat out against Mr. Bear's orders.

Edith and The Bears were ready to escape New York's blistering summer.

Edie on Ocracoke Island.

Dare was as beautiful and mysterious as any nymph or naiad on
Ocracoke's empty beaches.

Edie introducing Mr. Bear to an island dog.

Vincent Youmans flew his small plane to Ocracoke to help Dare set up some of the shots in *Holiday For Edith And The Bears*. Vincent gallantly held his breath under water while holding Little Bear's legs so the photo would be realistic.

An Ocracoke fisherman provided Edith's catch and balanced her against a piling.

Lunch was usually a picnic on the beach, and even Edith and The Bears took a well-deserved break. As she had done for *The Lonely Doll*, Dare made two pre-liminary mock-up versions of *Holiday For Edith And The Bears* before settling on the finished one.

As soon as they arrived Mr. Bear brought out a book.
"Now this," he said," will tell you all about Ocracoke."
"Read it to us, read it to us! cried Edith and Little Bear together.

"Bare feet felt so good that she left her shoes off all day, and then the day after, and then all summer long."

I had petitioned my mother for a dog since I was five and was still pleading my cause at the age of ten. I offered to adopt an ancient, arthritic poodle that walked with the gait of an animated card table from a friend's grandmother, or even settle for a cat. Nothing succeeded. Dare later borrowed my animal hunger for Edith in *The Doll And The Kitten*.

My parents and I went to Maryland for Thanksgiving 1957. It was a departure from our holiday tradition of having Thanksgiving dinner at a mock-Colonial restaurant in New York where children were served the crème de menthe frappé as a special dessert. That seventy-two-proof snow cone guaranteed nausea in the taxi ride back to our apartment, a blinding headache and a long, fitful nap to sleep the liquor off.

As we bumped up the potholed lane, I saw a large dog sitting on the kitchen step. He bounded up to me as I raced out of the car, and I embraced his skinny ribs. Mostly Doberman and missing an eye, he was the most perfect pet I could have imagined.

"Pete" and I had four days together. He slept on my bed and raced me to the dock. When we got into the car to drive back to New York, Eugenia told me Pete would not be coming with us. He would be left at the rural shelter for disposal.

Fifty years later, I found a draft of my mother's memoirs where she wrote,

"I watched Brook's large tears dropping on the dog's neck as she sobbed while we drove to the shelter."

That Christmas Tallulah gave me a poodle.

"Damn it, the child deserves a dog!" Tallulah bellowed, after hearing about Pete. Like Dare, Tallulah was never dispassionate about my welfare.

I named my poodle Tally after my benefactor, and Dare made me a book titled *Brook and Tally* to celebrate. Tally was my first pet that did not come with a short expiration date.

Holiday For Edith And The Bears was published in August 1958. It was featured in *Life* magazine and – just like *The Lonely Doll* – made The *New York Times* Best Seller List for children's books.

Many reviewers liked it even better than *The Lonely Doll*. The somewhat grumpy New York *Knickerbocker News* columnist, Duane La Fleche, enthused, "It is only now and again that a children's book comes my way that I can call 'lovable.' This is one of those times. So I sing the praises of *Holiday For Edith And The Bears* which is both a book of photographs beyond compare and a story that is just right; a story that is just big enough and just small enough, that is just adventurous enough and just quiet enough, and, above all, that is warm and honest and has in it that loving forthrightness of childhood."

Edith was now popular enough to be featured in a Bufferin advertisement, using a photograph from *Holiday For Edith And The Bears*.

Brook and Tally.

Edith and The Bears visit Ocracoke Island in Dare's second book *Holiday For Edith And The Bears*. In an ad featuring a new child-proof cap for children's Bufferin, Edith asks, "Why can't I get the bottle open, Mr. Bear?"

Edith: Mr. Bear, what's new Bufferin for Children?

Mr. Bear: It's medicine, Edith, but it tastes orange.

Edith: Is it *just* for children, Mr. Bear?

Mr. Bear: Yes, Edith. You see, it's in the safe, 1¼-grain dosage Doctor says is perfect for little aches and pains—fevers, cold miseries, teething. Sleeplessness, too.

Edith: Will it make me feel good right away?

Mr. Bear: Well, big Bufferin, like I take, works twice as fast as aspirin—for millions. And Bufferin adds Di-Alminate* to its aspirin, to help soothe upset tummies.

Edith: Oh. Why can't I get the bottle open, Mr. Bear?

Mr. Bear: Because Children's Bufferin is guarded by a child-proof safety-cap. So you won't get at them when you don't need them.

Edith: Can I take one now, Mr. Bear?

161

Mary Rennels Snyder, who had met Edie back in the 1920s when she was writing for *Cleveland Topics*, now had a column in the Gary, Indiana *Post-Tribune*. She visited Dare in New York and championed her talents with the same enthusiasm as she had Edie's.

Miss Wright is that rare combination, a young sophisticated modern woman working in a competitive field and city, and a lady who gives the impression of having been reincarnated from Madame de Stael. *It is her setting that suggests the latter, but listening to her preferences one sees that she is as current as Rice Crispies. She is shy, and the only thing that frightens her is "selling myself" to publishers and editors. Her luxury is to go out and leave all the lights burning…Miss Wright has the sensitivity and warmth to picture the mind of a child…that is what will give her the extra dividend of youth long after her own passes.*

The Madame Alexander Doll Company brought out their first Edith doll in 1958. Edie commented on the touching back-story:

Madame Alexander at first refused to copy Edith because she has always designed her own dolls. Then one day she called Dare to say she had changed her mind. Her granddaughter recently had died, and Edith had legs that reminded Madame Alexander of her granddaughter's

legs. This convinced her finally that she must duplicate that doll in memory of the child who had died and to please all the little girls in the world who wanted an Edith.

Other than her costume, the 1958 "Edith" doll by Madame Alexander hardly resembled Dare's real Edith. Her wig wasn't blonde, or even straight, and the body type mirrored a much older child.

29

The Lonely Doll and *Holiday For Edith And The Bears* established Dare as a successful and respected author. She had forged a new medium in children's literature, and the challenge would be coming up with new ideas for future books.

Ready to try something different in 1958, Dare left Edith and Little Bear in a Manhattan bank vault and took her tiny bisque doll named Persis along with Mr. Bear up to her brother Blaine's Butternut Island in Walton, New York. Like Edith, Persis had been one of Dare's favorite childhood dolls and had her own distinctive personality.

The Little One tells the story of Persis' rescue from a deserted old house by a turtle, who pushes open the door and finds the little doll covered in dust. He leads her out of the house and Persis runs down the lane basking in the sunlight.

Persis is an original innocent, much like Dare herself. When a butterfly suggests Persis would be more comfortable without her clothes, off comes her pinafore, dress and petticoat.

She is found sleeping under a Mayapple by Nice Bear and Cross Bear – a grumpy looking version of Mr. Bear that Dare borrowed from a friend.

Persis revels in the beauty of nature, talks to butterflies, crows and turtles and cannot understand why Cross Bear won't be her friend.

Nice Bear takes good care of Persis, feeding her honey and berries, and tucking her to bed on a mossy mattress under a blanket of leaves.

He bathes her in the brook and makes a new little dress of leaves and ferns each day. Although the doll's body was bisque, her feet were made of composition and began to soften in the water. Like Edith and The Bears, Persis acquired a few scars from her location shots.

When Persis falls from a tree while trying to surprise her bears with a gift of honey, Cross Bear is the first to care for her.

"I love her," he tells Nice Bear.

Persis hears him and wakes up.

"Turtle," she called, "did you hear?" Cross Bear loves me. They're both my very own bears now. I shall stay with them forever and ever...."

It was a marvelous time for Dare and Blaine. They set up many of the shots together, and Blaine acted as the official animal wrangler. Dare scrubbed the turtle with a nail brush and polished him with baby oil to make him shine.

The crow was supposed to be tame but Dare found that even tame crows dislike posing.

Both siblings had an uncanny ability to charm any animal. They could remain still, without any sudden movements, until an animal approached them. Dare had acquired this talent by posing for her mother at an early age. Blaine had been a restless child, who had to learn it from the animals themselves.

Blaine wrote me this letter, two years after *The Little One* was published. It was typed with many cross-hatches and a problematic space bar after I had sent him Gavin Maxwell's memoir *Ring of Bright Water*. The book described Maxwell's rescue of a wild otter, and his efforts to bring it into his household.

Dearest Brooky:

I thank you ever so much for "Ring of Bright Water". How did you know that it was just the right kind of book for me?

I think I will never have an otter (barring Dare) even though I know where to get one.

As Mr. Maxwell says, when you capture or otherwise come into possession of a wild animal, you cannot be sure that you are right in keeping it.

Once upon a time I caught two teeter-peeps. Their kind is called so because they spend all their time teetering and peeping. Their dictionary name is Solitary Sandpiper. Dare did some sketches of them. Someday I will show you.

There was another day when I kidnapped a wood-duck. If your thumb had foolish fluffy feathers, it would look just like my baby duck. It was early October when he left me. He was the fattest drake to go South that year.

I had a woodchuck once, called Grumpy (he was full of complexes and would bite anyone he could reach) and I turned him loose in the North Woods of New Hampshire.

I've been on intimate terms with crows, mice, red squirrels, hawks, monkeys, muskrats, raccoons, possums, worms and wolves. I have scars to prove it.

But one of the best, who had no name, is probably number one on my list of four-footed and two-winged friends.

KIYUTE. Or coyote. At that time I was working on a ranch in the Powder River country—the foot-hills of the Big Horn Mountains. That part of Wyoming had been the scene of the Johnson County war. I talked with old men who had survived it. Real fine bloody horse-opera. Not quite like TV, for those ancient gentlemen had not had blank cartridges in their six-shooters and 44-40 Winchesters.

My duties on the ranch included the building of barbed wire fences (what a job for a cowboy!) the digging of ditches, and one super and superb business. Every morning when the sun rose I had to get up and go out and bring in all the horses to be used that day. A fair-sized pasture it was – maybe a thousand acres.

But we must get back to el coyote. I lived in a little tent fifty feet from a little brook in which I washed and sometimes brushed my teeth. Just halfway between my tent and the brook lived the little prairie wolf with three feet. He couldn't live with his fourth foot, for it had been somehow lost. Trap?

Anyhow, one of the boys had roped him for fun, and he was staked out on a six-foot chain, which according to the old notion of Pie Are Square, gave him in his circle exactly 113.0976 square feet of roaming room. And he knew every decimal of that space.

Occasionally somebody would toss a little garbage in his direction, and so he ate and lived. Cattlemen and sheepmen do not like Senor Coyote. The dudes we had on the ranch were afraid of him; for put one sixteenth of a toe inside the magic ring and that was how much toe you would lose.

But the miserable pup (he was not much over one year old) did, as we know, live between my tent and my bath. He lay on his dirty bare sun-baked patch with his yellow eyes full of fear and hatred.

After a while I was tired of walking around the premises of that junior delinquent wolf. In a great burst of courage I said to me "I will walk over him. If he bites me I will bite him right back."

And so it came about that we bit each other. But I bit better. Have you ever chewed on a wolf's ear? Don't try. You get hair in your teeth.

After that one fight (which was not fair because I was much bigger than the pup) we talked reasonably and became very good friends. All the fights we had after that were in pure fun.

Having acquired a friend (who gave him things to eat) the pup went back to being a pup. Just as obnoxious as any young dog. Or perhaps worse. Senor Coyote had an absolute passion for toothpaste. I owned the only tube of toothpaste in Johnson County. The nearest store was in the village of Buffalo, thirty dirty miles away.

When I went to the brook to brush my teeth, I always carried the toothpaste in my right hip-pocket. Little Senor El Coyote knew my habits, and it was his dearest ambition to get that toothpaste. He would frolic with me, but he always had one eye on my old hip-pocket. And one day he was too fast for me—or maybe I was too slow — AND HE GOT THE TOOTHPASTE.

Have you ever seen a toothpaste tube with a million wolf-tooth holes in it? At that moment I retired from the ranch, and I have never seen Senor El Coyote from that day to this. But he was my friend.

I cannot put up with children save those who send me good books.

Thus you have again my thanks, and you must tell your mother and father that I appreciate their child.

This typewriter is Italian, and since I try to write English, there is constant conflict, and we wind up with many mistakes. You forgive, please?

If so, I would say love at you.

Blaine

Dare brought Persis to our farm in Maryland for a few more book photos. My father and the little doll seemed to get along quite well. Eugenia stayed in New York.

The Little One was published in 1959. Although it received some lovely reviews, Dare's Persis books were never as popular as her Lonely Doll series. It was impossible to please all the reviewers.

The *Kirkus Bulletin* considered Persis a great improvement over Edith: "Lacking the inappropriate sophisticated quality of the last doll heroine, Persis emerges as tender and appealing a heroine who ever wandered clothed in leaves throughout a sunny expanse of field. Expertly professional photographs suggest poignantly even the smells, sounds, and textures of the Catskill countryside and the vivid personality of the toy people who inhabit it. Unique, even in terms of its preceding books."

The *New York Times*, however, sniffed that Persis had "...nowhere near the style of her predecessor... The Bears are delightful, and the background of rocks, grasses, and tree-trunks is beautifully photographed – only Persis seems a little commonplace."

Doubleday publishers wanted another Edith and The Bears book, and Dare's next project was *The Doll And The Kitten.*

For some time, Dare had been unhappy working with Doubleday, where they were demanding a more formulaic approach to her stories. She told the *Walton Reporter*, "They want a series like *The Bobbsey Twins...* and I don't."

When the publisher sent Dare a letter justifying their change of color on *The Doll And The Kitten* book jacket, Dare wrote herself a memo about the contested shade of red: "It's not dreadful. It's just undistinguished. Next contract I'm going to get a guarantee of final word on the jacket." That would be the last of Dare's books published by Doubleday.

As she had for *The Little One* a year earlier, in 1959, Dare photographed *The Doll And The Kitten* almost entirely around Blaine's home. She set up the shots at Robert and Betty MacGibbon's farm a couple of miles south of Walton, New York. Blaine's Butternut Island was surrounded by the MacGibbon farmland, and their red Guernsey cows show up in the background of Dare's earlier photographs. The MacGibbons later switched to the less-photogenic Holsteins when American tastes moved away from the rich Guernsey milk.

Local children Brenda Doane and her sister Louise loved to hang around the barn when Dare was photographing the book. Brenda was in awe of Dare's beauty, and said she had the aura of a magical being. She remembered Blaine as always smelling good.

Persis with Brook's father Don.

Dare on the porch of Blaine's cabin.

In The Doll And The Kitten, Mr. Bear takes Edith and Little Bear to stay at an old-fashioned farm.

Edith is desperate to have one of the farm animals for a pet, and Mr. Bear stops her from leading a calf out of the barn. "He's going home with me when we leave," said Edith, "so he has to learn to stay in a house."

When she's told the calf is not an option, Edith tries for something smaller.

"Dear Mr. Bear," said Edith, "do you like lambs?"

"Lambs? Lambs?" said Mr. Bear. "Of course I like lambs."

"Then you wouldn't mind if I took a little, little one home with me?" asked Edith.

"I certainly would!" said Mr. Bear. "Lambs grow into sheep and sheep need green fields. You cannot take any of the farm animals home, Edith. Don't ask again!"

"Mr. Bear is horrid," Edith confides to Little Bear.

Edith finds a kitten in the barn, but there never seems to be a good time to ask Mr. Bear if she can keep it.

Mr. Bear has to rescue both Edith and Little Bear when they attempt to get the kitten down from a barn beam, and Little Bear ends up dangling from one end of a rope when he hoists Edith up in a basket.

Blaine was nearby on kitten watch.

Edith is allowed to keep her kitten, and the vacation concludes without any more drama.

Dare was fearless about balancing on barn beams or hanging out of a loft window. She once slipped balancing on an attic joist in our Maryland farmhouse, and I watched her espadrille-clad foot punch through the ceiling below along with several chunks of plaster.

That fall, I was knocked down at school during an overly-spirited game of Red Rover. My head hit the bricks, and I was hospitalized for a week with a concussion. Dare slipped into my room telling the nurses she was my aunt and presented me with very special get well photographs from Edith, Little Bear and Mr. Bear.

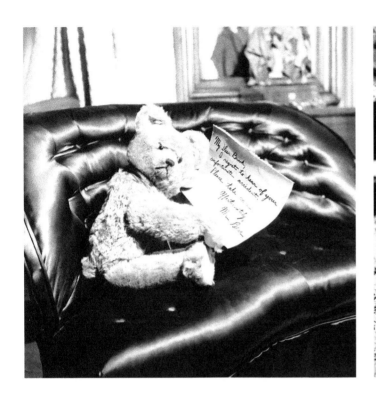

30

Edie had wanted to paint my father's portrait for several years. She finally persuaded him to begin sitting for her late in 1958. Edie rented a Scottish kilt for Don, and Dare made herself a complimentary outfit. My mother knew that Don was being painted, but she was unaware of the subtext.

The three met at Dare's apartment so that Dare could take photographs for Edie to base the portrait on.

When both Dare and my father were in costume, Edie coaxed them to model together with Dare's Victorian horse, Folly, as a prop. Edie had neglected to rent an ascot, so Dare wrapped one of her petticoats around my father's neck. Dare was flirtatious, Don was gallant, and Edie's agenda was quite clear.

Edie worked on my father's painting as well as a "companion" portrait of Dare that was framed identically and intended to be displayed as a pair. The concept of companion portraits – dating back centuries – was that the paintings would allow the couple to remain together forever, even after death.

Edie sent Don's portrait to Cleveland after my father finished posing at Dare's apartment. My mother had assumed the painting would be a gift to her and was furious at what she considered Edie's betrayal. Edie responded that the portrait had always been intended for her own collection and offered to paint another one for Eugenia.

Edie told a newspaper reporter that she and Dare enjoyed having drinks next to the portrait when Dare visited Cleveland. My mother's anger at Edie and, by extension, Dare was all-consuming. It seemed to be fed by a primal wellspring that was unrelated to the precipitating event. She wrote a mocking song about Edie and Dare and sang it around the house. I had spent my childhood learning to deflect Eugenia's wrath, but there was nothing I could do to stop it now.

Edie painted companion portraits of Dare and Brook's father Don so they could remain together through the ages.

Edie went ahead and painted a second portrait of my father. Although Eugenia eventually accepted it, she never forgave Edie or Dare for denying her the original.

An article about Edie, described the portrait, "Elegantly posed, red-haired and blue-eyed, with mocking smile and slender hand, [he] typifies our romantic dream of a Bonnie Prince Charlie."

Dare used a newly acquired movie camera to shoot a sequence in Edie's Cleveland penthouse. The film pauses at the nameplate on Edie's door, then moves inside and pans across her studio, lingering for a moment on my father's portrait.

The camera closes in on Edie, speaking silently to Dare as she puffs a cigarette. The smoke swirls around Edie's head, growing denser until she is as milky and mysterious as a glass of absinthe.

Don's second portrait by Edie. It did not appease Eugenia.

Edie, with paint brushes in hand and a cigarette to her lips, pauses in the window of Dare's terrace.

31

Later in 1959, Edie and Dare took a trip to the Virgin Islands, where they met Claire Booth Luce. Luce was enthusiastic about spear fishing, and persuaded Dare to try Gyotaku, the Japanese art of fish rubbing. Dare gave us a print she did on that trip and told me how awful she felt pressing down on a still living fish.

Dare switched to Random House publishers in 1960 after my father introduced her to Bennett Cerf. With no expectations from them to produce Bobbsey Twins clones, she decided to try an entirely different type of book featuring a child's visit to London.

At thirteen, I really was too old to play the role. Nevertheless, I was stuffed into clothing more appropriate for a child five years younger and in the summer of 1960, we set off for a month in Great Britain.

Eugenia refused to join us during the photography. My grandmother, who adored both Dare and Edie, came along to celebrate her seventy-sixth birthday. She always felt a special bond with Edie, who was only a year older, and part of it might have been the way they both regarded my mother.

Brook departing New York and choosing a hat in London. Don gave Dare a meaningful glance when they attended a horse race.

My grandmother had brought a heavy electric iron in her suitcase to take care of my limited wardrobe of a couple of blouses, a wool suit fit for a dowager and a smocked dress that any six-year-old would have rejected. The morning we arrived at our hotel, grandmother plugged the iron into a British socket and blew the fuses for the entire floor. I was an equally inept innocent abroad and looked quizzically into the hotel bidet as I turned the faucets. My outfit for the day was soaked, and I had to dry my hair over the heated towel rack.

Poor Dare had to contend with photographing a "child" for her book who was five foot six and painfully self-conscious. Dare undoubtedly wished she was accompanied by the lively, whimsical girl I once had been and not the slope-shouldered adolescent I'd become.

I hated the way my hair looked, my grandmother refused to let Dare put any mascara on my invisible lashes and I slogged through a damp London in a shapeless raincoat and clear plastic shoe covers. The cloudy-bright days bothered my sensitive eyes and Dare had to count to three so I could open them when she clicked the shutter.

She was infinitely patient with my self-loathing and caught a couple of nice candid shots when I was not posing.

Colin Keith-Johnston, who had known Dare since they performed together on Broadway in *Pride and Prejudice* came by for tea with his little boy. It was clear that Colin was still madly in love with Dare, and she blossomed as he recited some of Mr. Darcy's lines.

We took a day off to visit the charming village of Marlow on the River Thames with the family of my father's British law partner. Their son, Richard, was almost fifteen and I wanted desperately for him to like me. We took two boats out punting on the river before returning to the inn for tea. The day turned uncharacteristically sunny, and we settled our rickety folding chairs on the sloping lawn while balancing plates of cucumber sandwiches.

A rare smile from a sullen teen.

Brook at the gates of Buckingham Palace.

Richard Gardner, before Brook's humiliating tumble.

Dare and Don on the Thames.

Dare took some lovely photographs of Richard just before my chair went over backwards in the soggy soil and I turned upside down with my white cotton underpants facing the sky.

I went right back into my cocoon. It was not that I expected to become a butterfly. I would have settled for being a moth as long as I had wings.

My mother arrived in London after photography for the book was completed and made no effort to disguise her contempt of Dare. It was not helped by the fact that my father had bought Dare a beautiful pair of antique earrings with tiny seed pearls set on gold thistles. Don thought he had his bases covered by having the same jeweler who crafted tiaras for the royal family copy the earrings for Eugenia, but overlooked the fact that my mother never wore earrings.

Our charming Victorian hotel was not large enough to contain her rage.

Date With London was not a success and plans to make a series of books in other European capitals were scrapped.

Random House's president, Bennett Cerf, was besotted with Dare, and never held the book's failure against her. He sent frequent mash notes to Dare over the years she was represented by him. One read, "I only wish the droit de seigneur rules were still in effect…" and another begged, "Come in one day soon and let your publisher kiss you!"

The book reviews expressed some puzzlement as to the target audience. The *New York Times* described me as "piquant" which wasn't exactly insulting, but still sounded like a better adjective for tartar sauce than young teen. Fortunately, I didn't read the *Indianapolis Star* and missed their reviewer's soul-shattering assessment.

"Brook is the girl, and though she isn't pretty she has a mobile, glowing face that is better than mere prettiness."

The teenage awkwardness that saturated, and perhaps sank, *Date With London* proved to be an advantage when I was cast as the sensitive Southern girl, Mick Kelly, in the film version of Carson McCullers's *The Heart Is A Lonely Hunter* opposite Montgomery Clift. Filming was delayed while the producers tried to find a company to insure the troubled Clift, but no one was willing to take that chance. Another producer would make the film several years later, but by then I had outgrown the part along with adolescence.

Dare caught a bit of that vulnerability when she photographed me as an ivy-nibbling nymph a few months after we'd shot *Date With London*.

Brook as a nymph.

Dare's author photo for
Date With London.

32

Dare began working on *The Lonely Doll Learns A Lesson* in 1961 as soon as she had completed *Date With London*. The story was shot almost entirely at her apartment and gave her a bit of breathing space before setting off on her most ambitious book project.

In *The Lonely Doll Learns A Lesson*, Edith neglects Little Bear to focus on her new kitten. She learns how much she misses Little Bear when she's confined to bed with measles and only her kitten for company. Dare was not averse to getting Edith dirty or dampened during a photo shoot, but she carefully taped a cardboard thermometer to Edith's mouth rather than poke a hole in it.

Even though Little Bear accidentally cuts half of Edith's hair off in a misguided attempt to remove a tangle, Edith buys him a puppy with her savings and everyone learns how to get along together.

Dare and I went to the ASPCA to borrow a puppy for a weekend of photography. It might not have been their policy to act as a canine lending library, but the person at the desk was willing to let us choose a beguiling mixed breed for a few days. We brought the puppy back to my block on East 84th Street for an exterior shot, then took the little guy over to Dare's.

The puppy considered Edith a lovely soft chew toy and had to be prised off her arm several times during the shoot.

I was in school when Dare returned it, and glad to miss the farewell.

Dare with the feisty kitten.

33

Dare's childhood fascination with myths and enchantments, as well as her own perception of being not quite real, found their way into her next book, *Lona, A Fairy Tale.*

This was a story for older children, and even adults, and Dare's dry humor was evident from the first sentence:

> *Once upon a time, when magic was common and princesses were plentiful, there were three kingdoms. They were happy kingdoms. All their wars were done, and all their kings were wise.*
>
> *One of the plentiful princesses was a baby named Lona of Yarmalit, who was captured by Druth, the evil wizard.*

Druth locked Lona in his castle until he could perfect a princess spell. Princes, however, were easy to enchant, and Druth turned young Prince Rogain of Muirlan into a toad simply for spite.

Dare had featured two of her childhood dolls, Edith and Persis, in her earlier books, and now it was time to bring out another. Lona was an Italian doll manufactured by the Lenci Company who had also made Edith. But whereas Edith was created to resemble a young child, Lona was a long-limbed lady "boudoir" doll originally dressed as Madame Pompadour. Lona was never intended for childish play, and she was pristine when she joined Dare and Edie in 1961 on their worldwide photo shoot.

Before they left, Dare and Edie sewed matching costumes for Lona and Dare. In the story, the wizard Druth casts a spell on the grownup Lona, turning her into a doll-sized princess. Dare would photograph herself and the doll as the large and tiny versions of the princess.

They traveled around France in the summer of 1961, with Dare driving a stick shift on an underpowered Simca as Edie exhaled smoke clouds out the window.

Dare as Princess Lona.

Dare's childhood doll Lona played the diminutive Princess after she was shrunken by an evil wizard's spell.

A rather foppish young Frenchman dropped by the photo shoot to chat with Dare.

Dare as Princess Lona.

A mirror in a small French hotel reflects Edie bathing in her pearls.

Dare wrote Blaine about the gray weather and challenging plumbing.

Dare sent Blaine a letter in August 1961, which she began in Pontivy, Brittany and finished in Vitré. They had left Beg Meil three days earlier and were driving back to Paris with stops at all the towns with castles that might work in the book. Fougeres, Laval and Chateaudun were next on the list. Dare wrote:

> *We now know what it's like to stay in a third-class French provincial hotel. You need a flashlight, a map, and a compass to find the bathroom.*
>
> *[After dealing with food poisoning in Paris and a bungled car rental]…we could not get reservations anywhere we'd planned to go, and finally ended up on the coast of Brittany for a month. There were magnificent beaches alternating with stretches of great rocks, and we were very happy when the sun shone. Unfortunately it did not for eleven solid days. And it was colder inside than*

out. But we did get a rest – in a dull sort of way, and I shot three sequences for Lona.

> *The place I was mad for was Pointe du Van which is land's end for France. There's a moor with gorse, and thyme, and heather and a steady buzz of bees. Then cliffs and rocks dropping 340 feet to the sea, and little white waves curling around their base, and white gulls flying which you had to look down on instead of up at.*

Dare assured Blaine, "I haven't run into any bogs or knocked down a single sign yet. I'm expert at negotiating medieval streets that go straight up, are too narrow to pass in, and madly cobbled, and full of babies, bicycles, cats, chickens, and people who never look behind them."

As for the book's magical theme, Dare told a reporter, "It is hard for caretakers in lovely old castles to understand why you want to photograph a toad on the turret."

Pointe du Van on the coast of Brittany.

Dare sculpting the enchanted toad.

Dare's doll Lona contemplates the view from the backseat.

Edie and Dare brought Lona to Ocracoke to shoot the beach scenes and employed "Young Jake" Alligood – the son of the island's original taxi driver – to help them.

Dare contrasted Young Jake with his late father:

"Big Jake was a good talker, but Little Jake is a cautious one with words. Tall and lean, and slow to speak his mind is Little Jake. Some of the flavor went out of Ocracoke when they buried Big Jake, but Little Jake is still there to greet you with his slow smile."

Back in New York, toads, dragons and princesses took over Dare's apartment.

Dare fashioned a two-headed dragon out of clay and had Edie blow cigarette smoke so it could seem to breathe fire. Edie used a lighter I had bought her as a birthday present several years earlier. She had been charmed by the unusual tribute from a small child.

Dare photographed herself nude for the shot where Lona is transformed back into a full-sized princess, but she blurred the photo in the final print.

She asked her literary agent, Bill Berger, to play the prince. Bill was a good-looking man with an often bitter view of life in general and clients in particular. His skills in negotiating Dare's contracts were less than stellar, but Dare did not see Bill's shortcomings. He was quite pleased to dress up in tights and chain mail for the book, and Dare used an illustration from her childhood King Arthur book as inspiration for his costume.

Edie blowing smoke for the dragon on Dare's tabletop.

193

Dare's apartment was a welcome refuge for me as she worked on Lona through 1961 and 1962, and I enjoyed being part of her creative process. There were problems at home that I could not mention to anyone. Eugenia had discovered a cache of love letters between Don and a beautiful blonde actress and had sequestered herself in the bedroom with a bottle of Bourbon and a prescription for Seconal. Don wisely fled to an attic room at the all-male Players Club. I was very fond of the woman who wrote the letters. She was elegant in her pencil skirts and peplum jackets, perceptive about my adolescent angst, self-assured in her career and also married. They continued their affair through the following decade in different cities and continents, even when my father branched out to comely British actresses and worked his way through most of the leading women in the Royal Shakespeare Company.

At fourteen, I was old enough to say, if anyone asked or cared where I was going, that I'd be with a friend. More often than not, I went to Dare's. Although she knew something was very wrong, Dare never pried or tried to get me tell her what was happening. Instead, she let me model the clay dragon with her or suggest poses for the self-absorbed Bill Berger as he puffed out his armored chest.

Although the reviews were generally favorable, *Lona* was not a commercial success. The text was too long for the young children who had fallen in love with *The Lonely Doll* series.

One reviewer commented, "I fear Miss Wright has tried to write all the world's great fairy tales rolled into one.

Dare was not trying to combine all the world's great fairy tales—only those that had affected her childhood and continued to resonate through her adult years. *Lona* had elements dating back to Dare and Blaine's forced childhood separation, the forbidden "Little Green Door" in her schoolgirl story, the elusiveness of true love, honor, courage, sacrifice and the never-answered question of how to become "real." Is the enchanted Lona played by Dare's doll any less real than the full-sized Princess Lona portrayed by Dare?

When Lona is turned into a toad at the end of the story, the Prince tells her, "Toad or Princess, I love you." She is as real to the Prince in amphibian form as she was as a beautiful Princess.

Lona could have become a classic in the era when Dare and her teenage peers had read complex fairy tales, but that time had passed.

Blaine's former girlfriend, Dorothy Tivis, arranged for *Lona* to have a tie-in with Vanity Fair lingerie. The campaign featured princess-appropriate adult nightgowns with castle backdrops. It seemed an odd matchup for a children's book.

Dare passed the complimentary nightgowns the company sent her along to me. She made her own gowns from fine cotton lawn and antique lace. Vanity Fair manufactured theirs from the most flammable of man-made fibers.

Dare posing as Princess Lona for a *Vanity Fair* lingerie promotion.

34

The Saturday Evening Post featured Dare in their "People On The Way Up" article in May 1962.

> *With the gracious cooperation of her doll friends, Dare Wright, 35, produces unusual children's books. 'I don't think of Edith as a doll', says Dare. 'She was my friend when I was a child and now she supports me. She's a personality in her own right.'*
>
> *The RAF pilot to whom she was engaged died in a crash, and Dare is still single – though not resolutely so. When she goes on vacation, she locks Edith and the bears in a bank vault. Once one of the bank officials, to whom the stuffed creatures in the vault seemed more animate than some of the stuffed shirts he knew, warned Dare: 'We won't know what to do if they cry!'*

Dare was actually 47, not 35, and she and Edie both needed a vacation after working on *Lona* for two years. They stayed at Bermuda's Castle Harbour Hotel in the summer of 1962 and were interviewed by the *Royal Gazette*.

The newspaper wrote that Mrs. Wright was hesitant about divulging much personal information she picked up while painting Sir Winston Churchill but mentions his complimenting her on the excellent likeness.

Churchill actually did not sit for Edie – she painted him from photographs – but Edie saw no reason to correct the reporter's assumption. He had, after all, written her a charming letter of gratitude.

Edie's painting of Dare against a
Bermuda backdrop.

Edie was close to eighty and still taking portrait commissions. Some of the paintings she did in the 1960s show an experimentation with more modern technique than her earlier ones, although the results seem less timeless.

Edie returned to Cleveland in respiratory distress, and her young physician, Dr. David Schultz, had her hospitalized for a severe lung infection. He later told his wife, Betsy, that Dare's visits to see Edie in the hospital always caused a stir. The staff was in awe of this gorgeous woman.

After Edie recuperated, she painted David Schultz's portrait to thank him. Dare took a set of photographs at Edie's Cleveland penthouse for her to work from. The handsome and then single doctor was smitten with Dare and visited her in New York, but she politely rebuffed his advances.

My father said that men mistook Dare's shyness for coyness, and that was a frequent reason they misread her signals. Potential lovers were bewildered when what they perceived as an invitation from Dare to proceed physically turned out to be simple friendliness. She was as innocent and guileless as her Edith or Persis dolls, and as unaware of her seductiveness as a five-year-old.

The anomaly of a brilliant and talented woman whose capacity for a mature physical relationship was arrested in her childhood might also hold the key to her success as an author. She could write from a child's point of view, because, like J.M. Barrie, the author of *Peter Pan*, she never outgrew the perspective of childhood.

David Schultz was Edie's physician and Dare's potential suitor.

Edie did a nude sketch of Dare in red charcoal at the same time she painted David Schultz's portrait. The men who came to Dare's apartment for cocktails or posed in Edie's studio had no idea what happened after they left.

35

Dare traveled to England by herself in June of 1963. It was a nostalgic trip to visit Philip Sandeman's younger brother Brian and his large family in Guilford as well as Philip's mother Marie. Brian's children adored Dare—the aunt they would have known if things had worked out differently.

There was another wistful meeting with Colin Keith-Johnston, her dear friend from the days they had acted together in *Pride and Prejudice*. They spent time in the country with Colin's nine-year-old son, Hugo, whom Dare had first met when she shot *Date With London* in 1960. Although he was sixty-seven, Colin bicycled around his garden with Hugo on his shoulders exhibiting, as always, the best of English gallantry. It was the last time they would see each other. Dare took a photograph of herself when she returned to New York and superimposed it on a background of the English countryside to send him as a memento.

Dare in England with her late fiancé's brother Brian Sandeman.

Colin Keith-Johnston with his son Hugo.

"For Colin."

Edith And Mr. Bear was Dare's next book. She returned to the original characters and familiar settings, shooting it entirely in New York in 1963. The plot centered on Edith's anguish after lying to Mr. Bear about breaking his valuable clock.

Dare created the scene where Mr. Bear arrives home with the packaged clock by placing two photos she had taken on a worktable and photographing them together for the finished picture. It was a technique she had begun with Lona and would often employ again. Dare made certain that the perspective worked just right when she combined the photographs.

Dare photographed the background…

then shot Mr. Bear on her terrace…

and created a blended photo for the book.

Edith does not intend to get into mischief, but she cannot stop herself from climbing up to investigate Mr. Bear's new purchase. The pile of books she's stand-ing on begins to wobble, and Edith and the new clock come crashing down.

She lies to Mr. Bear when he asks whether she or Little Bear broke the clock and feels miserable afterwards. Edith cannot even enjoy her birthday party, and quarrels with Little Bear over his artwork.

Little Bear calls Edith "horrid" after she stomps on his drawing.

"I am horrid," she muses, "I get horrider every day. Pretty soon nobody will like me. Maybe I should run away."

Edith slips out of the house and runs and runs until the streets around her are all unfamiliar. Cold and tired, Edith cries herself to sleep beside an ash can.

Dare shot those scenes on Tallulah Bankhead's block of East 62nd Street. Dare herself had run across that neighborhood one night in the mid-1950s, escaping from a date that had turned violent. Dare had gone back to a man's apartment for an after-dinner drink and had to fight him off when they were inside.

She broke away from his grasp and raced across town leaving her small clutch purse behind. Losing her shoes as she ran through the streets, she tumbled to her knees on the rough concrete. Dare's feet were bloody and her eye was blackened when she phoned my father for help.

Dare initially refused to reveal the man's name, and the purse was delivered to her apartment by messenger the following day.

Blaine asked my father to hire a private detective to track the man down. He also said that he needed to retain my father's legal services as he planned to kill Dare's attacker.

Dare's assailant turned out to be someone we all knew. He was a cocky, arrogant young man who had insinuated himself into Dare and Edie's world as the protégé of one of their dearest friends. They had welcomed him to their cocktail parties and Dare even took a series of photographs of him as a gift, but all her talent couldn't soften the sneering curl of the man's upper lip in the pictures. He moved through what would be a long life with the voracity of a sea lamprey, attaching himself to beautiful, famous and often wealthy quarry. Attracted by the glittering phosphorescence of his prey, he scraped away at their golden aura, taking enough of it to nourish himself while giving his victim the impression of being groomed.

In *Edith And Mr. Bear,* Edith returns home after realizing that she has to tell Mr. Bear that she was the one who broke his clock. He gives her a bath and a glass of hot milk, saying, "I wouldn't have punished you for an accident if only you had told me the truth."

Although Edith cannot seem to avoid getting into more trouble, she never lies to Mr. Bear again.

Book reviewers were happy to see Dare return to more familiar subject matter. The *Atlanta Constitution* commented, "There's magic in Miss Wright's books about a doll named Edith, and her friend Mr. Bear. The author's superb photography lifts all her story books into the realm of art."

Dare's jacket photo for *Edith And Mr. Bear.*

Towards the end of *Edith And Mr. Bear*, Edith decides that cooking a surprise for Mr. Bear might make amends for her naughtiness.

"You're making an awful mess," Little Bear comments.

"All good cooks make messes," Edith replies covered in flour.

Ignoring Mr. Bear's warning about using the stove, Edith convinces Little Bear to help her light the matches. In reality, the tiny kitchen in Dare's apartment didn't even have a stove – just a sink and minuscule refrigerator with four burners perched on top. And the workspace where Edith and Little Bear mixed up the batter was a wooden board that Dare could remove when she needed access to her closet darkroom.

Dare brought Persis, her little bisque doll, back for a 1965 book titled *Take Me Home*. She photographed most of the story near Blaine's home in Walton, New York, added some unused pictures she had taken in 1959 for *The Little One*, and shot the rest of the book in her apartment. The tiny doll, called Robin in this story, lives happily in the woods among the wild creatures. Wearing dresses made of leaves, or nothing at all, she lives on honey, berries, and sunshine. One day, as Robin is napping near a path, a little girl picks her up and takes her home with her. "Put me down, put me down," Robin shouts, "I live in the woods. It's my home."

But the little girl wasn't able to hear dolls talk.

The woods were very quiet without the small doll, and all the birds and animals missed her very much. When Robin's friend, Crow, flies to the house where Robin is living, she begs him to take her back to her woodland home. Along with a small stuffed bear belonging to the little girl, Robin escapes the confines of living indoors and wearing a dress, and they run to freedom through the snow with Crow flying overhead like a protecting black shadow.

Dare was fifty when she wrote and photographed the story. Like Robin, she had chosen a lifestyle that was different from conventional expectations, but rewarding in its artistic freedom.

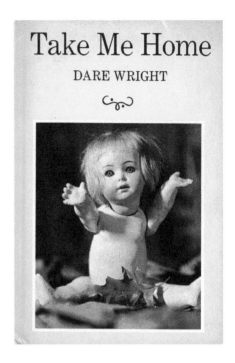

36

Dare photographed me in a long black dress before the 1965 Brearley School Senior Dance. It was well before the time when teenagers wore black, and the color stood out in the swirl of pastels on the dance floor. I'd chosen the dress because of its resemblance to the one in Dare's 1939 portrait, and borrowed her silk stole. I took a date with silver hair and felt uncharacteristically soignée.

The Sixties were in full swing and Dare and Edie shortened their skirts to match the era. With none of their sewing skills, I made myself a shiny silver minidress to wear at a discotheque party with Andy Warhol and his "Superstar" muse Edie Sedgwick. Edie was only in her early twenties, and as vulnerable and fragile as a fawn. Ravaged by her childhood, Edie was spun to iridescent powder when she stepped into Warhol's orbit. That evening, Edie swayed slowly in a dance floor spotlight while girls wearing go-go boots danced in cages hung from the ceiling. A loud and very large woman – one of Andy Warhol's indispensable assistants whom I'll call Moira – wove frenetically through the crowd.

Wealthy, privileged and addicted to amphetamines, Moira was known for giving drugs to Warhol's acolytes with the same dirty syringes she used on herself. I didn't even drink and had no desire to experiment with drugs. Only eighteen, I was younger than most of the crowd and ready to go home. On the way out, I stopped in the ladies room and was about to exit my bathroom stall when I heard Moira's voice on the other side.

"Want a poke?" she yelled as her hand, holding a syringe, came under the stall door. I jumped up on the toilet seat, balancing on my slippery heels to keep from falling into the bowl. Moira's hand moved like a blind snake, trying to find where I was hiding, and I felt a seam of my shiny, and poorly sewn silver dress rip up the side. Frustrated, Moira withdrew her hand, leveraged herself up with a groan, and took the syringe back to the crowd.

I carried the dress over to Dare's apartment a few days later and although she showed me how to bind the seam so it wouldn't split, it felt too tainted to ever wear again.

Brook with Dare's borrowed stole.

Dare and Edie beneath Brook's portrait.

Dare had entered her fifties with no shortage of suitors. Her dates still followed a predictable pattern of courtship. A man became infatuated, they had cocktails at Dare's apartment, they went to dinner and then everything fizzled. If it had been surprising to find that Dare was a virgin back in the days of the 1949 Cooper Marsh trial, it seemed implausible in 1965.

The British actor, Dennis King, was a gentleman much in the style of Colin Keith-Johnston. There was an exceptional gallantry to these British actors born in the final years of Queen Victoria's reign. A recent widower and her senior by seventeen years, Dennis proposed to Dare but ruefully accepted her friendship instead of marriage. Dennis had starred in a successful Broadway operetta *The Vagabond King* thirty years earlier, and often serenaded Dare with songs from the production when she went to his apartment. The bathroom was just off the living area. When Dare first asked to use it, Dennis told her, "There's not much privacy, so I shall sing quite loudly while you are in there."

Dennis King, an actor and consummate gentleman.

Brook as a college freshman.

At eighteen, I began dating a series of older men. There was a six-foot five fledgling actor named John Phillip Law, who would soon find Hollywood fame co-starring with Jane Fonda in *Barbarella,* and the writer, George Plimpton, who had graduated from Harvard the year after I was born. George and I took Dare to dinner with us at the fabled Elaine's restaurant one night. She mesmerized the bawdy, misogynist crowd not only with her ethereal beauty, but also by speaking quietly and intelligently on the current literary market. Even George's pal Norman Mailer, who had stabbed his second wife only five years earlier and usually expressed a strong, if not quite so violent, rage toward female authors pulled his chair closer to Dare and took a piece of chicken off her plate. George, for all of his erudition and editorial acumen, was given

to repeating the story of his legendary boxing matches with Ernest Hemingway once too often of an evening.

Dare and Edie traveled to Virgin Gorda in the British West Indies in 1965, spending several weeks at the Little Dix Bay resort. Dare brought her movie camera, and Edie captured her daughter's luminous smile and bout of giggles when she tripped over her flippers emerging from the ocean. It was a time of regeneration in a seductive climate.

They filmed each other with the movie camera walking amidst the lush foliage, bathing in the ocean and in their spacious hotel room. In one short segment, Dare films Edie in front of the dressing table rolling her hair for the night. There's a brief moment where Dare and her camera are reflected in the mirror. Dare is completely nude.

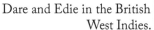

Dare and Edie in the British West Indies.

37

A Gift From The Lonely Doll proved to be one of the most popular books in Dare's *Lonely Doll* series. Published in 1966, the story tells how Edith knits a very special, if ridiculously long, Christmas scarf for Mr. Bear. Dare went back to Walton for the location photography and made a country-themed set at Edie's Cleveland penthouse to finish the interior shots. *American Weekly* magazine featured a color photo from the book on its cover.

In the book, Edith keeps her knitting a secret from Mr. Bear and tucks it into a basket as she finishes a row. When Edith unfurls Mr. Bear's Christmas scarf, it's clear that she's made it way too long. Little Bear, quite unnecessarily, points that out to her.

Edith is miserable but solves the problem by cutting the scarf into three smaller ones so Mr. Bear and his cousins would each have one.

That same year, Edie painted a portrait of herself and Dare standing by an easel. Edie's expression holds a touch of sadness and Dare's face is, as always, mysterious.

Edie surprised my grandmother with a painting of my late grandfather, Justice A.A.F. Seawell. Grandmother and Edie had met several times over the years, and she and Dare had bonded during our *Date With London* trip. She took Edie's side against my mother in the battle over Don's portrait.

Grandmother wrote Edie after she'd received my grandfather's portrait in the summer of 1966. She said she had, "…a quiet feeling that the judge has come home, and a great wonder and delight that you were able to capture so perfectly not only his likeness but his spirit. I believe that, as you say, he must have talked to you. Dare's initials beneath your name--the fact that she too worked upon the portrait — make it all the more precious to me…You both have a thousand-fold my deepest love and appreciation." She added a postscript, "Eugenia says she is not coming to see us. Why?"

Dare and Edie in 1966.

Edie painted Don's late father from black and white photographs and duplicated Don's skin tones to achieve a remarkable likeness.

38

Dare and Edie had been contemplating a move to a drier climate since the early 1960s. Edie's continual respiratory infections, most certainly not helped by her smoking, and Dare's recurring sinus problems had them considering Arizona or Colorado as possible choices. Edie still lived in Cleveland, but the discussions presumed that she and Dare would move out west together. Edie could leave her Ohio commissions and paint landscapes anywhere, but what would the move do to Dare's career and social life? Edith and The Bears were grounded in New York, even if their books often took them to rural settings. Dare's life was also woven in the fabric of the city. It was one thing to travel with her mother to exotic locales like Sicily and Virgin Gorda, but very different to uproot their separate lives to begin a joint one in another part of the country.

I was a sophomore at Columbia University when I married in 1967 and left New York for Washington DC. It was wrenching to be apart from Dare and not be able to stop by her apartment whenever I wanted to talk.

We played dress up one more time when I brought my wedding dress over for a bridal portrait. Dare loaned me her gloves, and we bought a bouquet of daisies from the corner store. I hoped I looked all of my nineteen years.

Eugenia was not pleased to be sharing the spotlight with a bride. I had, quite unwisely given that it was only two days before the wedding, planned on cooking dinner for my future in-laws.

Don and I were in the kitchen waiting for the doorbell to ring when he asked me to go check on my mother.

I knocked on her bedroom door and opened it a crack. The lights were off and Eugenia lay on the quilt with her arms stretched in a crucifixal posture.

"I've had a small stroke and I've gone blind," she whispered dramatically from the dark. "Go on without me…I will probably be well by morning."

I walked back to the kitchen and told my father with an emotionless delivery, "She says she's had a small stroke and has gone blind but should be well by morning." There was only the briefest of beats before Don responded. "Right…will you help me with this tray?"

I wasn't surprised at Don's reaction. Acknowledging Eugenia's eccentricities was strictly forbidden. Don did catch me by surprise two days later as he walked me down the aisle. Although I hadn't told anyone, I had almost canceled my wedding the week before. The strains of "Trumpet Voluntary" wafted over the guests and I saw Dare and Tallulah's smiling faces as Don leaned his head towards mine.

"It's not too late to back out," he stage-whispered with absolute sincerity. "We'll just turn around right now."

Dare photographed Brook as a bride-to-be.

Dare had to give up her apartment at 29 W. 58th Street in 1967 when the charming old building was slated to be demolished. She photographed Edith and The Bears there for the last time, standing in the emptied room amidst the rolled-up carpets and moving boxes.

Her new apartment at 11 E. 80th Street was carved out of an upper floor of the former Bloomingdale mansion. It was an elegant address, but Dare's little sliver of the building seemed oppressive. Unlike her previous flat, there were no tall windows or terrace to let in a breeze and it was a less-inspiring backdrop for Lonely Doll photography.

In an era of decorative overload – explosions of flowers on fabrics and even patterned toilet paper – Dare brought simplicity to design and fashion. She copied the shelving and couch from her previous apartment and made cushions to place on luggage racks for extra seating. Dare also saved the fireplace mantle from 29 W 58th Street and installed it in her new living room.

Edith and The Bears bidding goodbye to 29 West 58th Street.

Dare went to Colorado that summer of 1967 to continue a new series without Edith and The Bears. *Look At A Colt* would be the second title intended to bring children closer to the natural world. *Look At A Gull* had initiated the series showing the life of a seagull from egg to flight.

The colt was three weeks late being born, and Dare was in the barn when it finally arrived at 2:00 a.m. Dare's natural shyness did not extend to squeamishness, and she photographed the colt as it emerged from its mother.

The series received excellent reviews, but never came near the success of Dare's earlier books. The photographs were beautiful but needed the dolls and bears to capture the reader's interest.

My father was now spending most of his time in Denver, while my mother preferred to stay in New York with her theatre work. Don had been asked to move to Denver to take over as legal counsel to *The Denver Post*, and would later become its president and then move on to founding The Denver Center For The Performing Arts.

Dare stayed with Don in Denver before he drove her to the ranch to await the colt's birth. They would no longer see each other as much as they had in the past when Dare often dropped into his New York law office for advice or a chat.

The end of the Sixties was an unsettling time for Dare. I had left New York, Don was only there occasionally, Edie's health was less robust, and political and social unrest thrummed in the background.

Dare and Edie revisited Colorado as a possible place to relocate. My father arranged for Edie to paint the late Frederick Bonfils, one of the founders of *The Denver Post*, and introduced her to Bon-

fils' daughter Helen. Helen, then President of *The Post*, did not warm to Edie or her painting. She remembered her father as being much taller than Edie portrayed him. Edie had the last word in an interview, where she mentioned that famous men always gained several inches in height after their deaths.

39

Dare brought Edith and The Bears back for her next book *Edith And Big Bad Bill*.

Random House's publisher, Bennett Cerf, wrote Dare in 1968 that he thought the book was charming and might be her biggest success yet, adding that New York's Mayor John Lindsay wanted to go into the book publishing business after seeing how pretty Dare was.

In the story, Mr. Bear takes Edith and Little Bear to visit his cousins Charles and Albert in the country. They are warned to keep out of the dark wood where a notoriously bad black bear is living.

"They say he's big, and he's a different color," Cousin Albert says.

"Is that bad?" asks Little Bear.

"Everyone knows that all proper bears are brown just like us," Cousin Charles tells him.

Naturally, Little Bear coaxes Edith into exploring the dark wood. They are captured by Big Bad Bill, who ties Edith to a tree to stop her yelling. Little Bear explains that Edith is just frightened, and Bill quickly unties her.

Although Bill seems threatening, Edith and Lit-tle Bear soon realize it is just bluster. Little Bear loves staying at Bill's cabin and learns to whittle and build fires just like the big bear.

Neither the cantankerous Bill nor Little Bear think Edith is much good at anything, but she proves them wrong when Bill accidently chops his foot.

As Little Bear calls for help Edith impudently parrots his words back, "How can I help? Girls aren't good for anything."

While she takes charge of Bill's wound, she muses to Little Bear, "You know...I don't believe Bill is bad at all...I think he's just lonely the way I was before you and Mr. Bear found me. It makes people cross and mean to be lonely."

Dare intended the book to be viewed as an old-fashioned melodrama, but it was not received that way. Edith's being tied to a tree was supposed to remind readers of *The Perils Of Pauline* silent movies or the more recent "Dudley Do-Right" episodes of *The Rocky and Bullwinkle Show* where the heroine was roped to the railroad tracks.

Only one reviewer mentioned the book's civil rights position: "There is a small lesson in integration in this book as they find that, in spite of being different in color (the other bears are all brown) [Bill] is not at all bad—only lonely."

Edith and Little Bear argue with Mr. Bear's cousins that Big Bad Bill should not be judged by his looks, and Edith accuses them of hating Bill because he's a different color.

"I think black and white bears are nicer than just common brown bears, so there!" she cries.

Mr. Bear agrees and convinces Charles and Albert to invite Bill to dinner.

The book ends with Bill showing up at their door for the meal and the promise of future friendship.

Dare photographed the book around Blaine's home in Walton, NY. Big Bad Bill was a large Steiff bear that Dare had colored with shoe polish. He had to be handled carefully, as the polish rubbed off.

I can hear Dare and Blaine's own playful voices in the banter between Big Bad Bill and Edith, but it did not translate to a successful book.

Dare's Random House editor forwarded two letters they had received. One told Dare to stop writing children's books if she continued presenting Edith as a stereotyped weak female. The second was attached to a copy of *Edith And Big Bad Bill* and had several pages underlined in red pencil, "Your betrayal of the female sex is infamous, doubly so as you are a member, if your photograph is to be trusted. I have marked the passages which I found injurious to my daughters' image of True Womanhood."

Dare's editor tried to soften the outrage by writing, "Ever since women's lib started up, we at Random House have occasionally received letters castigating us for the image of women that various back-list books present. Who would have guessed that poor little Edith would ever have provoked such a violent reaction! Well, there's no pleasing everybody."

If Dare could not control the public opinions of *Big Bad Bill*, she could at least refashion her Edith doll. She and Edie wiped the old eyes, mouth and brows off, then repainted Edith with new features to face an increasingly critical audience.

Edith in mid-repair.

Edie repairs Dare's Edith doll with the precision of a surgeon as her lit Chesterfield sends a wisp of smoke wafting above the operating table. The patient received new felt on her limbs and freshly painted facial features.

40

Tallulah died in December 1968. Although she had become increasingly frail, I was unprepared when I found out by hearing a college classmate casually mention her death. Eugenia had kept the news of Tallulah's final illness from me. She was never good at sharing.

Dare came with us to Tallulah's memorial service at St. Bartholomew's on Park Avenue, and we sat in the front pew as family. Tenor Robert Merrill sang her radio theme song, "May The Good Lord Bless and Keep You". My legs buckled – a phenomenon I had only read about – and my father caught me before I fell.

Tennessee Williams, whom Tallulah had me call "Uncle Tenn" when I was a child, described her as "a fantastic cross-breeding of a moth and a tiger."

Edie and Dare returned to Ocracoke for a final vacation. The beach was now too crowded for nude sunbathing and the slow-paced island lifestyle was disappearing. They had been aware of its fragility from their first visit two decades earlier and did not want to witness any more of its erosion.

Dare would look back on that earlier time in a private book she wrote titled *Ocracoke In The Fifties*.

Wearing Don's "I Love You" charm bracelet.

Ocracoke children.

The 1970s were a difficult time to live in New York. It was a dirty and crime-ridden city that pulsed to a menacing back-beat. Dare was pushed off a curb and hit her head on the sidewalk. She spoke of moving to California, but instead wrote *Edith And Little Bear Lend A Hand*, which celebrated the positive potential of the city she had lived in for four decades.

In the book, Mr. Bear decides to move Edith and Little Bear away from the dirty city so they will have clean air and room to grow.

"The city is bad for you," Mr. Bear tells them when they come home from school. "It's crowded, dirty, noisy, and the air's not fit to breathe…You'll love the country."

"No, we won't, because it isn't home," they protest.

When they realize that Mr. Bear is not going to change his mind, Little Bear comes up with a plan, "If the dirt and noise and bad air all got cleaned up, I bet he'd let us stay."

Edith and Little Bear write the Mayor asking what they can do to improve their city. He responds by telling them that nobody's too little to help in the cleanup. They begin picking up every candy wrapper, old newspaper, paper cup and bottle cap dropped in the street. Edith dials a special number the Mayor has given to report smoking chimneys and Little Bear discovers a recycling center for their old bottles and cans.

Their efforts persuade Mr. Bear to reconsider leaving the city.

"Promise we won't move away," begs Little Bear.

"No promises," answers Mr. Bear. "But since you care so much, and you've worked so hard, we can stay for now."

Edith and The Bears on Dare's block of East 80th Street.

The trio take a boat trip past the almost completed Twin Towers of The World Trade Center in *Edith And Little Bear Lend A Hand*.

41

I brought my baby daughter Brett up from Washington in the spring of 1972 so Dare could meet her. I had wanted to name her after Dare but knew the fallout from my mother would be too intense.

Dare held Brett tenderly and gave her own baby bracelet to her. Brett fell asleep in Dare's arms, as comfortable in her presence as every baby, child or animal I'd ever seen Dare touch.

Dare often came down to our Maryland farm with us. There was now electricity and running water and even a swimming pool, but the old house was not all that changed from when she and Edie had stayed there in the Forties. Mice still ran across the baseboards and snakes startled guests on a regular basis.

Once Dare arrived with her hand wrapped in a bandage.

"I was getting the roaches out of my alarm clock, and the knife slipped," she explained. "A rather New York story," she added with a smile.

Edith and Little Bear's hopes for a cleaner and safer New York were not coming true. There was an effluence of evil flowing through the crime-ridden city. A friend suggested that I tuck my long hair under a newsboy cap when I walked the cross-town blocks after dark so that I could pass for a boy and not be attacked.

Brook with her daughter Brett.

Gayelord Hauser, whose friendship with Edie had lasted over four decades, wrote her from Sicily in the summer of 1973 after the death of his partner, Frey Brown.

Life has to go on, but it is difficult in so many ways. I live in this paradise which Brownie [Frey's nickname] created, but it's quite empty now and I'll probably sell this place next year. Brownie loved you and Dare and he resented the fact that life pushes us on & on not being with our friends. Now I realize what is important, alas too late. Life is so short and one should be with the few people we love. During Brownie's memorial...I had your dear portrait of him on the fireplace. He looked so alive, gentle & kind thanks to you, darling Edith. Just think how much joy you have given to people whose beloved ones you painted & who have passed on. It's the opposite of a grave or tomb, your portraits are a promise of life everlasting.

Dare went up to Walton to photograph *Look At A Calf* in the summer of 1973, leaving the dolls and bears behind to tell the story of calves and cows and how a dairy was run. Edlyn Chytalo was the freckled faced little girl drinking milk in one of the photographs and remembers Dare's kindnesses. Edlyn and her brother Edward often spent time with Blaine, fishing and learning to identify birds along the Delaware River.

Dare gave Edlyn Prince Rogain's jewel from *Lona* and jokingly lamented how beastly older brothers could be.

Around this time, a mutual friend witnessed my mother verbally attacking Dare when they'd crossed paths at a party. Dare was shocked and wounded by Eugenia's outburst and asked an old friend, the actress Erin O'Brien-Moore, for help in restoring the friendship.

Erin knew both of them well. Eugenia had introduced Erin to Dare back in the 1930s, and Erin and Blaine had a brief fling before he left for the war. Erin wrote back that none of it was Dare's fault. She said Eugenia was a narcissist who would never think of anyone but herself, and only saw the world as, "me, me, me."

Dare phoned my father to say she thought it would be better if she stopped seeing him. She asked if they could spend a day together that she would always remember. Dare and Don had lunch together then took a long walk in Central Park. They went back to Dare's apartment and spent the rest of the afternoon going over old photographs Dare had taken of our family.

She asked Don if he really loved her, and he answered that he did, although he would always remain married to Eugenia. Dare said that was enough for her – knowing that Don loved her – because he was the only man she had ever truly loved.

Don with a wineglass in Dare's apartment.

42

In 1974, Edie left Cleveland to move into Dare's tiny apartment. Dare made artistic morsels to tempt Edie to eat, and helped her with the full makeup, false eyelashes and the wig that she now wore when she went out.

Patty Hearst, whose father was publisher of *The San Francisco Examiner*, had been kidnapped in early 1974 by a group called The Symbionese Liberation Army. The FBI believed my family was also in danger, as my father was publishing *The Denver Post*, and that summer the FBI kept all of us under protective surveillance.

It was a surreal and claustrophobic time, and we were not allowed to tell anyone outside the family what was happening.

The last time I visited Edie in New York, she told me that she wanted to paint my daughter, Brett. "Dare will make her a blue taffeta dress," Edie said softly, "It will go so beautifully with her red-gold hair." There wasn't enough time left for it to happen.

Edie shared Dare's single bed in a narrow hallway off the living room. On the morning of July 29, 1975, Dare woke up to find her mother had died beside her. Edie was ninety-two.

Dare fled to Walton after Edie's funeral. Blaine had moved off his island to a small rental in nearby Downsville, New York on the east branch of the Delaware River. Dare stayed with her old friend, Florence Wakeman, whose home was featured in several of Dare's books.

Dare sent the contested original portrait of my father to my parents, but Eugenia remained unappeased.

Edie never mastered the technique of photography in spite of her many artistic talents.

I flew up from Washington to check on Dare when she returned to the city. We had lunch at a French bistro on Madison Avenue, but Dare only took a few bites of her omelet. She moved a bit of egg to the side of her plate. "It doesn't seem real," she said very quietly, "But perhaps I'm not real either."

I showed her how I had finally gotten my ears pierced, and we laughed about how I had taken my little daughter with me to get the courage to do it. The following week I received a delicate pair of Dare's gold earrings with a note congratulating me on getting my "silly ears" pierced.

She asked about Nana, and I told her I was concerned about the crowd around the methadone clin-

ic that had just opened near Nana's apartment at 216 East 85th Street. The neighborhood was deteriorating, as were so many in the city, and Nana had to walk past menacing young men loitering in front of her building.

Dare phoned me on a Sunday morning in January 1976. She had seen the front-page headline on a New York tabloid that read, "Bound, Gagged, Tortured – Spinster Is Murdered." There was a cover photograph of Nana's body being loaded into an ambulance. She was eighty-four years old.

The last surviving member of Nana's group of German friends – the women who had lost their fiancés in the First World War – arranged her funeral.

Dare was sick for much of that winter with a respiratory infection that turned into pneumonia. Her lungs had always been delicate. Perhaps it was a legacy from Edie's chain smoking.

Dare never really recovered from the profound loss of her mother. Dare had forged her own successful career in a different part of the country, but she and Edie shared an artistic talent and sensibility that stretched beyond their sometimes-indistinguishable painting style. They were each other's closest friend for sixty years.

Edie and Dare.

43

Dare returned to Walton in the summer of 1976 to photograph *Edith And Midnight*.

In the book, Mr. Bear has acquired a country home where Edith and Little Bear can spend their vacations, and Edith is determined to tame a wild black pony she spots running in the moonlight. Little Bear helps her look for the pony that Edith has named Midnight, although his heart is really set on fishing. They lure Midnight towards a fence with apples, and Little Bear manages to rope him.

"He's scared. Let's let him go," Edith cries as she sees the pony struggling. "If he liked us, we wouldn't have to catch him. We'll bring him nice things to eat. We'll make friends with him."

Their patience pays off, and Midnight learns to trust his new companions. Mr. Bear is astounded but agrees that Midnight does indeed belong to them.

Dare also had a new friend, Jerry Mayro, who owned The Burlington Bookshop on Madison Avenue around the corner from Dare's apartment. Jerry watched and fussed over Dare, making certain she ate enough and providing company and books when she was lonely.

Dare wanted to photograph a story for Brett and brought Persis to our Maryland farm in the summer of 1979. I did not know that it was the first time she had seen my father since their day in Central Park five years earlier. Don and Dare walked down to the dock together, and Dare asked him why they had been apart for so long. Don reminded her that she had told him not to see her again.

"I guess I didn't mean it," Dare confessed.

We spent a marvelous week photographing the book. Dare wore a striped leotard when she swam in the pool, and she and Brett made up stories about pirate's treasure buried in the cove, just as she had done with me.

Jerry Mayro in The Burlington Bookshop.

Brett and Persis.

An overly friendly four-foot-long black snake began showing up wherever we went. He draped himself over Brett's bicycle, curled up on the kitchen step waiting for us to open the door and raised himself against the screen on the back porch to see what we were doing. We named him Horace and concluded he must be the reincarnation of a golden retriever.

Dare called the book *Make Me Real*. In the story, Brett's mother brings her a little doll she found in a trunk. Brett is not very interested and tells her, "What I want is someone real who'll play with me. A real, live friend."

Brett goes back to reading her book until she hears a small voice tell her, "My name is Persis. I've been shut up in that trunk for years and years. Don't put me back there where nothing ever happens…You have to keep me. If I belong to you I can be real, and we can be friends."

Brett and Persis spend the summer riding a bicycle, picnicking and swimming in a pool. They go out in a little rowboat and catch a small fish.

Brett and Persis on the dock that Dare and Don built twenty-four years earlier.

230

Brett asks why her mother cannot hear her new friend, and Persis tells her, "Only the little girl I belong to can hear me. I'm just a doll to everybody else."

She promises Brett that they will remain friends forever but tells her sadly that Brett will not be able to hear her when she grows up.

> *"Will you find me another little girl someday?" Persis asks.*
>
> *"I don't want you to have another little girl," Brett replies.*
>
> *"But I'll need a little girl to make me real again. Please," Persis begs.*

Dare wrote the bittersweet ending:

> *They had a long time, filled with fun and adventures, but at last a day came when Brett stopped hearing the sound of Persis' small voice.*
>
> *Brett was grown up, and Persis was just a doll again.*
>
> *Brett never stopped loving her. She never, ever put her away anywhere.*
>
> *Persis is sitting on a shelf where she can see and hear everything that goes on around her.*
>
> *She's waiting for her next little girl. Will it be you?*

There is a photo in the book where Brett is sewing Persis a new wardrobe. Dare had balanced Persis next to Brett on the arm of the rocking chair., and the doll was accidently knocked to the floor. Brett, Don and I looked with shock at Persis' broken head. The only sound was a wasp batting itself against the screening.

Dare touched Brett's hand and said softly, "It's all right, Brett. I'll fix Persis."

She asked my father for a straight pin and some glue. Putting a thin bead of glue on the point of the pin, she slowly pieced Persis' head back together.

When Dare returned to New York she realized that she needed one more shot of Brett on the dock. Going through old negatives, she found a photograph she had taken of me as a child on the same dock and used it as the first picture of Brett in *Make Me Real.*

Dare didn't think anyone would notice when she substituted an old photo she had taken of Brook as child for one of Brett in *Make Me Real.*

Brook's daughter Brett sewing an outfit for Persis.

Don and Dare walked down to the dock each evening. Sipping their gin and tonics, they sat and spoke by the glassy creek as the fairy lights of fireflies swirled about them. Past and future were suspended in the timelessness of familiarity, and whatever lay ahead was impossible to imagine.

Don lived another thirty-six years to reach a hundred and three. His careers included theatrical attorney, Broadway producer, newspaper publisher and head of a performing arts center. He received the Order of The British Empire from Queen Elizabeth, won a Tony Award for producing a Broadway musical and was recognized by B'nai B'rith and the Anti-Defamation League for his contribution to the Jewish cause. In spite of his many affairs, Don stayed married to Eugenia until her death, always crediting their marriage as the secret of his success. A month before his death, he blew a kiss to the portrait of Dare in his apartment.

Dare's final book, *Edith And The Duckling*, was published in 1981. The lesson of learning to let go of something you love reflected Dare and her mother's complex relationship, and also foreshadowed Blaine's death.

She used the Walton, NY home of Blaine's friend, Florence Wakeman, to portray Mr. Bear's summer house. In the story, Edith and Little Bear bring an abandoned duck egg into the house and keep it warm until it hatches. They find that it is not easy following the little duckling as he gets into every corner of the house and even sends Mr. Bear tumbling down the stairs. Mr. Bear helps them build an outdoor shelter, and the little duck learns to swim in an old tin pan.

All too soon, the duck is grown and ready to fly south for the winter.

"I didn't think he'd leave us. We're his mother," said Edith. "I don't want to watch him fly away."

"Edith, ducks belong to the water and the sky," said Mr. Bear. "You've raised a fine duck. Can't you be happy to let him go where he belongs?"

Mr. Bear tells Edith that he cannot promise it, but the duck will probably return in the spring.

"This is his home, and you're his family. I think he'll be back."

Edith, with tears in her eyes, answers, "All right, then. Goodbye, our duck. See you in the spring, dear duck. Oh, Mr. Bear, why is spring so far away?"

Blaine took the joyful book jacket photo of Dare.

Blaine took Dare's author photo for *Edith And The Duckling*.

In December 1981, Dare received a visit from a long-forgotten acquaintance. Alton Ballance met Dare briefly as a child growing up on Ocracoke years before and had never forgotten her or Edie. He recalled their magical reunion.

Looking back on my first trip to New York, I believe during Christmas, 1981, I can't remember now why I decided to connect with Dare. Perhaps it was knowing that she lived in the city and her association with Ocracoke

I took a cab over to her East Side apartment. It was all a dream-like evening surrounded by the glow of Christmas. I had never spent a Christmas off the island. Walking into the apartment I was intrigued by the paintings on the wall, her many possessions, and this legendary woman from my childhood and Ocracoke's past (I would later think of Miss Havisham from Great Expectations). Of course she showed me Edith and the bears.

Eventually she shared the scrapbook with the Ocracoke in the 50s photos and texts, neatly pasted under or beside the photos. She asked what I thought about them being published and I encouraged her to pursue this. I also asked if she would ever return to Ocracoke and she said no, that it wouldn't be the same without her mother – as well as knowing how much the place had changed.

Our visit went several hours, and eventually we walked out together onto 5th Avenue. A man walked by wearing a long mink coat. I thought, "I am in New York City and it's Christmas Eve." The air was sharp, with only light traffic moving by. During a moment of silence before I hailed a cab, Dare said, "Oh…it's Christmas Eve."

I will never forget this.

Dare as a Christmas angel.

44

Blaine's health was failing. His life-long cigarette habit caused circulation problems in his legs, and he was in the early stages of lung cancer. He broke his hip in a fall, and Dare went up to nurse him.

A Downsville local, Edward Chytalo, remembers Blaine as a happy man whose modest income from the "Phoebe" fishing lure allowed him to live as he wanted. As a young boy, Edward was impressed by Blaine's diet of raw hamburger and mayonnaise with a side mixture of honey and beer atop corn kernels. Blaine taught Edward to fish, although he always threw the fish back.

Edward and his sister Edlyn learned the names of birds from Blaine as they floated downriver in his boat. Blaine seemed to have an infinite knowledge of the natural world that he preferred over the man-made one.

Blaine in his later years.

Blaine in the 1950s.

Edward took his driver's test in Blaine's Rambler wagon, and Blaine came to the high school to watch Edward inducted into the honor society. Blaine was always available to sit and talk on his cabin porch. The sensitive boy from the small town learned that the RAF fliers were given a special drink – Blaine called it "Kickapoo Joy Juice" – to loosen them up when they returned from a bombing mission so they could talk about the horrors they had witnessed.

Blaine drank in the evenings as he read by his stove. He drank alone, and perhaps he drank a bit too much, but he was never a staggering drunk.

Edward adopted Blaine's "uniform" of khaki pants, a white shirt and Stan Smith sneakers to wear in Blaine's honor into his adulthood.

Blaine withdrew as he grew weaker, seeking a quiet place to die much as an animal would do. Edward and his family left food and books on his porch and went back later to see that Blaine had taken them inside.

Dare spoke to Blaine on the phone. He did not want her to see him, and she agonized whether she should go anyway. In the end, she remained in New York. Blaine died on July 23, 1985 at the age of seventy-three.

Edlyn Chytalo, Edward's little sister, spoke about an incident on Blaine's river: "I went for a canoe ride after Blaine died and took the jaunt that Blaine and I did often. A red wing blackbird sat on the end of my canoe; I knew it was him. I will always treasure the knowledge he taught me on the fine art of birding. I was blessed to have Blaine and Dare a part of my childhood."

45

Blaine's death was a defining moment for Dare. Her brother had vanished once from her life when their parents divorced. Now she faced the same void she had known as a two-year-old, but without her mother's strong presence to buffer the tragedy.

Dare and Edie had enjoyed a single cocktail before dinner. Now Dare began having a second one, and dinner became a cracker or two. Jerry Mayro and a few other friends brought Dare meals, and I sent boxes of easy-to-prepare foods from Washington. We saw her grief, but it took a while to recognize the extent of Dare's drinking. Like Blaine, she hid her pain well.

Jerry and my father arranged for Dare to enter a small facility on the Upper East Side where she could be helped. She went voluntarily but left after a couple of days. Dare could not find her street clothing and walked back to 11 East 80th Street in her nightgown.

May 17, 1988 was an oppressively steamy day. I made several calls to Dare from my home in Washington, DC, but she never picked up. Dare did not have an answering machine, and the phone just continued ringing. By early evening I was worried enough to fly to New York. She did not answer her door, but I thought I could hear faint noises behind it. I ran out to a corner phone booth and dialed 911. The police came quickly and broke down Dare's door. She was lying in a pool of blood moaning softly.

The coffin-sized elevator was too small for a stretcher, and the ambulance crew had to carry her down three flights of marble stairs. I rode in the ambulance with her to New York Hospital. The admitting physician said Dare had lost so much blood that she would not have lived until morning.

Jerry Mayro and I went back to Dare's apartment to figure out what had happened. Dare must have fallen and hit her head on the bronze bust of Voltaire sitting on the hearth. I'd always disliked Voltaire's smirking expression; now it leered through a wash of blood.

Dare had tried to clean her wound--the bathtub was filled with blood—and then stumbled around the apartment as she became weaker, leaving smears on

Dare in lower Manhattan in the 1940s.

the walls and furniture.

We brought mops, buckets and masks to clean the apartment. Jerry had severe asthma, and we both had to retreat to the hallway when the ammonia fumes from the disinfecting solution got overwhelming. I found a plumber in the Yellow Pages who removed the congealed clog from Dare's bathtub and drained the bloody water without a comment.

Jerry and I threw out Dare's stained bedding and all the liquor bottles. We scrubbed the bust of Voltaire and I bought new sheets and towels for her at Bloomingdales. We wanted it to be welcoming when she came home.

It was clear that Dare would need help when she left the hospital. She came home with a marvelous woman named Christine Corneille. Christine was not a nurse, but Dare did not need one. Under Christine's gentle care, Dare began eating regularly and never even commented on the absence of liquor. The apartment was immaculate.

I moved to California in September 1988 convinced that Dare was in perfect hands.

Dare's number was listed in the Manhattan phone book, and she was always happy to see fans who called her. Most were sincere, but Christine, who would leave Dare alone while she had visitors, sometimes noticed items were missing when she returned. Precious pieces of jewelry disappeared as did the copy Dare had made of Edith called Replica.

Dare's ingenuous and trusting nature, coupled with her increasing fragility, made her an easy target. One woman tried to get Dare to sign over all the rights to her books for a hundred dollars. After that incident, Christine remained in the apartment when someone new came by.

Christine's niece, Marie, often helped out, too. She was just as gentle and caring as her aunt. They saw that Dare had everything she needed when they left Dare on her own over the weekend.

Dare was happier than she had been in years. With Christine and Marie's care, Dare could stay in her apartment surrounded by the paintings and photographs she and Edie had created. There would be walks in the park, nourishing meals, companionship and the promise that she could remain dignified and comfortable for as long as she lived.

But fairy tales have ogres and monsters lurking behind the sheltering trees. What seems innocuous and enticing can, in an instant, become a maelstrom of evil.

Marie phoned me one Monday with horrific news. She had arrived just as a derelict man was running out of Dare's apartment. Dare had been beaten, bloodied and raped at the age of seventy-six by a homeless man she had befriended in Central Park. Trustingly, Dare let him follow her back to her apartment.

All Dare could say was, "That monster! That monster!"

Dare with the bust of Voltaire.

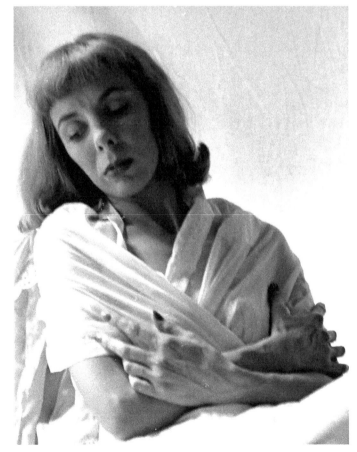

46

Dare was never left alone again. Christine and Marie took turns sleeping on the couch. They walked in the neighborhood with Dare, and she smiled at everyone she met. Christine's six-year-old niece came over to braid Dare's hair and make up stories with her. Dare was safe with her new family.

Dare retained her sense of humor, even as her mind began to wander. She spoke about doing another Lonely Doll book, and suggested the title *Edith And Little Bear Go To The Moon*. I promised to help her shoot it, wherever the location.

"Well, it must be on the moon, mustn't it?" she replied mischievously.

A moonlight scene in *Edith And Midnight*.

My mother also needed caregiving. She had been struck by a hit-and-run driver near her New York apartment and almost lost her legs. The accident precipitated the Alzheimer's that would eventually kill her, and my father brought Eugenia to live with him in Denver under a nurse's supervision. She became absorbed by images of fire, fearful that uneaten food would spontaneously combust and terrified that cold gazpacho soup could sear her palate.

Eugenia never lost the ability to remember the lines from her one-woman plays. Even when she no longer recognized me, she could still give a word-perfect half-hour performance. After she moved to a nursing home, she embellished the shows by stripping naked and running down the hallway.

Dare had a bout of pneumonia in the spring of 1995. Her physician chose to perform an invasive bronchoscopy in his office rather than prescribe the usual antibiotics. Dare went into immediate respiratory distress and was taken to Lenox Hill Hospital. A physician there told me they would put her on a ventilator so that she could breathe more easily. He assured me that it was "…only for a couple of days."

The doctor made a tracheotomy incision in Dare's throat and inserted a breathing tube. He attached it to the ventilator machine, which began blowing air into Dare's lungs.

She would never breathe on her own again.

The days became weeks, as Dare became increasingly dependent on the machine. The Lenox Hill staff made several attempts to wean her off the ventilator so that I could bring her to California with me, but none were successful.

The hospital would no longer keep her after she was classified as a chronic care patient. New York City has several long-term care facilities, but I had no choice in deciding where Dare would be sent. A Lenox Hill Hospital social worker told me they were transferring Dare to Goldwater Hospital on Roosevelt Island.

No one would choose to put a loved one in long-term care, but choices and options evaporate in the face of medical necessity. The reality is that most of us are only a medical error away from ending up in a public hospital. Dare was on life support and there was no place else that would take her.

Goldwater Public Hospital rested on a former island of the damned, separated from Manhattan by the treacherous currents of the East River. The City of New York bought the island 1828 and built several institutions to house its outcasts. These included a penitentiary, workhouse, smallpox hospital and lunatic asylum. Destitute women from the island's almshouse were pressed into service to care for the city's foundlings, who usually died in their care. Goldwater Hospital was built there in 1939 as a chronic care facility. The architect designed the spaces to bring in light and air, and there was still a weathered beauty in the bronze balcony doors and tall windows. Sunlight refracted off the East River and the wards were clean and bright. Dare entered Goldwater in 1995 and died there in 2001.

Hospital time runs differently from real world time. In Dare's case, it initially went very quickly. There was a brief window where she might be rescued from remaining ventilator-dependent. The longer the machine had been breathing for her, the less likely it was that she could ever be weaned from it. Her weeks at Lenox Hill had almost closed that possibility.

At first, the staff at Goldwater offered some hope that they could succeed where Lenox Hill had failed. The physician overseeing Dare's case seemed exhausted by his workload but committed to rescuing Dare from the machine.

Ventilator weaning is a harrowing process. The doctor had to let Dare try breathing briefly on her own, while she panicked from lack of oxygen. There was no way to let her know that it was for her own good. What if a few more seconds of struggle could help her regain independent lung function?

In spite of their efforts, the respiratory team was unable to get Dare off the ventilator. I was told she would live six more months, but she lasted six years.

Edie had died in 1975, and Blaine in 1985. The ten-year pattern would have continued if Dare had died in 1995, but the machine, and Dare's reluctance to let go, didn't let that happen. Something akin to a spell kept her from opening the forbidden Green Door from her childhood story. She would be forced to endure heroic challenges of pain and fear before she was allowed to join her beloved Blaine and Edie.

At the end of Dare's fairy tale *Lona*, the princess forfeits her human form and allows herself to be turned into a toad by an evil wizard. It is only through this sacrifice that her kingdom can be saved from the evil. In the body of a small toad, Lona sets off on a long journey to find the magic to undo the wizard's curse. All the people in the kingdom were grateful for her unselfishness and wished the toad princess well in her quest.

As Dare wrote in the book's final paragraph, "There is a great power in wishing."

Christine tied Dare's hair up in a side ponytail, so she could rest her head against the pillow. Dare's mouth remained partially open, but she could make a kissing gesture with her lips when she saw me. The muscles in her arms retracted, and Christine kept a block of paper in each of Dare's hands so her nails would not dig into her palms. I brought replicas of her Edith doll and Little Bear and tucked them in her elbows.

The susurrus of Dare's breathing apparatus was an incessant undertone. I have read that the sound of the machine can drive you mad. But when it stops (and it often malfunctions) the silence means suffocation.

I flew out from California each month to be with her, spending Thursday through Sunday at the hospital. Dare's apartment rent was very low, and I did not want to break the lease if there was any chance that she could come back home. I asked the nurses and physicians at Goldwater whether there was a mobile ventilator that Christine could monitor in Dare's apartment. They told me that even if it were possible to have a ventilator in a private home, it would have to be maintained by a specialized team and no insurance would pay for that.

47

By the summer of 1997 it was clear that Dare would never live independently again. As Dare's legal guardian, I was responsible to the court, and could no longer justify holding on to her apartment. Taking two weeks off from work, I arrived in New York to go through Dare's possessions. Anything of worth would be sold to pay her bills; the rest would have to be disposed of. Sentimental value fell in between those categories. Dare had named me her only heir and although her savings had gone to pay the hospital bills, I cherished the albums, photographs, and letters she wanted me to have.

The apartment was almost airless under a duvet of heat. The building's heyday as the Bloomingdale Mansion was long past, and Dare's portion of the structure got little ventilation or light. The walls had been artlessly repainted so many times that the molding was obscured by thick layers of coating.

I enlisted the help of my friend, Winkie Donovan, to help me sort through Dare's belongings. Winkie and I had been classmates at The Brearley School and she had often come over to Dare's with me when we were children.

Dare had converted the apartment's big closet into storage for her mother's portraits, and the paintings were hung on an elaborate pulley system. As Winkie walked into the closet and tried to move a painting, a coil of rope dropped from the ceiling and wrapped around her neck in a noose.

We looked across the room at Edie's self-portrait. She did not seem pleased.

Perhaps Edie was trying to protect Dare from beyond the grave. We stopped our work, and I addressed Edie's portrait, "Edie, we understand that you think this is a violation of Dare and her belongings. Please know that we are doing this task with love and respect for her and for you. Winkie is now going to light a cigarette, and we will leave it burning in an ashtray for you to enjoy."

Winkie put the cigarette on the mantle, and we slipped quietly out of the apartment. When we returned the next morning, the cigarette was down to a stub. We worked cautiously all day, but there were no more supernatural assaults as we finished emptying out Dare's belongings.

Walking through Dare's empty apartment for the final time, I was aware of all the energies, both creative and destructive, that had followed her to this address. Marvelous books and paintings had been fashioned there, but Edie's death and Dare's brutal rape overshadowed any positive images. It felt as if I had spent the previous two weeks inhaling the dust and skin particles of all the people who had passed through the rooms. Their microscopic detritus filtered through my lungs and lingered in my chest as I closed the door and hurried out to the street.

Dare's mother Edie.

Edith and Little Bear in the window of
Dare's last apartment at 11 East 80th Street.

48

Dare's friends winnowed to a small cadre. Those who had made excuses to avoid seeing Dare in her apartment on East 80th Street would never cross the river to visit her at Goldwater. Their usual justification was, "Oh, I want to remember her as she used to be."

Christine Corneille continued to watch over Dare at Goldwater Hospital. Although there were no funds left to employ her, Christine arrived at the hospital when she finished her day job. She would bathe Dare, suction her tubing so she did not choke, braid her hair, and turn her to avoid bedsores. Christine's niece, Marie, also came by in the evenings to spend time with Dare.

We were the only people Dare seemed to recognize, and she cried when I came into the room.

"Ah, your mother is crying because she is so happy to see you. You two look so much alike," a nurse once exclaimed.

Christine, a native of St. Lucia, laughed. "Do you know that the day I brought Dare to Goldwater, the nurse asked if Dare was my mother? This white lady? I think they are all crazy here."

Jerry Mayro, Dare's friend from The Burlington Book Shop, remained loyal to Dare in spite of his own ill health. His lungs were so compromised from emphysema and asthma that he had to pause frequently on the walk from the Roosevelt Island tram station to the hospital. Still, he continued to visit her until his death in 1999.

Winkie was many decades younger than Dare, but only outlived her by two years. She would arrive at Goldwater with a bottle of scented lotion to massage the fragile parchment of Dare's arms.

"You are so beautiful," Winkie whispered, as Dare opened her eyes wide in delight.

Brook, Dare, Jerry, Christine and
Winkie at Goldwater Hospital.

Back in the early 1970s, Dare had taken Edith and The Bears on a boat trip around Manhattan for *Edith And Little Bear Lend A Hand* where they were photographed looking at the almost-completed Twin Towers of The World Trade Center. As the boat turned upriver, the shoreline of Roosevelt Island came into view and Edith, Little Bear and Mr. Bear looked excitedly over the rail as they passed by Goldwater Hospital.

For six years, the East River flowed outside Dare's hospital window, but she could not move to see it. Fruit trees along the river walk shed their blossoms in the winds Dare could not feel, and two thousand days and nights merged in a vortex of memories and sensations she could not communicate.

The three other beds on her ward changed inhabitants more frequently than the seasons. In some weeks, the deaths matched the rise of the river's tides. All the patients were ventilator-dependent, so there were no sounds other than the machines pumping air into their throat tubes. Their skin became smooth and waxy in the days before death.

Dare was floating in a stratum between life and death, tethered physically to the tubes and machines that drained and suctioned and pushed air into her lungs, but also by an intangible thread that would not let her leave the horror she was living at Goldwater.

I thought Dare might have been reluctant to let go because she did not want to disappoint Edie. Dare had always been her mother's "good and precious child," who never complained or gave up on a task.

She closed her eyes much of the day, unless Christine and I were talking to her. I hoped that she was back on the beaches of Ocracoke, lying nude in the surf or posing for a self-portrait in the old lighthouse with the warm breeze off the Atlantic against her tanned face.

Edith and The Bears with Goldwater Hospital in the background.

Christine spent the early evening of January 25, 2001 reading her bible to Dare. It did not matter to Christine that Dare had never been religious. The words, or perhaps just the lilting cadence of Christine's voice, seemed to soothe her. Closing the book, Christine smoothed Dare's hair as she left for the night.

The cold and moonless sky was felted to a deep charcoal as the high tide embracing Dare's island hospital rose against the decaying embankments. The invisible moon tugged at Dare as she slept, and at 8:20 PM she surrendered to its primal force. All expectations, anguish and constraints fell away and what was real, or only a fairy tale, no longer mattered.

Dare still held the Edith doll and small bear that I had tucked in her arms six years earlier.

Yet I know that good is coming to me – that good is always coming; though few have at all times the simplicity and courage to believe it. What we call evil, is the only and best shape, which, for the person and his condition at the time, could be assumed by the best good. And so, Farewell.

From Dare's childhood book *A Faerie Romance*

ACKNOWLEDGMENTS

This book would not have been possible without Grace Rachow's editing skills, and I am indebted to her discerning eye and gentle prodding. Ocracoke Island's Alton Ballance and the late Sherry O'Neal provided their marvelous memories of Dare and Edie both on and off the island. Edlyn Chytalo Flannery and her brother Edward Chytalo, who grew up near Blaine's cabin in upstate New York, were profoundly influenced by Blaine and Dare's kindnesses to them as children and shared their stories with love and gratitude. Brenda Doane, another upstate girl, reminded me of how nice Blaine always smelled. Brian Sandeman responded to questions about his older brother Philip with exceptional grace and candor.

The late and irreplaceable Aileen Robbins gave her invaluable editing advice and support from the earliest weeks of the book's gestation until it was almost hatched.

My daughter Brett was loved by Dare from the moment I put my red-haired baby in her arms. Watching Dare with Brett during the photographing of *Make Me Real* pulled me right back to my own childhood and photo shoots with Dare on our family farm.

The book's layout, format and photographic restorations are thanks to my husband John Ogilvie who transformed my garbled suggestions into a practical structure.

Edie's expanded story is on Dare's website. Someday she will get her own book.

And finally, my eternal gratitude to Dare for bestowing me with a childhood of wonderment, and whose magic continues to enchant through her books and photographs.

www.DareWright.com

Dare Wright Books

The Lonely Doll Series

The Lonely Doll, Doubleday, 1957; Houghton Mifflin Harcourt, 1997
Holiday For Edith And The Bears, Doubleday, 1958; Dare Wright Media, 2013
The Doll And The Kitten, Doubleday, 1960; Dare Wright Media, 2013
The Lonely Doll Learns A Lesson, Random House, 1961; Dare Wright Media, 2013
Edith And Mr. Bear, Random House, 1964; Dare Wright Media, 2013
A Gift From The Lonely Doll, Random House, 1966; Dare Wright Media, 2013
Edith And Big Bad Bill, Random House, 1968 *
Edith And Little Bear Lend A Hand, Random House, 1972; Dare Wright Media, 2013
Edith And Midnight, Doubleday, 1978; Dare Wright Media, 2013
Edith And The Duckling, Doubleday, 1981; Dare Wright Media, 2013

An Original Fairy Tale

LONA, A Fairy Tale, Random House, 1963; Dare Wright Media, 2013

The Persis Series

The Little One, Doubleday, 1959 *
Take Me Home, Random House, 1965 *
Make Me Real, Dare Wright Media, 2007

Dare's Animal Stories

Look At A Gull, Random House, 1967 *
Look At A Colt, Random House, 1969 *
Look At A Calf, Random House, 1974 *
Look At A Kitten, Random House, 1975 *
The Kitten's Little Boy, Four Winds Press, 1971 *

Dare's Other Books

Date With London, Random House, 1961 *
Ocracoke In The Fifties, Carolina Wren Press, 2006

* Currently Not In Print

Learn More About Dare's Books at www.DareWright.com

CREDITS AND PERMISSIONS

COVER CITATION

Ann Patchett's comments about *The Lonely Doll* were recorded in an interview conducted by the New York writer Catherine Hong who published the quotation on the popular children's book blog "Mrs. Little" on January 29, 2013 (https://mrslittle.com/the-list-ann-patchett/). It is reproduced with permission.

CONTENT PROVIDED BY DARE WRIGHT MEDIA, LLC

DARE'S FAMILY SNAPSHOTS AND PERSONAL MEMORABILIA

Reproductions from Dare's archives - 43 Images.

ART REPRODUCTIONS

Artworks by Dare Wright - 23 Images.
Artworks by Edith Stevenson Wright - 32 Images.
Canvases on which both Dare and Edie contributed to the portraits - 2 Images.

DARE'S PHOTOS

Dare's personal and professional photos - 299 Images.
Dare's photos and mockups that she created for her children's books - 116 Images.

CONTENT FROM THE AUTHOR'S ARCHIVES

P. 25 - Photo of the Lenci doll, Lona.
P. 32 - Vandamm Studio photo of Tallulah Bankhead and Eugenia Rawls in *The Little Foxes*.
P. 34 - Wedding photo of Donald Seawell & Eugenia Rawls with Tallulah Bankhead.
P. 38 - Photo of Donald Seawell in military uniform.
P. 39 - Photo of the actress Virginia Cherill.
P. 39 - Photo of Eugenia Rawls in *Cry Havoc*.
P. 120 - Sketch of Kim Stanley and Brook Ashley in *The Traveling Lady*.
P. 147 - Book cover of Dare Wright's *The Lonely Doll*.
P. 163 - Photo of Madame Alexander's "Edith" doll.
P. 204 - Book cover of Dare Wright's *Take Me Home*.
P. 206 - Photo of the British actor Dennis King.
P. 244 - Drawing by Donald White.

INTERIOR CONTENT REPRODUCED WITH THIRD-PARTY PERMISSION

P. 19 - Newspaper article courtesy of the *Toronto Star* / GetStock.com.
P. 33 - Photo of Tallulah Bankhead, Eugenia Rawls and Colin Keith-Johnston in *The Second Mrs. Tanqueray* courtesy of Getty Images.
P. 58 - "Silks Resurgent" article in *Town & Country* magazine courtesy of the Hearst Corporation.

P. 66 - Newspaper article and photo of Mary Marsh courtesy of the Hearst Corporation, New York *Daily Mirror*.

P. 67 - Photo of Mary Marsh courtesy of the Hearst Corporation, New York *Daily Mirror*.

P. 68 - Newspaper article and photo of Mary Marsh courtesy of the Hearst Corporation, New York *Daily Mirror*.

P. 70 - Newspaper article and photo of Fenimore Cooper Marsh courtesy of the Hearst Corporation, New York *Daily Mirror*.

P. 71 - Newspaper article and photos of Mary Marsh and Fenimore Cooper Marsh courtesy of the New York *Daily News*.

P. 72 - Newspaper article and photo of Mary Marsh courtesy of the New York *Daily News*.

P. 73 - Newspaper article and photo of Mary Marsh courtesy of the Hearst Corporation, New York *Daily Mirror*.

P. 82 - Maidenform ad reproduced with the permission of Hanesbrands, Inc.

P. 85 - Cover of *Cosmopolitan* magazine courtesy of the Hearst Corporation.

PP. 86 & 87 - Article in *Good Housekeeping* magazine courtesy of the Hearst Corporation.

P. 96 - Photo of Burr Tillstrom and puppets from the author's archives, courtesy of Getty Images.

P. 97 - Photo of Donald Seawell and Tallulah Bankhead courtesy of Getty Images, New York *Daily News*.

P. 98 - Photo of Donald Seawell and Tallulah Bankhead in snowbank courtesy of Getty Images, New York *Daily News*.

P. 98 - Photo of Donald Seawell and Tallulah Bankhead, seated, courtesy of New York *Daily News*.

P. 114 - Cover photo of Dare Wright and Lee Wulff courtesy of *Flying* magazine.

P. 150 - Newspaper photo of Dare and Edie courtesy of the Cleveland *Plain Dealer*.

Lightning Source UK Ltd.
Milton Keynes UK
UKHW052036010421
381379UK00002B/58

9 781733 431200

SEWING ACTIVEWEAR

HOW TO MAKE YOUR OWN PROFESSIONAL-LOOKING ATHLETIC WEAR

JOHANNA LUNDSTRÖM

COPYRIGHT © 2017 JOHANNA LUNDSTRÖM

AUTHOR: Johanna Lundström

COVER AND BOOK DESIGN: Johanna Lundström

COVER PHOTO: Sara Thalathaisong Sjöström

MAIN PHOTOGRAPHY: Johanna Lundström

OTHER PHOTOGRAPHY COURTESY OF: Jalie Patterns, Beverly Johnson, Fehr Trade, Anja Cederbom, Sara Thalathaisong Sjöström, Sheila Powell, Penny Schwyn, Gwen Gyldenege, Christopher Hansson.

AUTHOR PHOTOGRAPHY: Anja Cederbom

ILLUSTRATIONS: Johanna Lundström

TEXT EDITOR: Kylie Walker

sewingactivewear.com

thelaststitch.com

CONTENT

FUNDAMENTALS

PROJECTS

INTERVIEWS

Introduction

This book is born out of my passion for making activewear and the desire to share that knowledge with others—I want to help spread the joy that comes with creating our own athletic wear! The result of my quest is this book that covers all the basics and then takes you to the next level, showing you methods that are common in the ready-to-wear industry so that you can step up your sewing game even more.

I hope to both empower and inspire you on this rewarding sewing journey—as activewear maker Sheila Powell says in her interview in this book, making our workout clothes can even make us more motivated to exercise. So it's a double win for us creative fitness lovers!

Also remember to check out the accompanying website sewingactivewear.com for up to date information on activewear fabric vendors, patterns, and other helpful resources.

Happy sewing!

Johanna

CHAPTER 1
FUNDAMENTALS

Fabrics for activewear

Sourcing the right fabric is the first step on the road to a successful activewear project. Look for high-quality fabrics rather than cheap deals, unless you happen to find some great offer, because a fabric that doesn't keep its promise to transport moisture, keep the rain away, or just doesn't feel nice to the body is just not worth spending money on for your precious self-sewn activewear wardrobe.

FABRIC TYPES

For sweaty workouts, you'll want fabrics that transport moisture away from the body and keep your skin dry. Look for descriptions such as moisture wicking, functional fabrics and labels like Supplex, sports jersey and Dry-fit. Most functional fabrics are made of synthetic fibres, but there are also some natural fibres that have moisture wicking properties, such as wool.

Water and wind-resistant fabrics usually also have an added layer of coating or membrane, and often have a branded name such as Gore-Tex or Teflon. Another category that is becoming increasingly popular, especially with cyclists, runners, and walkers, is high-visibility fabrics that are fluorescent and reflective and are meant to make you more visible in the dark.

WICKAWAY LYCRA KNITS

A four-way stretch knit, usually jersey, which transports moisture away from the body and has excellent stretch and recovery properties. Perfect for tight-fitting garments such as leggings and tank tops. Common brand names are Supplex, Dry-fit, and Meryl.

BASE LAYER POLY KNITS

Base layer fabrics are stretchy polyester knits with a grid-like pattern. Base layer materials usually do a better job of keeping the body dry compared with wickaway Lycra (Spandex) jerseys. The perfect choice for underwear and running t-shirts. Less suited to form-fitting garments such as tight tops and leggings.

WOOL KNITS

Wool knits are a nice moisture wicking option if you are exercising outdoors in cold weather. However, wool doesn't transport moisture as well as synthetic base layers knits, so once the wool gets wet, it gets really wet. Thicker wool knits and felted wool knits are excellent options when making thermal jackets and can be used instead of polyester fleece fabrics.

NATURAL FIBRE KNITS

For workouts like yoga, BodyBalance, Tai-Chi, and Pilates, cotton, rayon, bamboo and modal knits are great alternatives, especially if they contain Lycra, as this will help the fabric keep its shape when you are moving around. These natural fibres, do, however soak up a lot of moisture so avoid them if you plan to break out a big sweat.

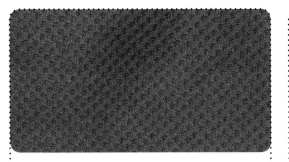

GRID FLEECE

This fabric is both warm and very breathable. It's a popular choice for activewear as it wicks away moisture better than regular fleece because of the structure of the grids. It has either mechanical stretch or a four-way stretch achieved with Spandex (Lycra). Perfect for cold weather workouts.

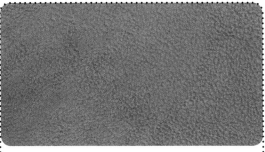

MICRO FLEECE

Micro fleece is a polyester fabric with a soft hand and small nap that usually has an anti-pilling treatment. It keeps the body warm and dry and is soft to the skin. Can be used in thermal underwear, base layers, hats, mittens and much more. It also wicks away moisture from the body.

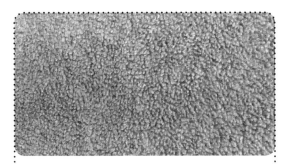

HEAVY FLEECE

This thicker winter fleece can be worn as a layering piece or an outer layer. Keeps the body warm and is primarily used for sweaters and jackets. Often has a thick, textured pile. These fleeces usually have the Polartec weight scale rating of 200 or 300.

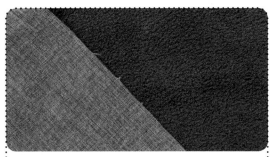

SOFTSHELL FABRIC

Softshell usually refers to a fleece material with a stretchy woven membrane attached, so it's two fabrics in one. Softshells are warm, water-resistant (not waterproof) and wind-resistant and are a good choice for aerobic activities in cold and damp weather. It is perfect for jackets and trousers and is sometimes also called Windstopper.

POWER MESH

A micro mesh that is soft, durable, breathable, and has an excellent four-way stretch. Ideal for insert details on clothing and for all applications where you need light support or lining.

POWER NET

This firmer Spandex micro mesh is perfect for bras, shapewear, waistbands, and other details that need to be stable. Has less stretch and is often thicker than power mesh.

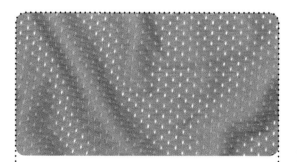

SPORTS MESH

This fabric has pierced holes evenly spread out on the fabric. It transports moisture and keeps you cool, so it's a good choice for cooling inserts on workout clothes. Can also be used for pocket and waistband lining. Sports mesh comes in many versions and can be firm or very stretchy. Sometimes called Airtech mesh.

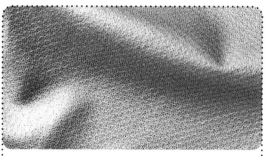

HIGH-VISIBILITY FABRICS

Often called Hi-Viz, these materials have reflective properties or a colour that is easy to spot, even in the dark, such as neon yellow and orange. The purpose is to increase the visibility of the person wearing it, especially for drivers of vehicles. Hi-Viz fabrics have become very popular in ready-to-wear activewear.

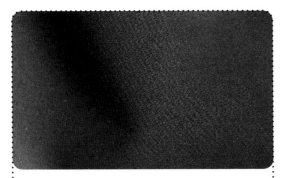

WATERPROOF BREATHABLE

These fabrics are made to resist water while still letting air out, which prevents you from becoming overly sweaty. Most materials in this category are very water resistant but will need sealed seams to be fully water proof.

The waterproof breathability function is because of a membrane that is bonded to the fabric to create a laminate. Also known under brand names like Gore-Tex and eVent and can be quite costly.

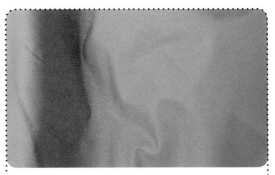

RAINWEAR FABRIC

Rain-proof fabric is often used for low to mid price rainwear garments. It's usually made of a polyester shell with a rain-proof inner coating, usually polyurethane (PU). Compared with the waterproof breathable fabrics, coated fabrics are typically cheaper. The main drawback with coated rain fabric is the lack of breathability. Sweat can't escape, so you can end up uncomfortably wet.

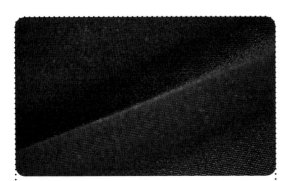

WOVEN WICKAWAYS

Quick-drying, breathable, synthetic woven fabric. Some are also wind resistant, have extra UV-protection, or are water repellent. Use for jacket, pants, shorts and other garments. Common brand names are Supplex and Taslan.

TRACKSUIT FABRIC

Perhaps more of a novelty activewear fabric these days, but still used by many big brands for jackets and track pants. Usually made of polyester, this knit has a shiny surface and a brushed backing.

STRETCHABILITY

Fabric stretch is an important factor when it comes to sewing activewear, as it enables the fabric to follow your movement. Garments without sufficient stretch may be uncomfortable to wear or could tear during use. Woven and knitted fabrics can both have some stretch. There are three main ways that stretch exists in a fabric; the first is the way the fibres are used to create the fabric—knits are stretchy by nature, because the threads are looped—an industrial version of handknitting.

The second way, found in both wovens and knits, is where stretch comes from the addition of Lycra (Spandex) or other stretchable material to the fibres used in making the fabric. Finally, there is mechanical stretch. Here, individual threads are tightly wound, giving them a small amount of stretchability.

Two-way stretch

Two-way stretch usually refers to knit fabrics that only stretch in one direction, generally crosswise from selvage to selvage. Knit fabrics that only have mechanical stretch, and no added Spandex, are usually two-way stretch. These fabrics have a stable feel to them and are an excellent choice for garments that aren't very tight-fitting. Because it only stretches in one direction, the two-way stretch is also referred to as one-way stretch.

Four-way stretch

Four-way stretch fabrics stretch both crosswise and lengthwise and usually have added Lycra to help with the stretchability. For tight-fitting garments with negative ease, such as swimwear and leggings, you need to use four-way stretch fabrics. Traditionally, in the fabric industry, the four-way stretch is called two-way stretch, hence, why it can be very confusing. But as four-way is the common term among fabric vendors we will use this definition throughout the book.

Stretch and recovery

For form-fitting clothes, such as leggings and tight-fitting tops, you'll need a four-way stretch fabric with at least 60% stretch, i.e. a 10 cm (4") long fabric swatch should be at least 16 cm (5 ⅖") long when stretched out. In addition, the amount of stretch will determine the result, which means that if you are making the same pattern but using fabrics with different amounts of stretch, you will get a different fit and feel. So, if your next fabric has less or more stretch than your previous fabric, you might need to adjust the size of the pattern to compensate for the difference.

Also, make sure that the fabric has good recovery so that it won't sag when you move your body. Recovery refers to how well the fabric bounces back after being stretched out. Test this by stretching out the fabric and see if it returns to its original size. If not, it will not be suitable for form-fitting workout wear.

Fabric weight is also important when you make activewear. For leggings, you'll want a thicker knit quality, as it will hide those underwear lines and hug the body in a more flattering way than a flimsy, thin knit would. These types of fabrics are usually referred to as medium-weight knits. Heavy-weight knits are more stable—sweatshirt fabric is a typical example of a heavier knit. In addition, if your top is very form-fitting and meant to be worn on its own, going for a very thin, light fabric might not be a good idea either. So, if you are in a store, stretch the fabric out over your body and see how it behaves. Another tip is to put your hand under the fabric and stretch the fabric over your fist to make sure the fabric isn't see-through—unless that is a look you are going for!

FABRIC WEIGHTS

VERY LIGHT	130 g/m² – 200 g/m²	4 oz/yd² – 6 oz/yd²
LIGHT	220 g/m² – 290 g/m²	6.5 oz/yd² – 8.5 oz/yd²
MEDIUM	300 g/m² – 390 g/m²	9 oz/yd² – 11.5 oz/yd²
HEAVY	400 g/m² – 475 g/m²	12 oz/yd² – 14 oz/yd²

The table above should be viewed as a general guide—there are no exact rules when it comes to fabric weight as it depends on several factors.

Weight matters for woven fabric too. A lighter fabric will feel more comfortable on the body and will usually wick away moisture better too. But a lighter material often wears down and rips easier, so if you want a woven fabric that is both light and durable, pick a rip-stop fabric.

Another thing to consider is pressure, especially if you are looking for compression and shapewear fabrics. The more pressure, the more the fabric will shape the body. The amount of pressure is, however, not usually listed in the fabric description, although some sellers will label their fabrics as "compression fabrics".

ACTIVEWEAR FABRICS,
OUR HEALTH AND THE ENVIRONMENT

In an ideal world, our makes wouldn't impact the environment or our health. But, unfortunately, that is not the case, and some materials will be more problematic than others, so it's good to be mindful of the choices we make. One potentially harmful material is synthetic fleece—a study by the University of California showed that fleece jackets release a substantial amount of microfibres during each wash. These microfibres are not biodegradable and damage our marine ecosystems.

Other problematic materials are the ones containing perfluorinated compounds (PFCs). These chemicals are often used to make our garments waterproof and dirt repelling and, in high doses, PFCs can be very toxic and damaging to our health. Fortunately, several manufacturers are now looking into alternative production methods and materials to reduce the environmental impact of these harmful fabrics.

More friendly options

What are the more eco-friendly options then? Certified organic wool fabrics are both sustainably produced and biodegradable and a good choice for workouts in cold weather. Cellulose-based fabrics, made from pulp, such as Tencel/Lyocell are also regarded as decent options as they are sustainably harvested and have a more eco-friendly production than traditional rayon fabrics; they wick away moisture better than cotton.

Synthetic activewear fabrics made from recycled fibres are also becoming increasing common, although it's still not as prevalent as one would have hoped. Other ways to think sustainably are to choose durable, good-quality fabrics that will last many years and mend your clothes instead of throwing them away if they show some wear and tear. Of course, the issue of how different materials impact our health and environment is too complex to cover within this book, but it's always good to be thoughtful about the choices we make.

JALIE

PATTERN VETERANS

For over three decades, Jalie Sewing Patterns has been designing patterns for an active lifestyle. They offer a wide variety of sewing patterns for activewear, including workout clothes for men and women, skating costumes, swimwear, bikewear, and much more. The company has been based in the family home since the beginning, and almost everything is still is done in-house in Canada. Here, Émilie Fournier gives us the inside scoop on their company and shares her tips on how to succeed with sewing activewear.

How did Jalie get started?

My mum, Jeanne, was on a tiny budget and would buy knit remnants that manufacturers would sell to fabric stores. Those were the cheapest fabrics available in stores at the time. Nobody knew how to sew those fabrics with regular sewing machines. **»**

JALIE

WHO: Canadian sewing pattern company founded in 1983 and run by mother daughter team Jeanne Binet and Émilie Fournier.

FAVOURITE EXERCISES: Kung-fu-stretches and barre (Émilie); Walks (Jeanne)

FIND: jalie.com

17

> ## MASTERING THE BASICS WILL GIVE YOU THE CONFIDENCE TO IMPROVISE.
>
> **ÉMILIE** JALIE PATTERNS

Jeanne loves challenges. She spent days figuring out a way to sew knits and elastics with her little Necchi machine, and she was able to make clothes for the whole family, including mini-versions of her own clothes—from underwear and swimsuits to even a denim jacket!

After a few years of people asking how to make swimsuits, underwear, t-shirts, and hats, she decided to start teaching from home. Just a few months in, more than 100 students would come each week to watch and learn her techniques in the humble sewing studio of the family's. The students began asking for patterns, which is what sparked the Jalie idea. It started with a copier in the bedroom, large sheets of paper and lots of work and patience.

How do you get your ideas for a new pattern? And tell us a little about the developing process?

Most of the designs are driven by customer's requests. We combine different requests together (for example, people were asking for a skating dress with spaghetti straps and others for an open-back dance leotard. We combined the two ideas to make the Violeta pattern, which turns out to be a great swimsuit as well. »

Share your best beginner tips!
Get good scissors and the right fabric. Be patient and trust the pattern. Mastering the basics will give you the confidence you need to improvise. It's always better to start with a basic t-shirt, and have fun improvising with colour blocking later on when you only have fabric scraps left, than starting with intricate designs. Also, starting with kids' sizes is a great way to learn without spending too much on fabric at first, and it will make a happy family member or neighbour!

**What are your predictions for
the future of DIY activewear?**
Custom print is increasingly popular, and PDF patterns make patterns accessible to anyone with a computer and printer. Some people will always prefer the feel and process of working with a paper pattern, but I think more and more people will switch to digital patterns. If the activewear fabric stores keep offering a good range of quality products, I can only see the number of people making their own gear going up because of how great it makes you feel to wear something that you created, in colours you chose, in a fit that is perfect for your body.

**And finally, why should
we make our own activewear?**
To feel fabulous and confident. For most styles, if you keep your pattern and fabric stash reasonable, it will you save a lot of money too!

jalie.com

Seams for activewear

Choosing the right seams is very important when making activewear. If you are sewing knit fabrics, you'll need to use a seam that has excellent stretchability so that it won't break under pressure.

Having a serger (overlocker) and a coverstitch machine will create seams that are better suited to stretchy knits and make your activewear look more professional. But if you only have a regular sewing machine, don't worry—you can still sew great activewear and in this book we'll cover a lot of tricks that you can use to achieve good results using a sewing machine.

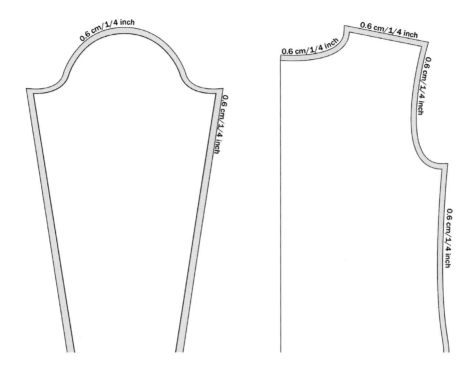

SEAM ALLOWANCES

For knits

Picking the proper seam allowance for knits often comes to down to preference. However, around 0.6 cm (¼") is a good choice for the side seams when sewing knits, as it corresponds to the width of most serger and sewing machine stretch seams and, thus, will both save fabric and eliminate the need to cut away excess seam allowances.

The trick when using a narrow seam allowance is learning how to control the pieces while sewing, which might require a little practice. If you are sewing on a serger, you can use the knife as a seam guide, just align the edges against the knife and cut only a tiny sliver of the fabric.

Some activewear patterns will have a seam allowance of 1 cm (⅖") or 1.5 cm (⅝") that you will need to remove at some point. If you are using a serger, you can cut away the surplus fabric with the knife while sewing. On a regular sewing machine, some stretch stitches will require that you remove the extra seam allowance before sewing.

For a serger flatlock seam, around 0.3-0.4 cm (⅛") is a good ballpark. However, it depends on the width of the flatlock seam, so do a sample to see how much fabric that ends up in the seam and then decide on the right seam allowance.

For woven fabrics

For activewear made of woven fabric, pick the standard 1.5 cm (⅝") seam allowance on all side seams to make sure you have a durable seam. If you have a serger, you can create a very secure seam in the following manner. First, sew the seams using a regular sewing machine straight stitch (do not overcast the fabric before you do this). Then overcast both layers of seam allowance in one go, using a 2-thread flatlock seam or a 3-thread overlock.

If you have a serger/coverstitch combo machine, you can also use the safety stitch, which sews a straight seam and overcasts at the same time. If some of your seams will be under a lot of stress, you can also use the 3-step security straight stitch on your sewing machine, if it has one, for those areas.

SEAM ALLOWANCE GUIDELINES

KNIT OVERLOCK SEAMS	0.6 cm (¼")
SERGER FLATLOCK SEAMS	0.3-0.4 cm (⅛")
WOVEN SIDE SEAMS	1.5 cm (⅝")
SERGER SAFETY STITCH	1 cm (⅖")
MOCK FLATLOCK	0.6 cm – 1 cm (¼–⅖")
FLAT-FELLED SEAM	1.5 cm (⅝") trim to 0.6 cm (¼") on one side

QUICK GUIDE: SEWING MACHINE STITCHES

STITCH	LOOK	USE	PROPERTIES
3-THREAD NARROW		• Light weight stretchy knits • Excellent for swimwear, Lycra workout clothes and sheers	• Very elastic • Durable • Easy to unpick • Non-bulky • Right needle + 2 loopers
3-THREAD WIDE		• On thicker and bulky knits (but works on lighter knits too) • Excellent for fleece, and sweatshirt fabric	• Very elastic • Durable • Easy to remove • More bulky • Left needle + 2 loopers
COVERSTITCH 2- AND 3-THREAD		• Hemming • Decorative stitches • Topstitching • Binding • Mock flatlock	• Great stretch • Durable • Professional finish • Keeps the knit from stretching out when sewing
3-THREAD SUPER STRETCH		• Stretchy Lycras • Light weight fabrics	• Great stretch and recovery • Not available on all sergers • Very secure
3-THREAD FLATLOCK		• Seams that need to lie flat on the body • For bulky knits • Decorative stitches • To mimic ready-to-wear garments	• Less durable than a regular serger stitch • No chafing • Good stretch • Non-bulky
2-THREAD FLATLOCK		• Seams that need to lie flat on the body • Hemming • Decorative stitches • For bulky knits	• Less durable than a regular serger stitch • No chafing • Good stretch • Non-bulky

STITCH	LOOK	USE	PROPERTIES
STRETCH STITCH ON SEWING MACHINE		• Seams on knits • Decoration • Flat joined seams	• Durable • Highly elastic • Similar seam allowance to a serger stitch • Can be difficult to unpick
ZIGZAG (LIGHTNING BOLT)STITCH		• Seams on knits • Topstitching • Hemming • Blind hemming	• Elastic • Durable when stitched twice • Versatile
TWIN NEEDLE STITCH		• Hemming stretchy knits • Topstitching • Decorative stitching	• Elastic • Durable • Can replace coverstitching
TRIPLE STRAIGHT SECURITY STITCH		• Topstitching • Edgestitching • Hemming	• Elastic • Durable • Difficult to rip • Often better for firmer knits than stretchy Lycras
3-STEP ZIGZAG STITCH		• Topstitching • Hemming • Side seams	• Very durable • Very elastic
DECORATIVE STITCHES		• Faux flatlocking • Decoration • Topstitching	• Durable • Good stretch • Difficult to rip • Can be used with decorative thread

SERGER OVERLOCK SEAMS

Serger (overlocker) seams are the best option for sewing stretchy knits because they have high stretchability and recovery, plus they are very durable. Also, thanks to the differential feed on a serger, you can easily control the tightness of the seam. So, if your fabric stretches out, you just increase the differential feed and if there are unwanted gathers, you can decrease the setting.

A good idea is to begin sewing a sample using the intended fabric, stitches, and thread to make sure the result will be satisfying. If your serger has manual tension, you might need to experiment with the settings to achieve well-balanced seams, especially if you are using speciality threads, such as woolly nylon, which can alter the tension.

In general, you don't need to secure regular serger overlock seams, such as the 3-thread and 4-thread overlock. Just start and finish with a thread tail. Most of the time you will then sew over the ends with another seam and that will automatically secure the overlock seam. When needed, you can also secure and hide the thread using a large needle. Thread the needle with the thread tail and attach the tail under the stitches and cut of the excess thread. Using a seam sealant is another way to secure the serger stitch.

3-thread wide serger seam sewn with woolly nylon

3-THREAD
arrow overlock with
woolly nylon

3-THREAD wide
overlock with
regular thread

3-THREAD OVERLOCK

The best overlock seam for stretchy Lycra (Spandex) knit fabrics.
It's durable, has great stretch and recovery and is not bulky. The
seam uses one needle and two loopers and comes in two versions:
narrow using the right needle and wide using the left.

The narrow stitch is an excellent non-bulky option for any tight-fitting Lycra
garment. The wider 3-thread is also a good choice for activewear, especially if
you want to topstitch the seam afterward as it provides a wider base to sew on.

Only the needle threads will be visible from the right side of the
fabric, so you can use thread that doesn't match in the loopers
You can use woolly nylon in all positions or just the loopers.

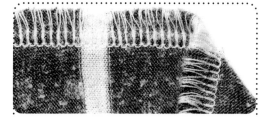

3-THREAD SUPER STRETCH

Some sergers will have this overlock
stitch that uses two needles and
the lower looper thread. It is often
called stretch overlock or super
stretch overlock and is intended for
sewing tight-fitting stretchy fabrics
such as swimwear and activewear.

Check your manual to see if this
stitch is available on your machine.

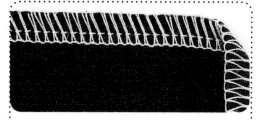

4-THREAD OVERLOCK

The 4-thread overlock is bulkier
and has less stretch compared
with the 3-thread version and is
better-suited for more stable fabrics
such as sweatshirt fabric, polar
fleece and wovens. It requires two
needle and two looper threads.

You can use woolly nylon in all
positions or just the loopers, but
using woolly nylon everywhere
will create a very bulky seam.

SEWING MACHINE SEAMS

You can also make activewear on a regular sewing machine. Most machines will have a seam that overcasts the edges and mimics the serger overlock seam. Those are often called stretch seams or overlock seams—check your manual to see which ones are recommended for very stretchy fabrics.

If your machine's manual doesn't suggest which stitch to use for stretch fabrics, look for stitches that are similar to an overlock seam and do a test on scrap fabric to see if it creates a suitable seam with plenty of stretch.

Also note that a different presser foot is usually needed when sewing stretchy seams, again check your manual to make sure you use the right one. Another option is to use a regular zigzag stitch, preferably sewing two rows for extra security. Both these methods will be expanded on in this chapter.

Sewing machine overlock stitch using a stretch seam presser foot.

If you are using a sewing machine to sew stretch garments, always do a test sample using your intended fabric and stretch stitch. Stretch the seam to make sure it recovers after being stretched out and that the stitches won't pop. If the seam passes those tests, you are all set to go!

If the fabric stretches out and gets wavy, increase the presser foot pressure (if your machine has that possibility) or try feeding the upper layer of the fabric towards the presser foot using an awl or a large needle and feeding it in an even rhythmic motion. Some people also like to use a walking foot to prevent seams from stretching out when sewing knits. I have personally not found the walking foot to be very good compared with the above-mentioned awl feed technique, but you can always give it a try and see if works for you!

MEDIUM zigzag stitch

NARROW zigzag stitch

TWO ROWS OF ZIGZAG

If your machine lacks a stretch stitch or if your stretch seam doesn't work as intended, you can also use two rows of zigzag. First sew the inner row using a narrow zigzag (or a lightning bolt stitch). Then finish the edges with a wider zigzag. Before you use this method, make a sample to make sure it the seam won't stretch out or pop when pulled.

Be aware though that the zigzag stitch doesn't have the same amount of stretch and durability as many stretch stitches. For more durability, use the 3-step zigzag instead (if available on your machine).

OVERLOCK STRETCH SEAMS

Most modern sewing machines come with several versions of this seam, so check your manual to see which type is recommended for your chosen fabric. This seam is durable and has excellent stretchability, and overcasts the edges just like serger overlock stitching does.

It is also easier to control compared to a serger seam, which makes the sewing machine stretch seam an excellent choice for tricky areas on knit garments. Usually, you'll need to switch to a special presser foot to make sure the seam hits the edge of the fabric.

There are, however, two drawbacks with these stretch seams: They can cause some fabrics to stretch out, and the stitches are also hard to remove with a seam ripper.

Seams for hemming

This chapter is primarily dedicated to hemming knits, which are usually where sewists struggle the most. The trick is to find a method that will prevent the hem from becoming stretched out and wobbly, while still being elastic and durable. Here, we will cover ways to hem garments on a regular sewing machine, a coverstitch machine, and even a serger

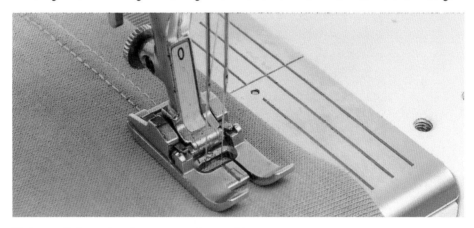

Twin-needle hemming done on a sewing machine

HEMMING ON A SEWING MACHINE

The best way to hem stretchy knits on a sewing machine is to use either a medium zigzag stitch or a twin-needle. Both stitches have excellent stretch and recovery. Hemming stretchy knits on a regular sewing machine does provide some challenges though, such as skipped stitches, tunnelling, broken stitches and wobbly, stretched-out seams. But with the right tools and techniques, you can achieve good results without having to invest in a coverstitch machine.

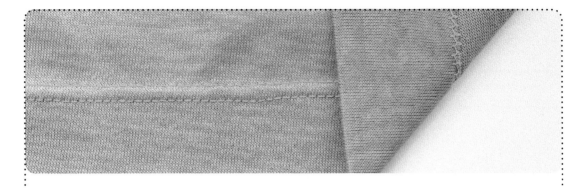

TWIN-NEEDLE

Hemming with a twin-needle is a way to mimic the coverstitch seam on a regular sewing machine. It creates two rows of straight stitches on the top and a zigzag seam underneath.

To perfect this stitch, you might have to experiment with the needle tension, stitch length, and presser foot pressure (if your machine has this option). You might also need to adjust the bobbin tension to prevent a ridge from forming between the stitches (tunnelling) when sewing with a twin-needle.

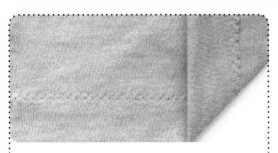

ZIGZAG

A regular zigzag is a versatile option for hemming knits as it stretches well and is available on most machines. If the hem will be stretched out a lot when worn, the 3-step zigzag is a better option than a regular zigzag, which might break under pressure.

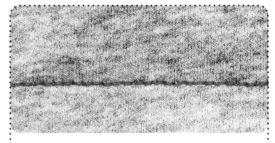

3-STEP SECURITY STRAIGHT STITCH

Also called triple straight stitch, this seam is great for sewing stretchy woven fabrics and can also work for some knit fabrics. It works best on materials that have some stability or when stitching over elastic. This stitch is found on most modern sewing machines.

Tips for hemming stretchy knits

Use a ballpoint needle
If you experience skipped stitches or your regular needle creates unsightly holes in the fabric, try switching to a ballpoint needle which is the best choice for sewing dense stretchy Lycra knits.

Stabilise the hem with water-soluble tape
The tape is sticky on both sides and prevents the fabric from stretching out when stitched. Just attach the tape on the wrong side of the hem and fold the hem. Fusi-Web and Wonder Tape are two versions of this double-sided tape.

Use spray starch to stabilise the fabric
Spray a generous amount and let it dry. The starch makes the fabric stiff and keeps it from stretching out; just rinse away the starch afterwards.

Sew over paper to avoid skipped stitches
If you get skipped stitches despite switching to a ballpoint needle, you can try sewing over paper and then tearing it away. It is best to use water-soluble stabilising paper, but wax or parchment paper will also work.

Adjust the presser foot pressure
If your machine has this option, experiment with the pressure to prevent the fabric from stretching out.

Feed the fabric
To keep the fabric from stretching out, you can also feed the upper layer of the fabric using a sharp object like an awl or a large needle. Push the fabric towards the presser foot while sewing; this motion will mimic the differential feed on sergers and coverstitch machines.

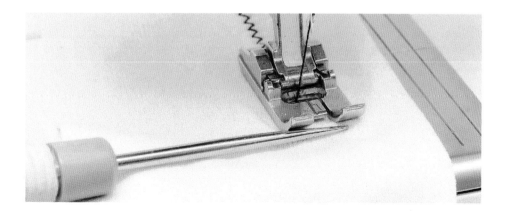

COVERSTITCH

A coverstitch machine will achieve the most professional-looking and durable hemming stitches and is what's used in the sewing industry. The chain stitch on the reverse side creates a durable seam with excellent stretchability and, thanks to the differential feed, you can prevent the hem from stretching out when sewing.

On most domestic coverstitch machines you can sew with 1, 2, or 3 needles, with the 2- and 3-needle stitch being the most suitable option for hemming knits. Coverstitch machines can, however, be tricky to master, and the machine has to be set up very carefully to avoid skipped stitches and other issues.

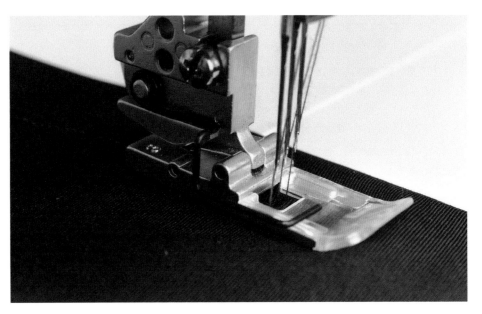

3-needle coverstitch seam

Tips for successful coverstitching

Use the right needles

The first call to action is to make sure you have the right needles. Check what type of needles your coverstitch manufacturer recommends and also ask the seller for advice.

When inserting the needles, make sure they sit correctly all the way in the needle bar slot before you start sewing.

Start with a clean machine

The next step is checking that the machine is clean. Look especially for lint or threads being stuck between the plates and you can remove threads with a pair of tweezers. If you have a combo machine that also works as a serger, clean out the lower compartment as well.

Thread the machine right

Before you start threading the machine, lift up the presser foot to release the tension plates. This is very important, as you won't get proper tension if the presser foot is down when threading. If you already threaded the machine, you can usually just attach the new thread to the old one with a knot. If you have a problem pulling it through the disks, you can release the tension even more on some machines by pulling up the presser foot lever even more.

When threading the machine, begin with the lower looper and again make sure that everything is clean and properly threaded. Finish off by inserting the thread in the needles and pull all the threads to the back, facing north west, making sure you have a decent thread length that you can use when securing the seams after sewing.

Do sample tests

Always do samples before sewing on the actual garment. You might have to adjust the tension, stitch length, differential feed, and even the presser foot pressure to achieve a perfect seam. So don't expect to get a perfect seam on the first attempt—especially if your machine is a little fickle.

Start and finish with a fabric scrap

Many issues with a coverstitch machine occur during the first few stitches. If you have a fickle machine and are sewing the garment flat and not in the round, I highly recommend that you begin sewing on a fabric scrap and then insert your garment and continue sewing. When you are done sewing your garment, insert another fabric scrap and finish the seam on that scrap. Then leave the scrap in the machine until it's time to coverstitch again.

Use the right coverstitch sewing techniques

Make sure the needles hit the fabric on the first stitch and then start sewing. You can sew the first few stitches slowly, but you'll get a better result if you sew with confidence and a decent speed after that, don't stop and start all the time to check the stitching!

Tricks for sewing over bulky seams

Most skipped stitches happen when sewing over thick seams. Here are a few suggestions to solve that problem:

- Clip the side seams at the fold of the hem and lay the clipped seam in the opposite directions.

- Hammer the seam flat. A rubber hammer is perfect for this purpose.

- Use a clearance plate (brand name Hump Jumper ®), which is a tool that helps raise the presser foot when sewing over bulky seams.

- Experiment with the speed when sewing over a hump. Experts I've consulted with recommend going fast over thick layers. Also, don't stop and start while sewing.

HOW TO **COVERSTITCH**

1   **Prepare for hemming.** Make sure the edges of the fabric are evenly cut. To make hemming easier over bulky seams, you can clip the side seams at the fold and lay the clipped seam in the opposite direction.

2   **Fold the hem.** On materials that can take a little heat, ironing the fold is recommended as it makes hemming easier. Don't pin when coverstitching. With practice, you'll be able to hem using just your fingers to keep the fold even, but you can also hand-baste the hem using large and loose stitches.

3   **Start sewing.** Always begin at the back of the garment, just after the side seam. Pull all the threads north west before you start sewing. Use a seam guide for an even hem if your machine lacks a built-in ruler. Gently guide the fabric and make sure it is evenly fed to avoid twisted seams.

4   **Finish the seam.** If you are sewing on the round, sew over the beginning stitches for a couple of centimetres (an inch or less).
Then lift the presser foot to release the tension. Check your machine manual for the specifics of how to release the threads and tension. See How to secure a coverstitch seam using the pull method (page 40) for the best way to secure the seam when coverstitching on the round.

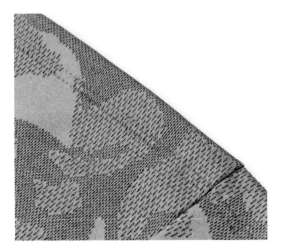

5   **The finished hem.** A coverstitch machine will achieve the most professional-looking hem on stretchy knits. Plus it has excellent stretch and recovery compared with many sewing machine stitches. For a neat finish, try to sew as close to the edge of the fabric as possible.

SECURE COVERSTITCH **SEAMS**

1 **Prepare for finishing the seam.** Close the seam by sewing over the
beginning stitches for a few cm (an inch or less). Then sew the last
stitch using the hand-wheel and stop at the highest point of the needle.
The needle needs to be high up for this method to work properly.

2 **Pull the thread.** Lift the presser foot. Then using a crochet
hook, tweezers, or any other narrow tool, pull the needle thread
towards you. Make the loop around 4–5 cm (2") long.

3   Clip the thread loop in the middle.

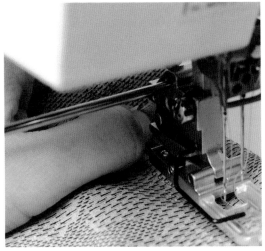

4   **Pinch the fabric.** Grab the fabric behind the presser foot and pinch the seam with your fingers.

5   **Pull the fabric.** Pull it firmly towards the back and then to the left or just pull it diagonally to the back. Test and see which direction works best for you. This pulls the needle threads to the reverse side and secures the stitch. Pinching the seam with your fingers helps prevent tunnelling when the thread is pulled.

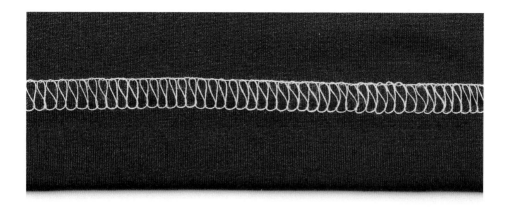

2-thread flatlock hem from the right side

FLATLOCK HEM

If you have a serger, but not a coverstitch machine, the 2-thread flatlock hem is a good option for hemming stretchy knits. This method takes some practice and works best on straighter hems. You fold the hem twice and then sew over the edge and pull the seam apart just like you would with a regular serger flatlock seam.

If you use decorative thread or woolly nylon, you can achieve a finish that mimics the hemming on ready-to-wear activewear. Moreover, this method is not just for hems; you can use the same technique for decorative stitching or attaching details such as pockets on a hoodie.

2-thread flatlock hem. It has ladders on the reverse side that catch the edge of hem.

SERGER FLATLOCK **HEM**

1 **Fold the hem.** Fold the hem twice, make sure the edge meets the fold. Set your serger on 2-thread flatlock and disengage/lower the knife.
TIP: You can keep the knife and cut just a smidgen of the fold for a very flat hem. The cut won't be visible.

2 **Sew the hem.** Place the fabric right-side up underneath the presser foot. The hem has to be sewn quite far away from the knife to create a flat seam when pulled apart. Also, make sure the needle hits the inner edge of the folded fabric.

3 **Pull apart the seam.** Do it just like you would with a regular serger flatlock seam. The right side shows the loops, and the ladders catch the edge of the hem.

4 **The finished hem.** The flatlock hem has excellent stretch and recovery. This method can also be used for decorative stitching; just fold the fabric and sew over it and pull apart. You might need to experiment with the settings to perfect this seam.

Flatlock seams

Flatlock is a seam where the fabric edges lie flat on the garment, so there will be no loose floppy seam allowance that can rub the skin. Flatlock seams are common in ready-to-wear workout clothes to create smooth, chafe-free seams.

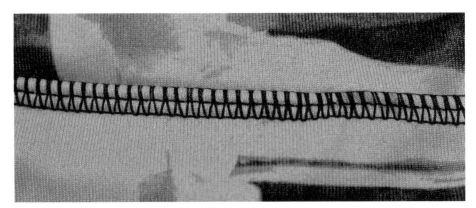

Industrial flatlock seam

However, those flatlock seams are made on industrial machines and you won't find that seam on regular household sewing machines. Luckily, there are several options for home sewists who want to recreate that look and this chapter covers these methods.

3-thread serger flatlock seam using woolly nylon in the looper

FLATLOCK ON A SERGER

On most sergers, you can usually sew a 2-thread or 3-thread flatlock seam. You sew together two pieces of fabric, wrong sides facing. Then pull the fabric apart to create a flat seam; the edges will butt under the stitches. The 2-thread flatlock is fairly easy to get flat when pulled apart. But with the 3-thread, you might need to experiment with the settings to get the fabric to lie flat.

For activewear, the 2-thread version might not be durable enough, so consider using the 3-thread flatlock seam instead. But be aware that the 3-thread serger version isn't as durable as the industrial flatlock.

How to succeed with 3-thread flatlock

The trademark of a successful serger flatlock seam is that it lies nearly flat when pulled apart. To achieve this, you might have to experiment to find the right combination of method and settings, especially if your serger has manual tension settings.

3-THREAD SERGER **FLATLOCK**

1 **Sew the flatlock seam.** It should be sewn right-side up, wrong sides facing. Make sure the seam catches both layers.

2 **The finished seam.** Ready to be pulled apart. In the photo woolly nylon is used in the upper looper thread.

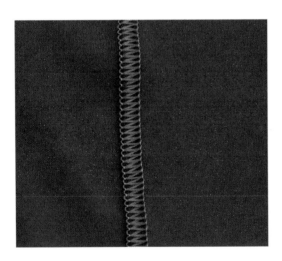

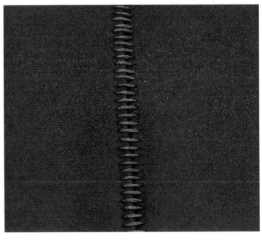

3 **Pull the seam apart.** This makes the seam lie flat.

4 **The reverse side.** The seam is very flat, which will minimise chafing.

10 tips for a successful 3-thread flatlock seam

1. Set the needle tension low and the upper looper tension high if your serger has manual settings.

2. Use woolly nylon or some other flossy stretch thread in the upper looper. This creates both a nice coverage and also adds tension in the looper, which helps the 3-thread flatlock lie flat.

3. Increase the cutting width and stitch length to create a wider and more dense looking flatlock seam. But beware that it might make the seam harder to pull flat.

4. Sew the seam with the right side up and wrong sides facing.

5. When sewing, make sure the fabric edges line up exactly; if one layer slips, you might not get an even and secure seam.

6. If you still can't get the seam to lie flat, try to move the edge of fabric away from the knife—but just a tiny bit, because if you sew too far out, the needles won't catch the fabric.

7. If you are sewing over three layers of fabric, for instance when attaching a pocket in the seam as well, place the double layers on top and the third single layer underneath. This creates a flatter seam.

8. Pull apart the seam as much as you can; it won't break if you have sewed it correctly. Ironing over the seam using a low temperature can make the flatlock seam lie even flatter, but can be risky when using heat-sensitive synthetic materials, so always do a sample first.

9. Flatlock seams sewn on a serger can snag sometimes. Wash your makes in a wash-bag and keep them away from bra hooks, zipper, and other sharp objects!

Mock flatlock seam on a sewing machine

SEWING MACHINE MOCK FLATLOCK SEAM

If you only have a regular sewing machine, you can mimic the flatlock seam using two sets of stitches. First, sew together the side seams with a stretch seam or a zigzag stitch. Then fold the seam and stitch over the seam with a second row of stitches on the right side, using a decorative stitch that has good stretchability.

Another option is to sew one row of zigzag stitches and press the seam allowances apart. Then, from the right side, you stitch over the seam. This option creates the flattest seam because it only sews over one layer of seam allowance on each side.

Stitching down a long inner seam on leggings or sleeves

To create non-chafing seams, it might be tempting to stitch down an entire inseam on a pair of tight-fitting leggings or a long-sleeve top. However, this is a tricky proposition since you won't be able to sew the fabric flat. Instead, you need to carefully guide the closed tunnel so that the stitch will be straight.

Generally, this method can't be recommended for long seams as there is a substantial risk that you'll end up with a distorted seam. If you want a flat inseam, your best option is to use a serger flatlock seam instead. But with practice, you might end up with an acceptable result when stitching over a closed inseam using a sewing machine.

MOCK FLATLOCK **SEWING MACHINE**

1 **Sew the side seams.** Use a straight stitch or a narrow zigzag stitch. The seam allowance should be narrow, around 1 cm (⅖") or less.

2 **Press the side seams apart.** This prepares the seam for the topstitching.

3 **Stitch over the seam.** Pick a decorative stitch that also has stretch. Sew from the right side, making sure that seam is in the middle.

4 **The finished seam on the inside.** This method is a great option to create a very flat seam on a regular sewing machine.

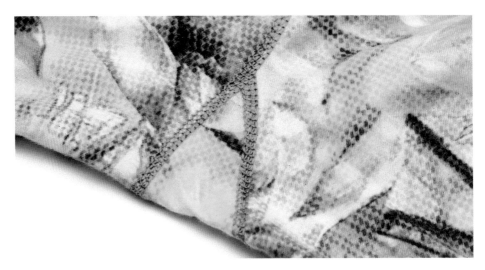
Reverse 3-needle coverstitch seam

FAUX FLATLOCK WITH A COVERSTITCH MACHINE

The reverse side of the 3-needle coverstitch looks similar to the industrial flatlock seam. So after you stitch a seam, you can sew a 3-needle coverstitch seam over the seam on the wrong side to create a decorative stitch in the right side. However, this is not always an easy seam to succeed with as the bulky seam increases the risk for skipped stitches and uneven feeding. In general, this method works best on thin and supple fabrics. Woolly nylon in the lower looper covers the seam nicely and makes it look even more like professionally made activewear. But it can also mess up the seam, especially if you are sewing over a bulky seam. So do a sample first to test if it will work on your chosen fabric.

Using a domestic coverstitch machine, the three rows of straight stitches will be sewn on the wrong side of the garment to achieve the flatlock effect on the outside. But there are also domestic machines that can do a decorative, reverse coverstitch seam on both sides of the fabric.

REVERSE COVERSTITCH **OPEN SEAM**

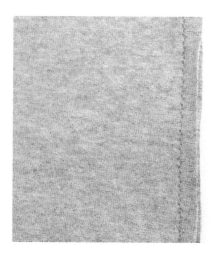

1   **Sew together the seam.** Use a narrow zigzag stitch and a seam allowance that is around 0.6 cm (¼"). Open up the seam, so that it lies flat.

2   **Coverstitch the seam.** On the wrong side, sew over the seam using the 3-thread coverstitch. Make sure the middle needle hits the groove where the seam is.

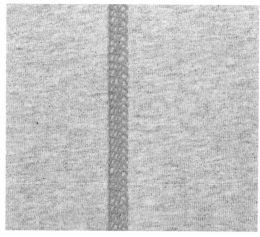

3   **The seam seen from the wrong side.** There are three rows of straight stitches on the wrong side unless you use a coverstitch machine that can sew reverse stitching on both sides.

4   **The finished seam on the right side.** In this example, a woolly nylon is used in the looper for a better and more decorative coverage.

REVERSE COVERSTITCH **OVER SEAM**

1   **Stitch the seam.** Use a wide 3-thread overlock with regular thread or a sewing machine stretch overlock seam. It's important to have a seam that is not bulky but wide enough for the coverstitch to properly grip the seam with the feed dogs.

2   **Coverstitch the seam.** On the wrong side, sew over the seam using the 3-thread coverstitch. The seam allowance should be folded to the right for better feeding and the left needle should hit just outside left of the seam. Gently pull the seam apart while sewing so that the seam will be flat when stitched over.

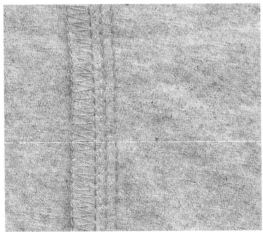

3   **The finished seam.** In this example, a regular serger thread is used in the looper.

4   **The seam seen from the wrong side.** Notice the three rows of stitches.

How to succeed with reverse coverstitching

1. When sewing over an overlock seam, folding the seam allowance to the right will usually yield the best result because it is gripped better by the feed dogs.

2. A clear presser foot or a foot with a center guide makes it easier to sew an even seam.

3. Make sure the fabric layers lie flat when sewing over them; you can achieve this by gently pulling the seam apart.

4. Adjust the tension. You might need to experiment with the tension settings of both the looper and needles, especially as the left needle only stitches through one fabric layer and the other two needles through three layers. Try decreasing the tension of the left needle for a balanced seam.

5. Reducing the presser foot pressure can help when sewing over bulky seams.

6. If you get skipped stitches or the fabric doesn't feed properly, switch to a larger needle, increase the stitch length, lower the differential feed, and try adjusting the presser foot pressure.

7. The seam allowance needs to be gripped by the feed dogs. If your seam allowance is too narrow, the feed dogs might not have a big enough surface to feed the fabric.

SHEILA POWELL

WHO: Sewist from USA who finds workout inspiration from making colourful, creative activewear.

FAVOURITE EXERCISES: Working out on my elliptical and finishing my workout power hooping with a 6.8lb hoop. I try to diversify and can be found on the treadmill or running in my backyard or aerobics.

FIND: www.sheilaz-ctk.com

SHEILA POWELL

MOTIVATION THROUGH CREATION

Sheila is a corporate gal during the day and a sewing and crafty gal at night. She works in the legal field, and between juggling clients, judges, clerks, and more for her attorneys, she daydreams about her next activewear project, and once in the sewing realm, she attempts to create motivating pieces.

How did you get into creating activewear?
Sewing my own activewear started out innocently. The majority of my activewear had seen better days and, secondly, the few that I'd recently purchased were already starting to show some wear and tear. As a sewing/crafty gal, I spontaneously decided I'd make my own and felt the need for vibrant colours to step up my workout gear. »

> MY BEST TIP IS TO CHOOSE THE RIGHT THREAD AND TENSION. EACH PROJECT REQUIRES ADJUSTING THE TENSION.
>
> **SHEILA** DIY CREATOR

How does making your own workout wear help you with exercise motivation?

Exercising in my me-made activewear creates a sure-fire boost to keep exercising. To heighten the workouts, the right fit and using bright colours brings up the motivation another notch.

Share your best tip when it comes to sewing activewear

Sewing activewear can be tricky. However, the best tip I've learned is to use the right thread and adjust the machine tension. Each project requires adjusting the tension.

www.sheilaz-ctk.com

Notions for activewear

Using good-quality notions is crucial when it comes to succeeding with your activewear. Your garments will be under a lot of stress so investing in things such as good-quality thread, elastic, and needles makes a huge difference when it comes to both the assembly process and the durability of the garment.

This chapter covers some of the most common notions such as different thread options, why you need to invest in specialty needles and what type of elastics are useful when making activewear.

Sewing on stretchy Lycra knits can be tricky sometimes, especially if you only have a regular sewing machine. Luckily there are some special tools and notions that makes this process easier, and those will also be covered in this chapter.

THREAD

Proper thread are vital to the success of your activewear projects. Also, don't skimp on quality when buying your threads, as you might end up paying later if the seams break or the thread causes your sewing machines to act up.

Sewing machine thread

Regular polyester sewing machine thread

On the regular sewing machine, use a good-quality polyester regular thread. The most important thing is that the thread is durable as the seams on activewear will be under a lot of stress.

Serger thread

Serger thread

Serger thread usually comes in cones, is more lightweight than regular sewing thread, and cheaper by the yard compared to regular sewing thread. For activewear use 100 polyester good-quality core spun serger thread. You only need matching colours for the threads that are visible from the outside. For the non-visible stitches, grey and off-white are great blending threads.

Woolly nylon

Woolly nylon

This thread is a must-have if you own a serger or a coverstitch and want to sew activewear. Woolly nylon is softer, more durable and has better stretch and coverage than regular serger thread. When sewn, the thread spreads out and covers the edges, which creates a soft and rub-free seam. You can use it in all positions, but the most common application is to use woolly nylon only in the loopers. Be aware that woolly nylon increases the tension, so you might have to loosen the tension settings when using this thread.

Woolly nylon comes in several versions and some threads are more flossy and offer more coverage than others, so you might need to try different brands to see which thread is best for your project.

Transparent thread

Often called monofilament thread, it's a lightweight thread made of either nylon or polyester. This transparent thread can be used in the needles and loopers for discreet stitches—a good option when hemming.

NEEDLES

Using the right needles are crucial when sewing activewear, as many fabrics in this category don't take well to regular needles, and you might end up with skipped and broken stitches.

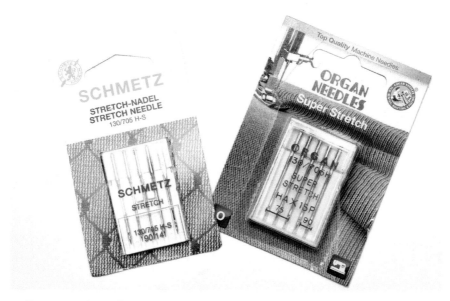

Ballpoint stretch needles

Sewing machine needles for knits

When sewing stretchy knits on a sewing machine, use a good-quality ballpoint needle to avoid holes and skipped stitches. For sewing machines, common stretch needle sizes are 75, 80, and 90, which will suffice on most projects. If you are sewing over thicker layers and are experiencing some problems, try switching to a larger ballpoint needle.

Ballpoint needles are usually labelled as stretch needles, and some brands also offer a jersey needle, which is a ballpoint needle but with a different shaped scarf and eye than the regular stretch needle. A jersey needle is best suited for regular jersey without Lycra (Spandex). So, for activewear, a stretch needle will generally be a better option than a jersey needle. A ballpoint twin-needle is another must-have for the sewing machine and can be used both for hemming and topstitching.

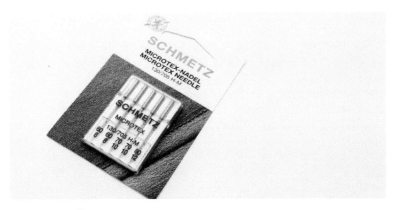

Microtex needles

Sewing machine needles for coated woven fabrics

If you are sewing on woven synthetic sports fabric, perhaps with some coating, a microtex needle is the best option. The microtex needle is slim and sharp and prevents unsightly holes and skipped stitches. Also, sewing over coated fabrics wears out the needle quickly, so switch often. If the stitches are looking wonky or you hear a click when the needle hits the fabric, it's time to change the needle.

ELx705 SUK-needles for sergers and coverstitch machines

Needles for sergers and coverstitch machines

Picking the right needles is crucial when using a serger or a coverstitch machine. Make sure that you use the needles that the manufacturer and seller recommend. If unsure, the ELX705 system needles are of good-quality and work with most machine brands, but again, make sure that they are right for your particular machine.

Basting glue pen

OTHER USEFUL NOTIONS

Basting glue

To get knits to lie flat and stay put, use a dab of washable basting glue for those tricky areas. You can also use regular stick glue, preferably a smaller one. The glue from a regular glue stick will also disappear when the fabric is washed.

Tailor's awl

An awl

A tailor's awl is your best friend when sewing knits. Use it to feed the upper layer of the fabric towards the presser foot when hemming knits on a regular sewing machine. This prevents the fabric from stretching out and mimics the differential feed on a serger or a coverstitch machine. If you have problems with puckering when stitching woven functional materials, an awl prevents this too.

An awl is also an excellent tool for marking, for instance when you are applying eyelets or zippers. Don't worry about creating visible holes, the small awl will just make a tiny hole and if you place it just inside the seam it won't be visible.

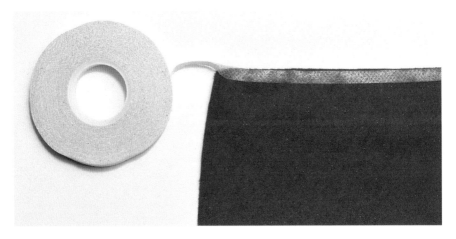

Water-soluble double-sided tape

Wonder tape

Water-soluble wonder tape helps the fabric stay put and is especially useful when hemming and topstitching stretchy knits on a regular sewing machine. The tape is sticky on both sides and disappears when washed. It can also be used for the lower edge of a collar and other areas where a neatly folded seam is essential.

ELASTICS FOR ACTIVEWEAR

When you begin making activewear you'll soon realise that not all elastics are created equal. In fact, there is a myriad of elastics to choose from and making the right choice is crucial to the success of your makes. In the guide on the following pages the most common ones and their uses are shown.

KNITTED ELASTIC

A basic elastic that can be used for a variety of activewear projects. Both soft and strong, knitted elastic is easier to stitch over than other more firm elastic, which is why it's a great choice when sewing activewear. Comes in many widths and is usually very cheap when bought in bulk.

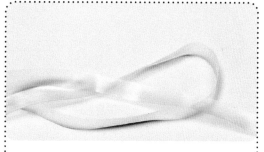

CLEAR ELASTIC

Lightweight clear elastic that can be used for any area that needs stabilization; shoulder seams, pocket openings, necklines, leg openings on swimwear, waistbands, and plenty more. This non-bulky, discreet elastic has fantastic stretch and recovery. See also How to stabilise a neckline using clear elastic (page 122).

PLUSH ELASTIC

An elastic that is plush on either one or both sides. Suitable for elastic waistbands and the bottom edge of a sports bra. It is sometimes also called bra strap or bra band elastic. The soft surface makes it comfortable to wear against the skin.

FOLD-OVER ELASTIC

Fold-over elastic can be used on everything from hemming fleece sweaters to covering the edges of a sports bra. It is knitted but has a stable center fold-line, and creates a non-bulky finish that works well for both knit and woven fabrics. See How to sew fold-over elastic (page 76).

ELASTIC CORD

Very common on activewear and
used for making adjustable elastic
cord drawstrings. Use it for garments
such as windbreakers, ski jackets
or fleece sweaters. Make sure you
pick a sturdy, durable cord for these
applications. See also How to make
elastic cord drawstrings (page132).

SILICONE-BACKED ELASTIC

Elastic with silicon grippers helps the
garment to stay put on the body. This
is commonly found at the hem of bike
shorts and on sports bras. It comes
in many different versions and sizes,
but try to find silicon-backed elastic
that isn't too bulky. Can also be used
to create a DIY workout hair band.

CHAPTER 2
PROJECTS

SLEEVES WITH THUMBHOLES

CUFFS WITH THUMBHOLES

Cuffs with thumbholes are a popular detail on activewear and this method is both quick and easy. These cuffs are a great option for the colder seasons. Another good thing with these is that they keep the sleeves from riding when you put on a jacket, which makes them perfect for layering.

>> **SUPPLIES**

- Ribbing fabric or another thicker, stretchy knit
- A sewing machine
- A serger (optional)

PREPARATION

For this project, we will use regular ribbing and the direction that has the most amount of stretch will go around the wrist just like a regular cuff would.

- Determine the width: Measure the circumference of the hand where the fingers begin. Then subtract 15% to get the width of the cuff and add seam allowance to the side seams.

- Determine the length: Twice the distance from the sleeve to the knuckles plus seam allowance.

- The recommended seam allowance is 0.6 cm (¼") or 1 cm (⅖").

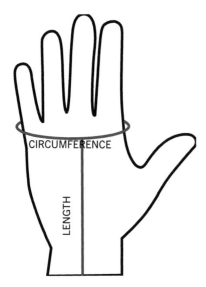

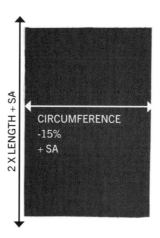

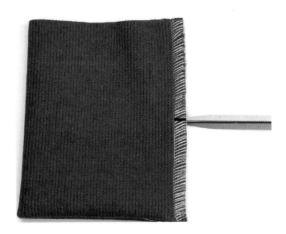

1 **Sew the side seams.** Fold the cuff lengthwise to sew the side seams using either a stretch stitch on your sewing machine or a 3-thread overlock stitch on a serger.

2 **Mark the length of the thumb opening.** Mark where the part of the opening should begin above the thumb. Cut notches with a pair of scissors. If you feel unsure about cutting notches in the seam allowance, you can just mark the fabric with a pen.

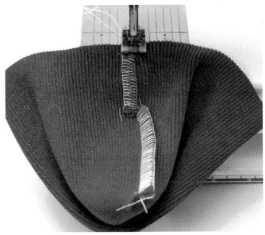

3 **Prepare the cuffs to create an opening.** Fold the cuffs, so the right sides are facing inward. If you have cut notches, fold the side seams in opposite directions to prepare for sewing the ditch seam.

4 **Sew together the sides of the cuff.** Sew a straight stitch in the ditch of the side seams down to the notch. Make sure to secure the seam properly, as this is an area that will be under a lot of stress.

5   **Turn the cuff outwards.** You can press the cuffs gently with an iron for a sharper fold before you close the lower edge.

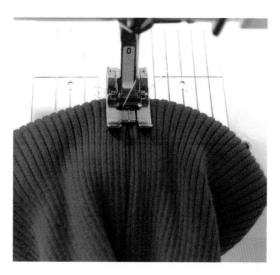

6   **Close the lower opening.** Do this by sewing a short-stitch-length bar tack zigzag along the cuff side seams for 1.5 cm (⅝") distance. Go back and forth 3–4 times to make sure the seam is durable.

7   **The finished opening.** Notice how thick the bar tack is; this creates a very durable seam. For extra security, you can stitch a horizontal row as well.

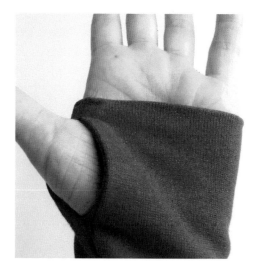

8   **The cuff.** Ready to be attached to a sleeve. You can use both ribbing and stable knits to sew this cuff.

SLEEVES WITH THUMBHOLES

You don't need cuffs to create a thumbhole opening on a garment. This tutorial will show you how to do a popular ready-to-wear activewear technique using fold-over elastic to cover the openings.

⟫ SUPPLIES

- Fold-over-elastic
- Sleeve pieces (cut but not sewn)
- A sewing machine
- A needle and thread for basting (optional)

PREPARATION

Cut the sleeve pieces but don't sew the seams as this method requires that you work on the flat. You'll get the best result using a narrow fold-over elastic for the thumbhole opening, as a wide elastic will create a bulky fold. For tips on how to attach fold-over-elastic, see How to sew fold-over elastic (page 76). If you are unsure about the placement or how big the opening should be, do a sample first to see what will work with the specific hand but a good starting number for an adult hand is 5–6 cm (approx. 2–2 ⅖").

1 **Cut the slit open.** Use a sharp pair of scissors or a hobby knife to cut a horizontal opening that is approximately 5-6 cm (circa 2–2 ⅖") long for an adult hand. The slit should be a straight cut.

2 **Attach the fold-over elastic.** Pull the slit apart so that it forms a straight line. Stitch the elastic using a medium zigzag. The elastic should always be shorter than the fabric and stretched out while sewing.
TIP: For instructions on how to attach fold-over elastic see
How to sew fold-over elastic (page 76).

3 **Close the opening.** Sew together the edges of the slit with a couple of rows of stitches close to the edge; this will ensure that the ends of the opening will stay closed when you sew the sleeve seam.

4 **Attach the sleeve to the garment and sew together the side seam.** On knit garments, it's usually best to first attach the sleeves to the arm holes on the flat and then sew the entire side seam starting at the hem of the bodice and sewing all the way up and around to the sleeve opening.

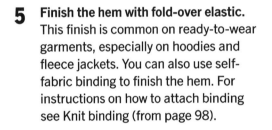

5 **Finish the hem with fold-over elastic.** This finish is common on ready-to-wear garments, especially on hoodies and fleece jackets. You can also use self-fabric binding to finish the hem. For instructions on how to attach binding see Knit binding (from page 98).

6 **The finished sleeve.** This method is an easy project that will yield a professional-looking result and can be applied on any kind of knit garment. **TIP:** You can also do a vertical slit for the thumb, starting at the hem and using the same methods as described in this tutorial.

BEVERLY JOHNSON

BRA-MAKING EXPERT

┌─ **BRA-MAKING SUPPLIES** ─┐

WHO: Canadian bra-making company
founded in 1996 by bra designer
Beverly Johnson

FAVOURITE EXERCISE:
"Pushing tables!"

FIND: braandcorsetsupplies.com
└──────────────────┘

Beverly Johnson is a real bra-maker veteran who has spent her professional life designing bra patterns for the fashion industry and for home sewing enthusiasts. Since 1996 she also runs Bra-Making Supplies which sells bra-making fabrics and notions—plus she holds bra-making classes around the world and on Blueprint.com. Beverly currently has two sports bra patterns in her collection, and here she shares her best tips on how to make your own sports bra.

You are a bra-making veteran. What made you venture into also designing sports bra patterns?
It was a natural progression from making supportive bras that fit, to making sports bras that support during vigorous activity. **»**

What are the secrets of a well-fitting and stable sports bra?

The fabric is the key; many sports companies spend millions of dollars researching the "right design", but when it comes down to it, we can make a no-bounce sports bra at home using the correct fabrics. Seriously. The fabric is the key.

For a supportive sports bra, what kind of notions and materials should we use?

Use a no-stretch fabric, or one with very low-stretch, such as Duoplex. Regular Spandex fabric is out of the question if you want support during vigorous activities. Power net for the back. A wickable lining is nice too.

I use our Active cotton to line sports bras, so it moves the moisture away from the body, keeping you dry. The one thing that is absolutely critical, for a sports bra is to keep the upper cup stable. That means no stretchy straps. You need to keep the upper half of the breast from moving—that's what will stop the bounce.

Why should we sew our own sports bras?

It's actually fun to sew a sports bra, plus the fit makes it worthwhile. This is one area where you can actually save money over the ready-to-wear offerings as well.

Does a larger bust require a different style of sports bra compared with one for a smaller bust? And if so, what are the differences?

The larger bust needs deeper darts, and I think a wickable lining is a must. But the fabric is critical as I said above. All breasts, even self-supporting ones, will bounce when you run. That's just a fact of nature.

braandcorsetsupplies.com

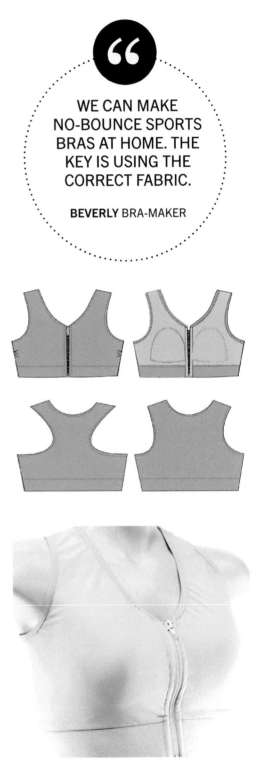

"

WE CAN MAKE NO-BOUNCE SPORTS BRAS AT HOME. THE KEY IS USING THE CORRECT FABRIC.

BEVERLY BRA-MAKER

FOLD-OVER ELASTIC

FOLD-OVER ELASTIC

Fold-over elastic is a great option for activewear and can be used on everything from hemming fleece sweaters to covering the edges of a sports bra. It is knitted but has a stable center fold-line, and the elastic creates a non-bulky finish which works with most knit fabrics.

Fold-over elastic, sometimes abbreviated FOE, comes in many different versions. Some are shiny on one side and have a plush surface on the other side. For activewear, you should use the plush side out. Other versions of FOE are thin, mesh-like, and slightly transparent—those are great to use on bulky fabrics such as fleece. A third kind is thick and knitted and is best suited for heavier fabrics and winter activewear.

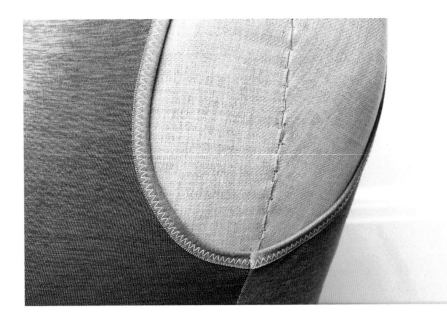

HOW TO SEW FOLD-OVER ELASTIC

Preparation

Decide if you want to attach the elastic flat or on the round. It's easiest to sew the elastic on the flat, which means that you leave one seam open, such as the side seam or shoulder seam. After you have applied the fold-over elastic, you simply close the seam and there is no need to sew the elastic as a closed loop. A neater option is to sew the elastic in the round, which means that you have already sewn the seams on the garment and you need to close the elastic by sewing together the edges. But you don't need to do that until you have attached the elastic with the first row of basting stitches.

Determining the length of the elastic

Fold-over elastic needs to be stretched out when attached, especially in the curves; otherwise, it will look wobbly. So, in general, the elastic needs to be shorter than your finished garment, unless the garment is very tight-fitting to begin with. Around 85% to 95% of the measurement of the edge where you are applying the elastic is a good starting point. But you can also stretch out as you sew; in which case you don't have to measure beforehand. Stretch more in the curves and less on straight areas.

Best stitch settings for fold-over elastic

A medium-sized standard setting zigzag stitch is a great option for attaching the elastic. Remember that the finished stitch will be wider and less narrow than it looks when sewn as it will bounce back after being stretched out. So, always test on a sample first. You can also use the three-step zigzag stitch if available on your machine. This stitch will make the seam even more durable and is a popular choice for sports bras. Some machines also have other decorative zigzag stitches that can be used for attaching fold-over elastic.

HAND BASTING **FLAT METHOD**

1 **Measure the fold-over elastic.** This step is optional but recommended if you are struggling with getting an even result. Make the elastic around 85–95 % of the distance you want to cover and mark corresponding marks on the elastic. Here, the notches are marked at the shoulder and side seams. Use the notches as a guide to know how much the elastic needs to be stretched when sewn. Trim off the seam allowance if necessary.

2 **Hand baste the elastic.** Fold the elastic over the edge and hand baste it in place, stretching it gently, especially around the curves. Don't cut the excess elastic until you have basted the seam. If you want to close the elastic before topstitching, leave sufficient room un-basted so that you can sew together the edges of the elastic.

3 **Stitch the elastic.** Use a medium zigzag. Stitch close, but not too close to the edge and stretch the elastic gently so that it shapes around the curves. The basting will keep the elastic in place.

4 **Sew the side seam.** Just sew over the elastic edges when sewing the side seam. This is the easiest way to close the fold-over elastic and is often used on ready-to-wear garments.

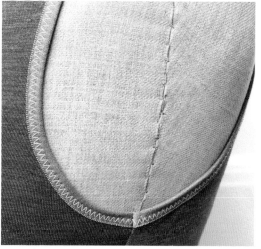

5 **Secure the seam allowance.** To keep the seam allowance in place sew a few tack stitches over the seam allowance from the right side. Remove basting stitches.

6 **The finished application.** Hand basting is an excellent way to achieve a pristine application when sewing fold-over elastic because it is both reliable and malleable. Recommended for beginners.

MACHINE BASTING **ROUND METHOD**

1 **Baste the elastic.** Place the open elastic on the wrong side, aligning the center with the edge of the fabric. Attach the elastic from the right side using a basting stitch and a contrasting thread. Stretch the elastic gently so that it shapes around the curves.

2 **Leave room for closing the elastic.** Don't cut the excess elastic until the elastic is basted. If you want to close the fold-over elastic, don't stitch the entire length. Instead leave around 2.5 cm (1") open on each side to sew together the edges.

3 **Close the elastic ring.** Sew together the trimmed edges if you want to create a loop. Remember to stretch out the elastic before you close it, otherwise, the seam will be stretched out and bubbly. You don't need to baste this part, as it will be easy to topstitch in place.

4 **Topstitch the elastic.** Use a medium zigzag and sew close to the edge. If you have stretched out the elastic while basting it, you will get a nice even result using this method.

5 **Remove the basting stitches.** Just pull the thread and remove. If you have picked a long enough stitch, this will be easy to do.

6 **The finished elastic.** Thanks to the basting method, the elastic will be flat and even.

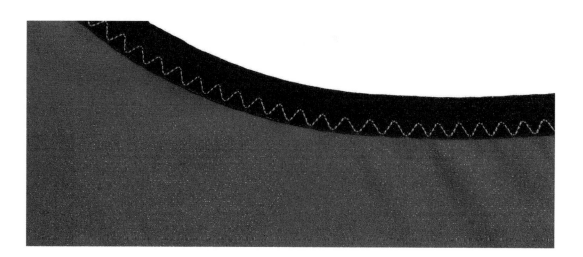

7 **Bonus tip.** Let the fold-over elastic be a design feature. By choosing contrasting thread and colour, you can add some interest to this application. In this photo, a 3-step zigzag stitch is used and it works very well for fold-over attaching elastic

CARD
POCKET

WAISTBAND CARD **POCKET**

Need a quick and easy way to make a pocket to store your gym card and locker keys? Then this little pouch attached to the inside of your waistband is the perfect solution.

━━▷▷ **SUPPLIES**

- ● Sports mesh
- ● A sewing machine
- ● A serger (optional)

SIZE OF THE POCKET

- ● Width: The width of a gym card + a tad extra ease + 0.6 cm (¼") seam allowance on each side.

- ● Length: Twice the height of a gym card + 2.5 cm (1") + 2 cm (¾") for the seam allowance.

1 **Overcast the edges.** Do this by either stitching the sides with a serger overlock or flatlock seam or a decorative sewing machine stitch. Another option is to turn the edges and topstitch them with a regular zigzag seam.

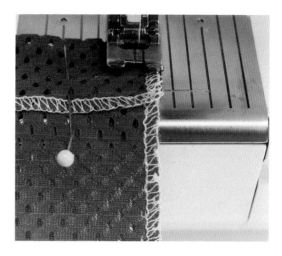

2 **Fold over the upper edge to create a pouch.** Use a card to find the right size. The edges should overlap about 2.5 cm (1") and you also need room above the card to use as seam allowance, approximately 1 cm (⅖") when folded.

3 **Close the pocket.** Stitch together the sides using a sewing machine stretch seam or an overlock serger stitch.

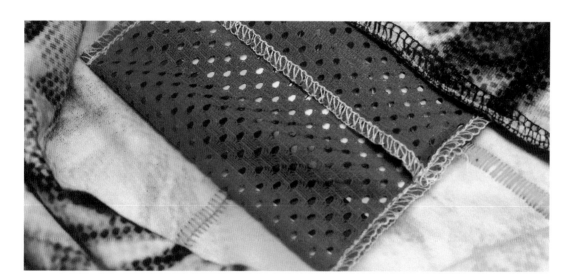

4 **The finished pouch.** Attach the pouch to the seam allowance of the waistband using a narrow zigzag stitch. Turn the waistband of the garment down to the outside so the seam allowance extends. Align the top of the pocket with the edge of the seam allowance.

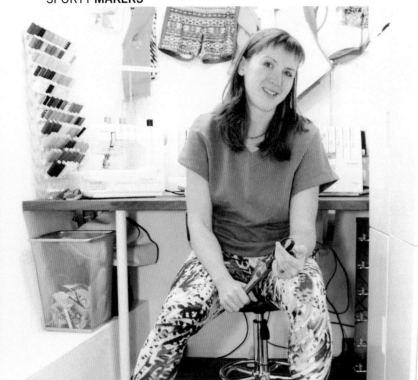

FEHR TRADE PATTERNS

WHO: British activewear pattern company founded in 2013 by athlete and sewing enthusiast Melissa Fehr.

FAVOURITE EXERCISES: Running, cycling, and bouldering (in that order)

FIND: fehrtrade.com

FEHR TRADE

ATHLETIC PATTERN MAKER

Runner Melissa Fehr started FehrTrade Patterns when she saw a gap in the market for functional exercise sewing patterns that went beyond the basics. She creates patterns for both men and women that are suited for activities such as biking, running, yoga, and much more. She is the also author of the book Sew Your Own Activewear (2018).

How did you get into designing activewear patterns?

I started sewing soon after I moved to London from Pennsylvania in 2002, and began drafting a few patterns here and there for myself about ten years later. I didn't begin drafting commercially, though, until I launched my pattern company in 2013. I started FehrTrade patterns because I had been made redundant from the tech job I'd had for over 12 years, and I saw that there was a huge demand for functional exercise sewing patterns that went beyond the basic shapes on offer. So, it was natural for me to combine my love of running and sewing and offer my expertise in both to a wider audience. **»**

Talk about your design process

For my first few patterns, my design starting point was a hole in my own exercise wardrobe—for instance, I thought, "I really want a pair of close-fitting shorts with integrated pockets to store my phone and gels", and so I went off and developed my Duathlon Shorts pattern. But some of my other patterns have been led by requests from my wonderful, active customers, like my Steeplechase Leggings pattern, which came about after some equestrians told me about their struggles to find no-inseam leggings that wouldn't chafe against the horse.

I usually start with an inspiration like this. Then it'll go through quite a few muslins in the design stage before I take it out for some on-the-road tests while I exercise, usually followed by a few more revisions, until finally, I'm happy enough that I send it off to my grader and start work on the pattern instructions and illustrations.

Picking the right fabric can be overwhelming when making activewear. What advice do you have?

If you're shopping online, knowing a few keywords to search for can make all the difference—many places will list activewear fabrics as "Supplex", "wicking", "sport", or even just "activewear", but it's worth having a look at the fibre content as well. »

SEW UP YOUR FIRST ACTIVEWEAR GARMENTS IN A CHEAP FABRIC WITH SIMILAR PROPERTIES TO YOUR GOOD FABRIC

MELISSA FEHR TRADE

Many new activewear sewists think that fabric must be wicking, but for me, as long as it's stretchy and not cotton (because it soaks up sweat like a sponge) a good-quality polyester or nylon Lycra can be fine for most workouts.

If you're looking for a good, all-around sports fabric that will work for bottoms as well as tops, then Supplex is a great choice. It's soft to the touch, has great stretch and recovery, comes in a million different colours, and most importantly—it wicks sweat and moisture away from the skin so it can evaporate on the surface. For winter running, I also love a good merino jersey, as it's lightweight, warm, and you can do a really hard workout in it without it smelling funky afterwards.

Your best beginner tip for sewing activewear?

My biggest tip is to sew up your first activewear garments in a cheap fabric, with similar weight and stretch properties to your "good stuff" and take it out for a spin! All of us are picky about what we wear, and you can really only judge how a garment will move when you wear it for your chosen activity. Check whether it moves around, rubs, or feel uncomfortable in any way, make those tweaks to your pattern, and then dive right into that gorgeous activewear fabric for your second version.

And finally, why should we make our own activewear?

Activewear is also one of the few areas where you truly can save money by sewing your own versus buying ready-to-wear, and you can really make garments that are better suited to both your body shape and activity - with pockets in all the right places, too.

fehrtrade.com

TIES AND STRINGS

ADJUSTABLE TIES IN THE SIDE SEAMS

Placing ties in the side seam is an easy way to create shirring on a garment—perfect for swimwear, tops, and gym shorts. This method is a ready-to-wear standard. The trick is to not use a stretch seam for the side seam. Instead, you sew the seam with a narrow zigzag, keep the seam allowances, and use those to create tunnels for the strings.

⟫ SUPPLIES

- Fabric for making the straps (you can also use pre-made strings)
- Loop turner or needle and thread
- Sewing machine
- Serger (optional)

PREPARATION

To make this method work, you need to have a seam allowance of around 1 cm (⅖") in the side seam where you want to add the strings. Hem the garment before attaching the strings but don't sew any other seams, because this method will work best when done on the flat.

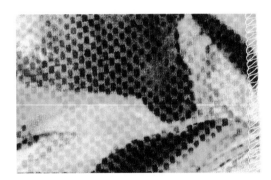 

1 **Overcast the edges.** This step is optional on knits, but it will keep the fabric edges from curling. If you have serger, use the 2-thread flatlock seam or the 3-thread overlock. On a sewing machine, use a zigzag or a decorative stitch.

2 **Hem the garment pieces.** This step is required before you attach the strings. Use a twin-needle on a sewing machine or a coverstitch machine for the best result.

3 **Sew the side seams together.** Use a narrow zigzag stitch. For extra security, you can add a second row of stitches close to the first.

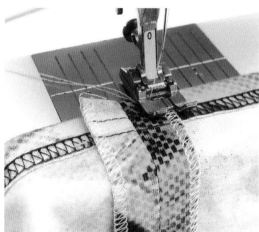 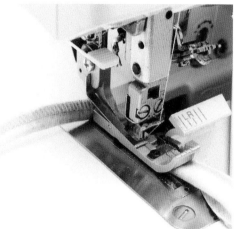

4 **Stitch the tunnels.** Press the seam allowance apart. Use a very narrow zigzag stitch and sew close to the edge of the area with the overcasting; this will create tunnels for the strings.

5 **Create the spaghetti straps.** Cut 2.5 cm (1") wide strips and fold them lengthways, right sides together. Stitch the strings using either a narrow zigzag or the 3-thread narrow overlock seam. The seam allowance should not be wider than 0.6 cm (¼").

6 Turn the spaghetti strap. A loop turner is great tool for this purpose. But you can also use a hand sewing needle and thread. Attach the thread to the top edge and then pull the needle through to turn the strap.

7 Insert the ties. Pull them through the side seam tunnels and leave a little extra outside the upper edge. Secure the ties by stitching over them close to the upper edge. One or two rows will usually suffice.

8 Close the strings. Finish by attaching the upper part of the garment, such as a waistband over the ties.
TIP: If your garment lacks a waist piece and is just folded and topstitched (such as a folded elastic waist) attach the strings close to where the waist seam will be.

TIES USING
A SHIELD

This method is perfect when you only want partial strings on your garment, such as at the hem of a pair of leggings or a top. It uses a shield and not the side seam for the ties, which means you can place he strings anywhere on the garment.

>> **SUPPLIES**

- Fabric for making the straps
  (you can also use pre-made strings)
- Loop turner or needle and thread
- Sewing machine
- Serger (optional)

PREPARATION

It's best to first hem the garment before adding the shield, especially if you want the ties to begin at the hem. Create the shield by cutting a rectangular piece of fabric that is wide enough for two straps. The length is up to you—make the piece the same length as the area you want to gather. You don't need don't need to add any seam allowance since you will attach the shield very close to the edges.

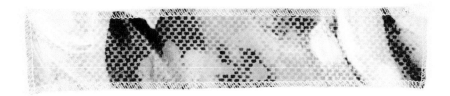

1   **Overcast the edges.** This step is optional on knits, but it will keep the fabric edges from curling. If you have serger, use the 2-thread flatlock seam or the 3-thread overlock. On a sewing machine, use a zigzag or a decorative stitch.

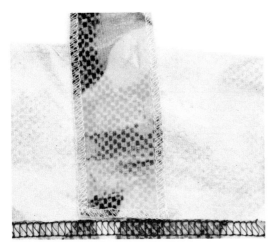

2 **Place the shield.** It should be placed inside the garment, right side facing up and either just above the hem or at the edge of the hem. If you are putting the shield over a seam, use the seam as a guide for the midpoint.

3 **Attach the shield.** Use either a straight stitch or a narrow zigzag. Sew the middle seam first, preferably using a seam guide that is attached to the presser foot . If you are sewing over a seam, stitch in the ditch, then sew along both the outer edges. There will be three rows of stitches in total.

4 **Sew the spaghetti straps.** Use the method explained in Create the spaghetti straps. Close the edges on one side and tie a knot.

5 **Pull the ties through the shield.** Leave a little extra of the strings outside the upper edge. The surplus will later be cut off once you have attached the ties.

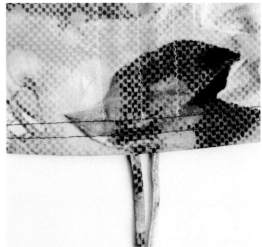

6 **Close the upper shield.** Stitch close to the edge, making sure you secure the stitch properly. Stitching a second row to secure the strings is good for extra safety. Cut away the surplus strings.

7 **Tie a knot in the strings.** Knot the end of the strings to prevent them slipping into the shield. Your shield will now look like this from the right side.

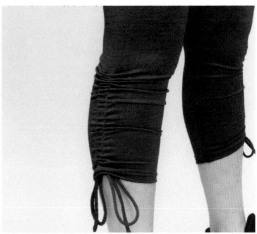

8 **Gather and tie the strings.** Adjustable ties are an excellent detail to add to your activewear. You can place them on the sides of your tops, at the hems of your leggings, or perhaps to spice up a pair of gym shorts! Plus they are easy to sew, and you can do them entirely on your regular sewing machine.

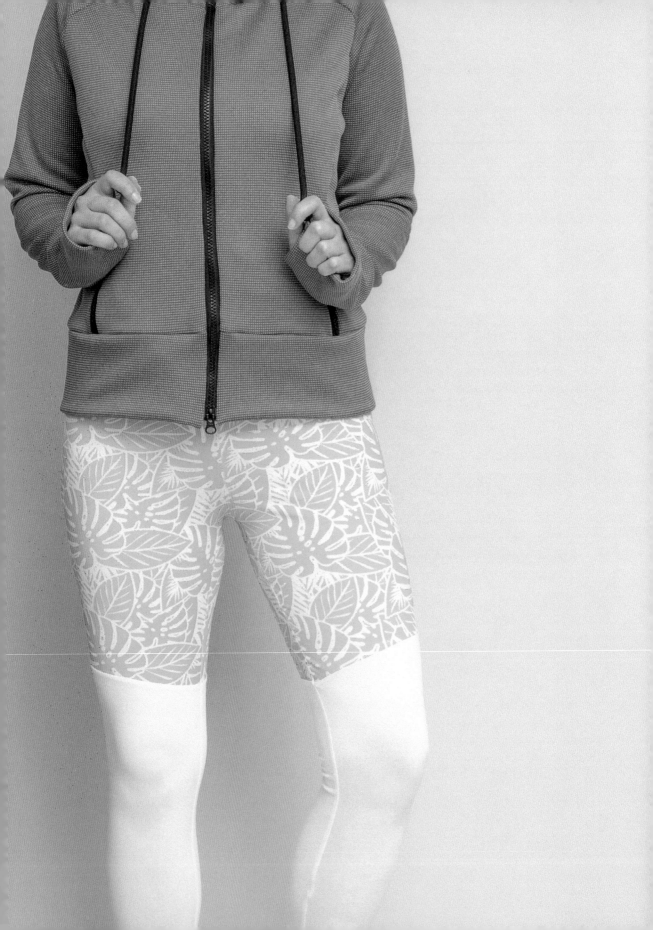

KNIT BINDING

BINDING WITH A TRIMMED EDGE

Pick this single layer binding option if you are struggling with getting an even finishing on the reverse side. With this method, you make the binding extra wide and then remove excess fabric after you have topstitched the binding. You can sew this binding entirely on a sewing machine, and it is also the least bulky binding method. Don't worry about using a straight stitch when attaching the binding. It will not pop, as you are securing the binding using a stretch seam.

>> **SUPPLIES**

- Knit fabric (both self-fabric and ribbing will work)
- Sewing machine
- Stretch twin-needle or a coverstitch machine (optional)
- Rotary cutter or a pair of sharp scissors

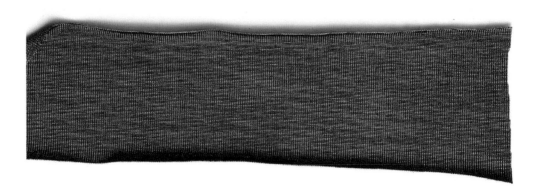

1 **Cut the binding.** Cut a rectangular strip of fabric crosswise that is both longer and wider than regular neckline binding. To calculate the width multiple the desired finished width of the binding by 3, then add around 3 cm (1 ¼") extra width or more; the excess fabric will be removed after sewing. The length of the strip should be the length of the area you are binding plus at least 5 cm extra.

2 **Attach the binding.** Use a longer straight stitch or a narrow zigzag and sew the binding to the garment, right sides facing. Stitch as far from the edge as you want the width of the binding to be. Stretch as you sew so that the binding will lie flat in the curves.

3 **Leave the ends open.** If you want to close the seam, you need to leave 2.5 cm (1") of the binding open on each side.

4 **Close the opening.** Sew the edges together to create a closed binding.

5 **Attach the remaining binding.** Sew right sides facing. You can also leave a side seam or shoulder seam and then sew over the binding edges to close it.

6 **Prepare for topstitching.** Fold over the binding and pin it in place. You can also baste or use basting glue to keep the fabric in place when topstitching.

7 **Topstitch the binding.** You can use either the stretch twin-needle or a zigzag stitch on your sewing machine or a coverstitch machine to stitch the binding in place.

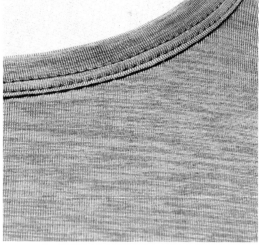

8 **Cut away the excess fabric.** Cut carefully, just below the stitch, using either a rotary cutter (it is not as scary as it sounds) or a sharp pair of scissors.

9 **The finished neckline.** This method is the least bulky of all binding finishes and can be done entirely on a sewing machine.

SINGLE LAYER
SERGED BINDING

This option is excellent if you have a serger but lack a coverstitch machine. The serged edge will create a neat looking inside and also helps control/the binding when topstitched. Use either a twin-needle or a zigzag to stitch the knit binding in place.

>> SUPPLIES

- Knit fabric (both self-fabric and ribbing will work)
- Serger
- Stretch twin-needle or a coverstitch machine

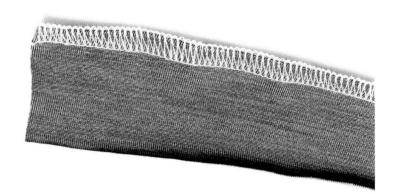

1   **Prepare the binding.** The width of the strip should be around 3.5 times the width of the finished binding plus seam allowance. Also, make the binding a bit longer than the neckline as it will make the binding easier to handle when sewing. Serge one side of the binding using either the 3-thread overlock stitch or the 2-thread flatlock seam.

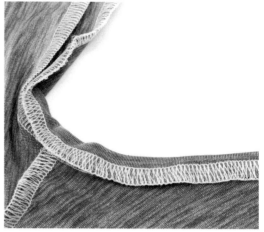

2 **Attach the binding.** Right sides facing, use a regular 3-thread overlock seam and stretch the binding gently as you sew, especially around the curves. Use the wider 3-thread overlock—you will use the seam allowance edge as your guide when folding the binding.

3 **Prepare for topstitching.** Fold the binding over the seam allowance. **TIP:** Hand baste or use basting glue to keep the binding in place when topstitching.

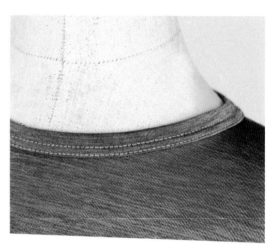

4 **Topstitch the binding.** Use either the twin-needle or a medium zigzag to attach the binding. Sew on the outside, close to the edge. For a closed binding sewn as a loop see page 99. You can also leave one seam open and close the binding by sewing together the seam.

5 **The finished neckline.** With this method, you will achieve a neat and non-bulky finishing without having to use a coverstitch machine.

DOUBLE LAYER
KNIT BINDING

Sometimes called French binding, this double layer binding technique is a finish that will closely mimic the look of ready-to-wear binding, but without having to use a binder attachment. It can, however, be bulky so only use this method on thin, lightweight knit fabrics. The biggest advantage with French binding is that it looks very neat on the inside as well, which makes it perfect for garments where the inside will be visible.

>> **SUPPLIES**

- Knit fabric (both self-fabric and ribbing will work)
- Sewing machine
- Stretch twin-needle or a coverstitch machine (optional)
- Rotary cutter or a pair of sharp scissors

1 **Cut a rectangular strip of fabric crosswise.** The width should be six times the finished width plus a little extra to compensate for what is lost when folded in many layers and stretched out. The extra width should be about 1cm (⅖"). Also, add some extra length to make the binding easier to sew. The binding will be stretched out when sewing so you don't need to figure out the exact length. You need to leave one garment seam open when using this method.

2 **Fold the binding.** If the fabric can handle it, ironing over the fold will make the fold more crisp.

3 **Attach the binding.** Use a 3-thread serger seam or a narrow zigzag on your sewing machine. Sew the binding, right sides facing. Stitch as far from the edge as you want the width of the binding to be. Stretch as you sew so that the binding will lie flat in the curves.

4 **Prepare for topstitching.** Fold the binding over the seam allowance. **TIP:** Hand baste or use basting glue to keep the binding in place.

5 **Topstitch the binding.** You can use either the stretch twin-needle, a medium zigzag stitch or a coverstitch machine to stitch the binding in place.

6 **The finished neckline seam.** As the edge consists of folded fabric the finish will look neat on the inside as well.

7 **Close the seam.** To finish the binding, you need to sew the seam that you left open. Hand baste or use basting glue to make sure the edge of the binding won't slip when you are sewing over it.
TIP: Using a serger when sewing over bulky binding layers can be tricky. If you have problems, stop serging just before the binding and use a sewing machine when sewing over the binding layers.

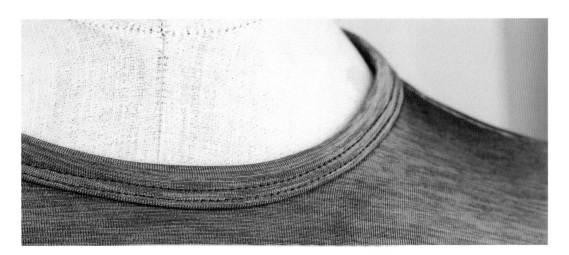

8 **The finished binding.** Using the French binding method is what will yield the most professional-looking results without having to use a binder attachment. Plus it can be done entirely on a regular sewing machine; just use an overlock sewing machine seam to attach the binding and then topstitch using a twin-needle.

BINDER ATTACHMENT
KNIT BINDING

This is the professional way to do a knit binding finish on clothes. The attachments do either 3-fold or 4-fold and will fold and sew the binding in one go. They are available for both coverstitch machines and sewing machines and will require some practice before you can fully master this tool.

>> SUPPLIES

- Knit fabric (both self-fabric and ribbing will work)
- Tape binder attachment
- Coverstitch machine (can also work on a sewing machine)
- Rotary cutter or a pair of sharp scissors

PREPARATION

Cut strips with the width recommended for your binder (the more exact you can cut them, the better the result; also, cutting them slightly too narrow is better than the strips being a little too wide). Generally, you should cut the strips along the direction of the stretch, but if your fabric is very stretchy and you struggle, try cutting them lengthwise instead.

Shape the edge of the strip as a triangle for easy insertion.

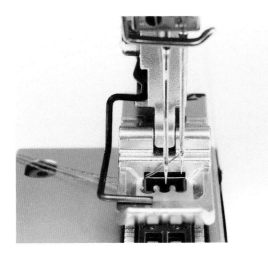

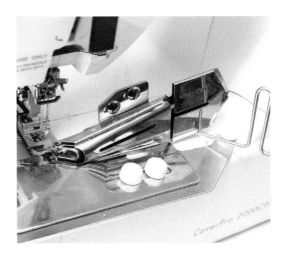

1 **Set up the needles.** If your coverstitch machine has three needles, use the middle and the right slot. Because you will sew through a lot of layers, picking a size 90 needle is recommended.

2 **Attach the binder.** Following the instructions of your particular model. If you have a generic binder, use blue-tac to keep it in place.

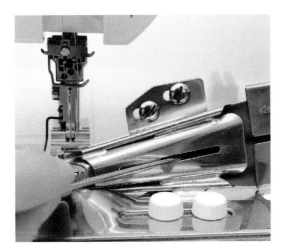

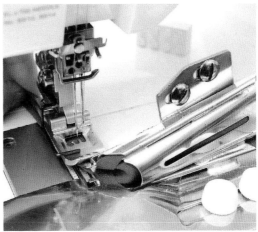

3 **Pull the fabric through the binder attachment.** Wrong side of the fabric facing you, use a needle, awl, or tweezers to pull it through the narrow tube opening.

4 **Place the strip underneath the presser foot.** Pinch the edge and then pull the binding underneath the presser foot. For best results, have around 2.5–5 cm (1-2") of tape behind the presser foot.

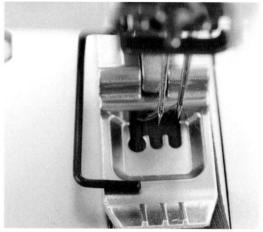

5 **Make sure that the strip is properly folded.** On some binder attachments, you can adjust the balance of the fold. I prefer the upper fold to be slightly wider than the lower fold, but test and see what works for you.

6 **Align the folded tape with the needles.** The edge of the tape should be slightly to the left of the middle needle.

7 **Start sewing the tape.** Don't insert the garment fabric until you have made sure everything looks okay. Make sure the binding doesn't slip. Insert the edge of the garment fabric into the fold. Resist the temptation to pull or jank the tape when sewing as it will mess everything up. Just gently guide the tape. If it is slipping, use an awl or tweezers to guide the binding straight again. You can also use a piece of Lego or a magnetic seam guide to keep the binding in place.

8 **Keep sewing over the edge.** When you are finished, keep sewing the tape; you will cut off the extra binding afterwards. Finish the application by closing the seam you left open, see step 7 of Double layer binding (page 105) for instructions.

 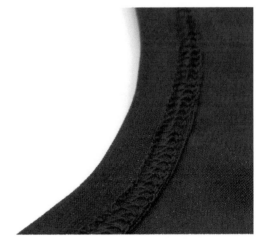

9 **The finished binding.** This method can be tricky to master, but the result will be very elegant. If you are using a coverstitch machine try to sew the reverse stitch as close to the edge as possible for the best-looking finish.

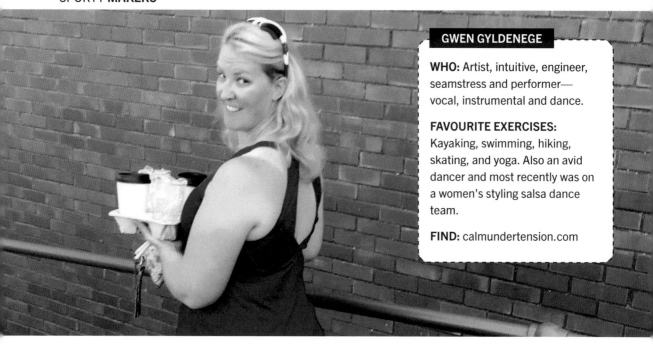

GWEN GYLDENEGE

WHO: Artist, intuitive, engineer, seamstress and performer—vocal, instrumental and dance.

FAVOURITE EXERCISES: Kayaking, swimming, hiking, skating, and yoga. Also an avid dancer and most recently was on a women's styling salsa dance team.

FIND: calmundertension.com

GWEN GYLDENEGE

AN ATHLETE DRIVEN BY A CREATIVE PASSION

Frustrated with the lack of appealing activewear for curvy bodies, sewist Gwen Gyldenege decided to take things into her own hands and start sewing athletic clothes for her various sporty pursuits. Now, she is also opening a sewing business offering clothes for athletes of all shapes and sizes. Here, she shares her best tips on sewing athletic wear and discusses how many big brands miss the mark when it comes to offering activewear for curvy athletes.

Talk about what made you begin sewing your own athletic clothes?
Spending hours in dressing rooms trying on as many as 20 items at a time, only to walk away with nothing became disheartening. Likewise, when I walked into my favourite store REI, it was extremely rare to find even a basic pair of black leggings that fit me well. »

> ## I GET TO MAKE GARMENTS THAT FIT ME EXACTLY, IN WHATEVER COLOUR AND PATTERN I DESIRE.
>
> **GWEN** ATHLETIC SEWIST

So, I figured that the time I'm not spending in a dressing room or scouring the store is time I should spend in my sewing room. There, I get to make garments that fit me exactly, are in a multitude of colours, and whatever pattern I desire.

There is a severe gap in the market for those of us who are both curvy and athletic. Now, thanks to my passion for sewing my own dancewear, hiking and skating gear, I'm opening my business to sew for athletes of all shapes and sizes. One of my favourite costumes was the one I made last year. I designed a costume to dress as the goddess Nike that also allowed me to salsa dance all evening long in comfort.

What are the benefits of making your own activewear versus buying?
One of the biggest challenges of buying activewear in the plus size market is that the colour I want or desire is rarely in style or on offer. If there is one available, someone else has likely already purchased it because the retailer has so few sizes in stock. »

I don't mind spending full price for a high-quality garment, but I also don't like to waste my time going in to find that there's nothing left for me. So when it's time to buy versus make, I choose to go for the highest quality products available.

Where do you find inspiration for your athletic makes?

I am inspired by the REI brand because of their attention to quality. I also use my Instagram queue, which is filled with many yogis and brands catering to people who enjoy yoga. I love to peruse surfing and stand-up paddle board magazines. I also have found that many people on the street or trails inspire me.

Share your favourite tips for sewing activewear

Some of my garments have required as many as 7 to 9 layers of fabric and elastic. That can be a bit tough for the standard at-home machine, especially if you've chosen an entry-level modern model. I like to use older machines personally. And when I am running that much through my machine I use a microtex needle and my walking foot.

I carefully push the fabric through with a screwdriver from the front, always being careful not to allow the screwdriver and the needle to meet. I have found the strongest lasting stitch to be the triple stitch zigzag. I use it to construct seams and I also topstitch using it. It is incredibly stretchy and strong and has helped me avoid wardrobe malfunctions that the regular zigzag allowed. I am very hard on my clothing, so I want to make something that won't require repairing.

calmundertension.com

RIBBING

RIBBING

Ribbing is perhaps the easiest way to cover openings and finish hems and can be used on everything from finishing armhole openings on a tank-top to creating the leg cuffs on a pair of casual sweat pants. Ribbing fabric has vertical ribs on both sides and has an excellent crosswise stretch.

1x1 ribbing

Picking the right ribbing

You'll get the best result if the ribbing fibre content matches your fashion fabric, which means that for most of your activewear makes, you'll need ribbing that is made of synthetic fibres. Some activewear fabric retailers also sell suitable ribbing so stock up on it when you find it, as synthetic ribbing can be harder to find than ribbing made of cotton.

1×1 ribbing is generally more elastic and is perfect for finishing lightweight fabrics, whereas the often thicker 2×2 ribbing has less stretch and is more suitable for finishing more sturdy garments such as sweaters.

2x2 ribbing

Determining the size of the ribbing

Generally, the ribbing should always be stretched out somewhat, so the ribbing piece should be shorter than the edge it is covering. However there are no steadfast rules on how much shorter the ribbing should be, it depends on factors such as where it will be applied, your preferences, and the properties of the ribbing, i.e. ribbing with less recovery needs to be shorter than firm ribbing in order to lie flat and stay true to size.

Here are some general guidelines on the length of the ribbing, but I strongly recommend making samples if you are unsure as there are no exact rules for ribbing. Also, remember to add seam allowances to your ribbing!

- Neckline: 65-75% (depends on the recovery of the ribbing and how curved the neckline is)

- Sleeveless arm openings: Around 80%

- Waist rib, hoodie or pants: 95 % (for a smooth finish that fits in with current fashion).

- Cuffs: 95% for a smooth modern finish, 80% if you want gathers like the old school college sweaters and sweatpants

TIP: If you want both a smooth finish and a narrow, tight-fitting edge, taper the rib cuff so that it becomes more v-shaped.

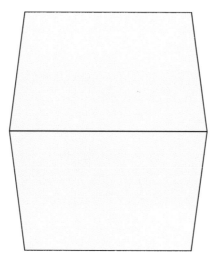

Tapered cuff with a v-shape.

Make notches for even applied ribbing

When attaching ribbing, it's a good idea to add notches on the ribbing that corresponds with the garment. For instance, on a neckline, add notches mid-back, mid-front and at the shoulder seams.

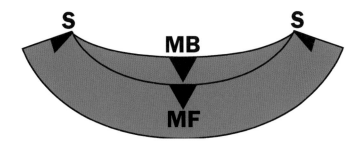

Just make sure you do the right calculations. For example, if your rib is 80 percent of the neckline, the notches on the ribbing should also be 80 percent of the corresponding distance on the garment neckline. For instance if your mid-back to shoulder distance is 10 cm on your garment, the corresponding ribbing length should be 8 cm.

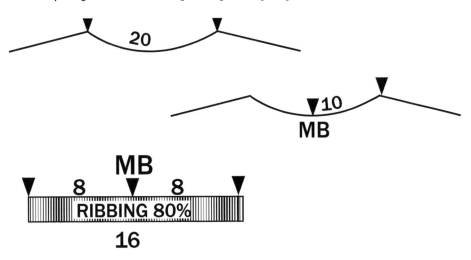

Ribbing will get narrower the more you stretch it

If you want a finished neckline rib that is 2.5 cm (1"), you'll need to add some extra width to the un-stretched ribbing. Just stretch out the rib fabric to see how much that is needed.

NECKLINE RIBBING
MADE EASY

The trick when sewing neckline ribbing is to use notches so that the ribbing will be distributed evenly across the neckline. The ribbing also needs to be substantially shorter than the neckline measurements in order to lie flat on the body. In this tutorial, we'll go through all the steps for a perfect ribbing application.

> **⟫ SUPPLIES**
>
> ● Ribbing fabric
> ● Sewing machine or a serger
> ● Stretch twin-needle or a coverstitch machine (optional)
> ● Rotary cutter or a pair of sharp scissors

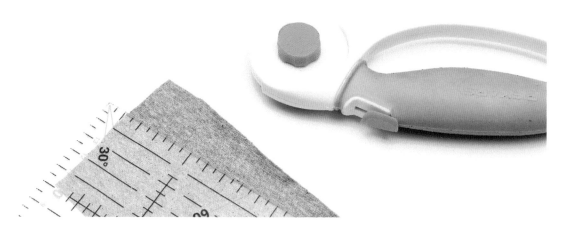

1 **Cut the ribbing.** Preferably use a ruler and a rotary cutter to cut the ribbing because it creates the most even ribbing piece. But of course a paper pattern piece and a pair of scissors will work too, just make sure the scissors are sharp! For a neckline, cut a ribbing that is around 65-75% of the garment measurement plus seam allowance. The length depends on the recovery of the ribbing, the width of the finished ribbing, and how curved the neckline is.

2 **Mark notches on the ribbing.** First, fold the ribbing. You can carefully press the fold with an iron on low heat to make the fold crisp. Then, mark notches that correspond to mid-back, shoulder seams, and mid-front. If your rib is 75 % of the neckline length, the notches on the ribbing should also be 75 % of the corresponding distance on the garment. Either clip the fabric or use a pen for the notches.

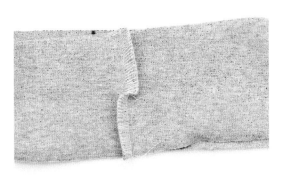

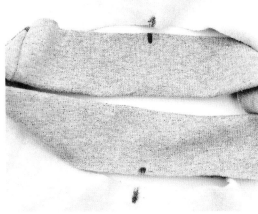

3 **Close the ribbing band.** Use either a 3-thread serger stitch or a sewing machine stretch seam. **TIP:** To create a flat fold, clip the seam allowance at the fold and press in opposite directions.

4 **Match the notches.** Mark the corresponding notches on your garment and align them with the notches on your ribbing. You can use needles or very loose hand basting to keep the ribbing in place.

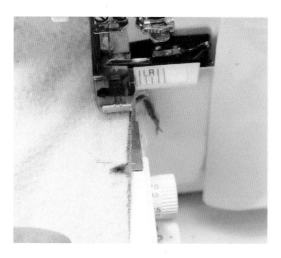

5   **Attach the ribbing.** Use either a serger or a sewing machine stretch seam to attach the ribbing. Stretch the ribbing while sewing, making sure the notches align.

6   **Press the ribbing flat.** After sewing, it's a good idea to press the ribbing on a low setting to make sure the ribbing lies flat and to remove any creases. Just test the fabric first to see that it can tolerate an iron.

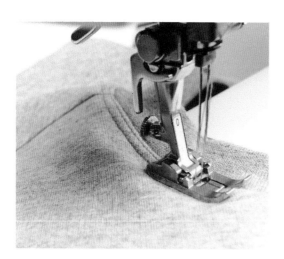

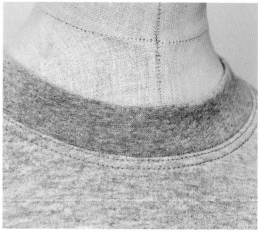

7   **Stitch over the seam allowance.** To create a flatter and more professional-looking finish, you can topstitch the seam allowance. Use a twin-needle, zigzag stitch, or a coverstitch machine for this.

8   **The finished neckline.** By doing the proper prep work, such as using notches and the calculating the right length you will get an even, flat neckline.

ELASTIC
OPENING

CLEAR ELASTIC OPENINGS

Finishing the edges on necklines, pockets, armholes and leg openings with elastic will keep them in place during activity and prevent the openings from being stretched out when sewing. In this tutorial, we'll use clear elastic to create a non-bulky finish. But regular elastic will also work for this method.

PREPARATION

If you are sewing a formfitting garment with negative ease, the ratio between the elastic and the garment length should be 1:1. But, on some projects, you might need to make the elastic shorter than the finished garment. In those cases, mark notches on the elastic that correspond to points on the garment, such as mid-back, shoulder seams and mid-front on a neckline. Then stretch the elastic out and pin the matching notches.

1 **Place the elastic.** Pin the elastic on the wrong side of the garment. If the elastic is meant to be stretched out, match to the corresponding notches on the garment. Depending on the project it might be easier if one seam is left open, and, in that case, you would close the seam after the elastic has been inserted. If you are sewing on the round, first close the elastic as a loop and then attach it.

122

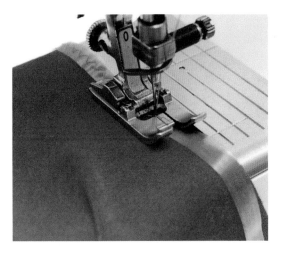

2 **Sew the elastic.** Use a medium zigzag stitch and sew close to the edge. Stretch out the elastic if necessary.
TIP: Clear elastic can slip or get stuck under the presser foot so start with a few centimetres (inches) extra so that the elastic extends behind the presser foot.

3 **Fold the edge.** Use the sides of the elastic as your guide when folding.

4 **Topstitch the elastic.** Use a medium zigzag stitch or a twin-needle, stitch with the right side facing up. Gently guide the fabric so that it will feed evenly.

5 **The finished opening.** This method is an excellent choice if you have problems with openings stretching out, especially when you are using a sewing machine. The clear elastic also makes the finish very discreet.

CHRISTOPHER HANSSON

FUNCTIONAL JACKET MAKER

Swedish sewist Christopher Hansson began sewing when he couldn't find cool training gear and casual garments that fit his style. He has a background in design and studied industrial design at the university. Now, he applies his design skills and his sewing knowledge to create high-viz jackets with very intricate detailing. He is also an avid rower.

You make complex, functional jackets. What inspire your designs?
I take inspiration from a lot of different places, but my main sources are from the heroic media, which include among other things, superhero-costumes, Tron, and Assassin's Creed. I believe that it should be possible to wear cool clothes in the dark while still being visible when passing traffic. »

CHRISTOPHER HANSSON

WHO: Industrial designer, rower and hobby sewist who creates intricate and functional clothes.

FAVOURITE EXERCISE: Rowing

FIND: @seamslikemagic on instagram

Installing zippers can be intimidating, share your best tips!

When I first started sewing, I pinned almost every five millimetres, which resulted in a very bulky seam. I once got an industry insider tip to free-hand the zipper (no pins, basting or glue), which gave a good result. My tip is to use only one pin to lock the starting position and then free-hand the rest of the way. I would also recommend starting from the bottom on both sides and also don't rush and keep the teeth pressed against the side of the presser foot.

What sewing tools have you found most helpful?

My serger, which I have outfitted with a seam guide and a piping foot plus an edge-guide-foot for my ordinary sewing machine. »

WHEN SEWING ZIPPERS, DON'T OVER-PIN. ONE IS ENOUGH AND FREE HAND THE REST

CHRISTOPHER
JACKET MAKER

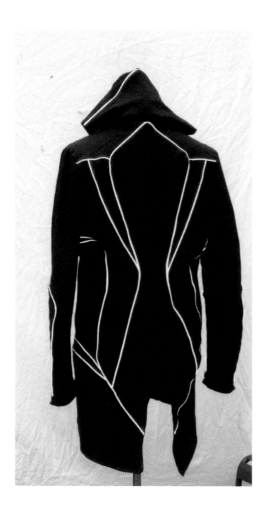

How do you create the reflective striping on your jackets?

I create the striping by buying piping and using a two-step process. I have fitted my serger with a piping foot which is a presser foot with a groove on the underside directly to the left of the left needle.
This groove guides the piping so it won't drift away. Then I just shove the piping between the two pieces of fabric, so the flange rests in the seam.

When I have fed the fabric through, I go to my ordinary sewing machine and topstitch on one side. I have folded the seam so the seam allowance is stitched during the top stitching. I am also using a special foot on my sewing machine, which is called an edge-guide foot. This foot is a bit higher on one side of the underside, which allows me to easily follow the edge.

I use speciality feet for my machines to increase my work speed and enhance the work flow. Before I acquired these tools, I used the regular zipper foot for the first step and the standard foot for the second step, which you can use too if you just want to try sewing piping in your clothes.

@seamslikemagic on instagram

CORDS AND DRAWSTRINGS

ATTACHING EYELETS ON KNITS

Adding eyelets (grommets) on stretchy knit fabrics can be a challenge as the fabric tends to pull away after a while and you might end up with a big hole and a loose metal ring. This method prevents that from happening and can be used on all sorts of fabrics because it resists stress well.

> **≫ SUPPLIES**
>
> - Firm nonstretch fusible interfacing
> - A scrap of knit fabric (optional, but recommended when using thin knits)
> - Eyelets/grommets and suitable tools

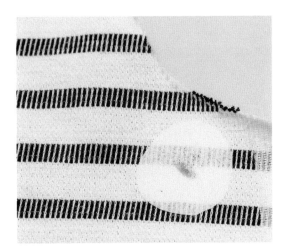

1 Interface the area. Place the interfacing, iron it on the fabric and mark where the hole should be.

2 Punch the hole. Make a hole that is slightly smaller than you would normally do. The knit fabric stretches out slightly so the hole needs to be smaller than what you would have used on a woven fabric.

3 **Insert the eyelet.** There should be a small amount of fabric covering the base of the eyelet. But too much fabric makes it hard for the washers to properly fit in with the eyelets.

4 **Add a fabric layer.** (Optional) This is needed if you are working with thin stretchy knits. The eyelets need some thickness to really "stick" to the fabric.

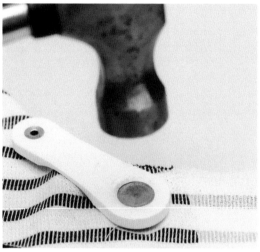

5 **Place the washer.** Check the instructions to see which side should be facing up. There are ridges where the eyelet attaches when pressed down.

6 **Secure the washer to the eyelet.** Use a dedicated tool such as pliers or a hammer. If you are using a hammer make sure it hits flat on the surface and hammer firmly but not overly hard.

 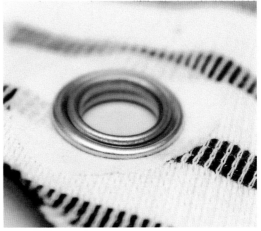

7 **Inspection time.** Make sure there are no glitches. The eyelet should sit tight to the fabric on the right side. The same goes for the washer on the wrong side. Use your nails or a needle and run through the entire eyelet to make sure it sits even and close.

8 **The end result.** This method is considerably more sturdy than a regular eyelet application and is therefore recommended for all your activewear makes and not just on knit fabrics.
TIP: If you are attaching eyelets on a waistband made of thin knit, interface the side that is closest to the body with a soft stretchy fusible, because the metal might rub against your skin and could also wear out the fabric.

ELASTIC CORD
WITH STOPPERS

Adjustable elastic cords are perfect for all sorts of activewear. They give your garments a very professional look, plus they are very practical too!

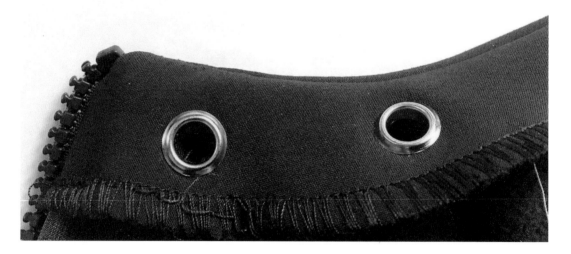

1 **Apply the eyelets.** Interface the inside area where the eyelets will be placed and then apply two eyelets fairly close together where you want the end of the cord to be placed. Repeat on the other areas of the garment where you want to add adjustable cording.

2 **Attach a stopper at one end of the elastic.** Then pull it along the cording to make room for the threading, around 10 cm (4"). Don't make a knot as you will thread the elastic through the eyelets.

3 **Thread the elastic cording.** Start with the outer eyelet (in this example, the one nearest to the zipper) and pull the cording inside the facing from the outside. Then take the other edge of the cord and pull it through the inner eyelet from the outside. The stopper will be sitting on the cording between the eyelets.

4 **Attach the cording to the seam allowance.** On the wrong side, sew the cording to the seam allowance. However, elastic cording can be hard to secure with a sewing machine because it is so dense. In those instances, use super glue to attach the cording to the seam allowance.

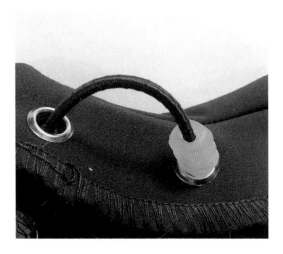

5 **The cord from the outside.** Repeat the process on the other side. Thread the cording under the facing to the other set of eyelets and repeat by threading it out through the first eyelet, sliding on a stopper, and then threading the cording through the last eyelet. Secure the cording to the seam allowance.

6 **Now close the casing.** Stitch over the facing to create a casing. As some functional activewear fabrics are hard to pin, use tape to keep the facing in place when topstitching.

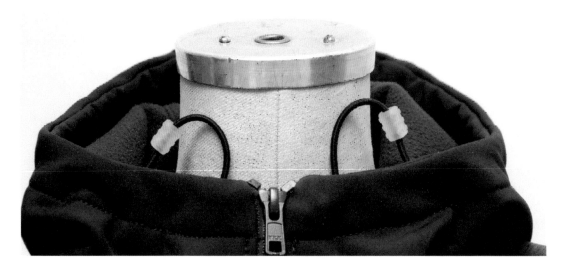

7 **Finished.** This method is an easy way to add a professional and very functional detail to your activewear.

BUTTONHOLES ON
KNIT FABRICS

Sewing buttonholes on stretchy Lycra knits can be daunting. However, with this method, you'll avoid both stretched out openings and skipped stitches. The trick is to use fusible interfacing, a larger needle, and a longer stitch length. Also, it's best to sew the buttonhole lengthwise as knits have less stretch in that direction.

>> **SUPPLIES**

- A ballpoint needle size 90
- Thin fusible interfacing with 1-way stretch
- Regular thread
- Soluble or tear-away stabiliser (optional, but helps prevent skipped stitches)

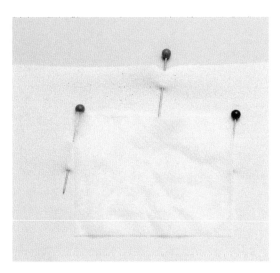

1 **Stabilise the wrong side with fusible interfacing.** Place the non-stretchy direction of the fusible lengthwise and iron using a low heat setting.

2 **Set up your machine.** Use a regular buttonhole stitch but increase the stitch length.
TIP: Do a sample to test your settings before you sew on the real thing.

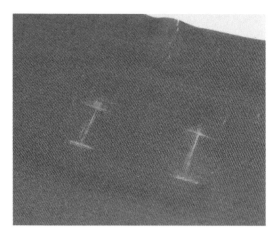

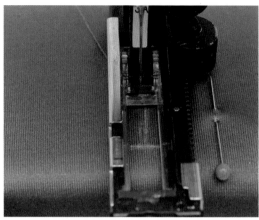

3   **Mark the buttonholes.** Use tailor's chalk to mark the buttonholes on the right side. **TIP:** If tracing on synthetic knits is difficult, start by marking the placement on the reverse side. Then transfer the marking to the right side by pushing pins through the fabric where the buttonhole starts and ends. Draw lines between those points.

4   **Sew the buttonhole.** Don't tug the fabric, let the presser foot do the job. Just make sure the buttonhole is straight. **TIP:** If you get skipped stitches despite using a size 90 ballpoint needle, sew over a soluble or tear-away stabiliser. You can also use parchment or baking paper.

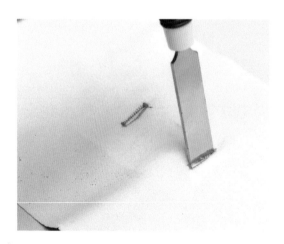

5   **Open the buttonhole.** A buttonhole cutter yields the best result, but a sharp seam ripper can also be used. **TIP:** Use a pin at the bars, this will prevent cutting through the edges if you are using a seam ripper.

6   **The finished buttonholes.** Use this method for drawstrings, elastic or other details on your activewear. It is very durable and also keeps the buttonholes from stretching out.

CROTCH
GUSSETS

ADDING CROTCH GUSSETS TO LEGGINGS

A crotch gusset prevents chafing and strengthens an area that will be under a lot of stress when you are moving around. There are four common crotch gussets: triangle, oval, diamond shaped and a long inner gusset that runs along the entire inseam.

If your pattern lacks a gusset, you can easily add them by doing some simple pattern alterations. In this chapter, we'll cover the two most common crotch gussets found in ready-to-wear athletic leggings; oval and triangle gussets.

Triangle crotch gusset on a pair of ready-to-wear leggings.

The basic principle of drafting crotch gussets is that you cut away pieces of the crotch area on your pattern and then shape the removed pieces into a gusset. This principle goes for all four gussets mentioned above, so once you understand the principle, you can draft any type of gusset.

When adding a gusset to a pattern, always do a test garment first to make sure that the altered crotch fits properly. If it is too big, you will get folds around the crotch area and if it is too tight, it cuts into the crotch and feels very tight.

A TRIANGLE
CROTCH GUSSET

This is the best gusset to begin with as it's both easy to draft and to sew. In this tutorial, we will only alter the back crotch, but you can extend the base of the triangle to the front crotch by applying the same drafting principles to the front inseam.

>> **SUPPLIES**

- Tracing paper and pen
- Scissors and tape or glue
- A serger and or a sewing machine

PREPARATION

This method requires both pattern drafting and sewing. But don't worry if you are new to making pattern adjustments, this is a very easy project. You will need pattern tracing paper and if you are using a PDF pattern, just print an extra copy of the back crotch, and you are all set to go. There is no exact rule of how big the piece should be, but a good starting point for a pair of women size M leggings is a finished triangle gusset that is around 6 cm wide (2 ⅖") at the base and the sides being around 7 cm (2 ¾") long.

Remove the seam allowances on the back crotch seam before you start drafting the gusset for a more exact fit. Then add the seam allowances back on the gusset and the crotch seam.

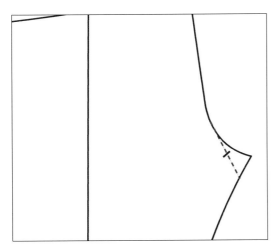

1 **Draft a slanted line at the back crotch.** It should run from the crotch curve to the inseam. This forms one half of the triangle gusset. Mark notches at the sides of the pattern.

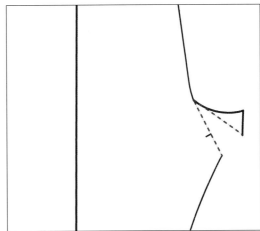

2 **Cut away the crotch piece.** Then duplicate it to create a gusset.

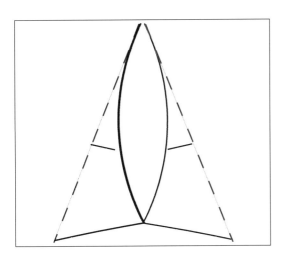

3 **Create a triangle.** Place the two pieces together to form a triangle.

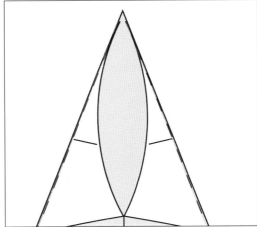

4 **Retrace the pattern pieces to form a triangle.** Also, add a notch at the midpoint of the triangle base; this will align with the mid-front crotch seam. You can also add a slight curve to the base.

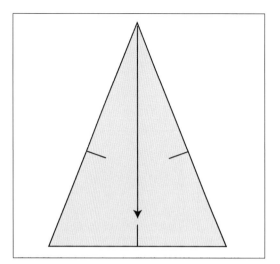

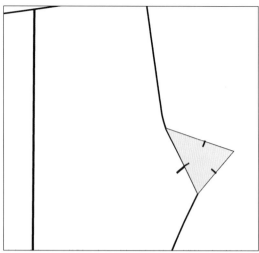

5 **Draft a lengthwise grain on the pattern.** Add seam allowances to the gusset and to the back crotch seam.

6 **Now the gusset pattern is finished.** The triangle will replace the removed crotch pieces.

1 **Attach the side of the gusset.** Sew the gusset from the base of the triangle to the tip using a stretch stitch. Stop sewing when you hit the tip of the triangle. This will be easier if the gusset layer is on top when you are sewing .
TIP: To prevent the edges of the gusset from slipping, use a dab of basting glue or just use a regular glue stick.

2 **Sew the back crotch seam.** With this method, you'll sew the crotch seam and the other side (leg) of the triangle gusset in one continuous seam. Place the back crotch pieces together and start from the base of the triangle and sew to the waist. Make sure the opposite seam allowance on the gusset is folded outwards.

3 **Sew the front crotch seam.** Sew the center front crotch seams together, right sides facing each other.

4 **Sew the inseam.** Start from the lower leg opening and sew the entire leg seam including the gusset in one continuous seam from leg opening to leg opening. Make sure the gusset's seams are folded outwards, and that the front crotch seam aligns with the triangle midpoint.

5 **The finished gusset.** This the easiest gusset to draft and sew. You can also use any of the flatlock methods to attach the gusset for a more chafe-free seam. Using woolly nylon in the loopers will make the seam gentler for the skin.

AN OVAL
CROTCH GUSSET

This gusset is an excellent choice for a chafe-free crotch gusset because it eliminates seams around the crotch area. It can be a little trickier to assemble compared to the triangle gusset so if you are new to sewing stretchy knits, practice on some scraps before moving on to the real thing.

> **>> SUPPLIES**
> - Tracing paper and pen
> - Scissors and tape or glue
> - A serger and or a sewing machine

PREPARATION

This tutorial requires both pattern drafting and sewing. You will need pattern tracing paper and if you are using a PDF pattern, print an extra copy of the back crotch and you are all set to go. There is no exact rule of how big the oval piece should be, and you can draft it to sit either vertically or horizontally. In this tutorial, we will draft a gusset that is widest in the horizontal direction.

Remove the seam allowances on the back crotch seam before you start drafting the gusset for a more exact fit. Then add the seam allowances back to the gusset and to the crotch and inseams of the leggings.

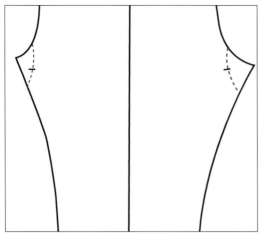

1 **Draft curved cutting lines on the back and front crotch.** Make sure that the inseam has the same distance on both the front and back crotch. Add notches.

2 **Cut away the crotch pieces.** Then duplicate them, so that you have four pieces in total for creating a gusset.

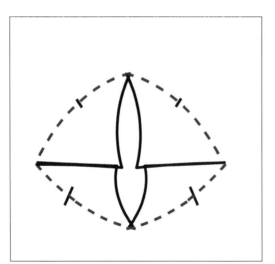

3 **Create an oval.** Place the four crotch pieces so that the inseam parts meet in the middle.

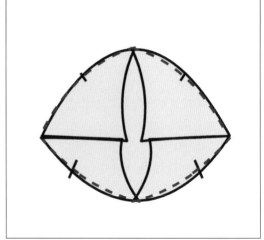

4 **Retrace the pattern pieces to form an oval.** Mark notches at upper and lower midpoint of the gusset. These will align with the mid-front and mid-back crotch seams.

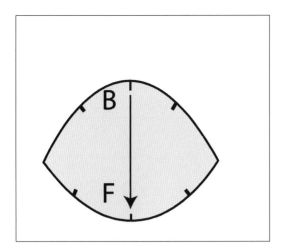

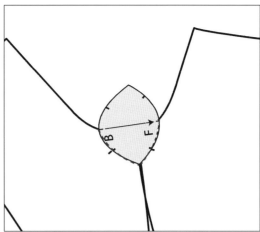

5 **Mark a lengthwise grain on the pattern.** Add seam allowances to the gusset and also to the back and front seams on the leggings.

6 **Now the gusset pattern is finished.** The oval gusset replaces the removed crotch pieces as seen in the illustration. The gusset should be cut crosswise for maximum stretch. But you can experiment and see what works best.

1 **Sew the crotch seams.** Sew the center back crotch seams together and then the center front crotch seams. A 3-thread flatlock serger seam is used in this example to create a smooth seam.

2 **Prepare for the gusset insertion.** Lie the back seam flat and make sure you have notches that match those on the gusset.

3 **Attach the back gusset.** Pin or hand baste the back gusset piece to the back opening, matching the notches.

4 **Sew the back gusset.** You can use either a serger or sewing machine overlock seam, a narrow zigzag or a 3-thread flatlock seam.

5 **Attach the front gusset.** Pin or hand baste the front gusset piece to the front crotch, matching the notches. Make extra sure that the midpoint gusset notch matches the crotch seam.

6 **Sew the front gusset.** Start from the lower leg opening and sew the entire leg seam including the gusset in one continuous seam from leg opening to leg opening. To make this easier, trim away the pointy edge where the inseam ends and the gusset begins.

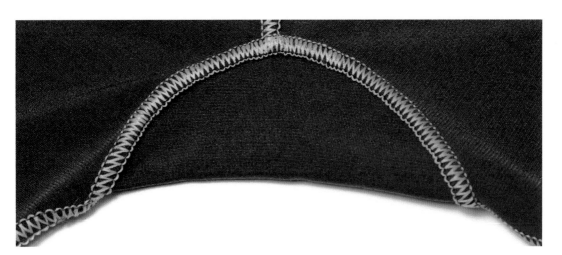

7 **The finished gusset.** This method is superior when it comes to crotch gussets for athletic wear. You can also use two layers of fabric for the gusset, for an even more secure and comfortable gusset. Another option is to use a stretch lining fabric for the inner gusset.

WHO: Owns a sewing repair business specialising in activewear and outdoor gear. Penny has also shared her sewing knowledge online since the dawn of the World Wide Web.

FAVOURITE EXERCISES: Mountain biking (she is a certified instructor) and snow skiing.

FIND: specialityoutdoors.com

SPECIALITY OUTDOORS

SEWING ACTIVEWEAR TRAILBLAZER

Since the 1990s, garment manufacturer and outdoor enthusiast, Penny Schwyn has shared her knowledge and resources online for those of us who want to DIY our activewear clothes. She runs her own business Speciality Outdoors which specializes in alterations and repairs of athletic gear.

You were a trailblazer when it comes to sharing sewing activewear knowledge online. What made you start your site and business?
I've been sewing all my life. I was exposed to outdoors manufacturing back in 1983-84, working for the original MountainSmith an outdoor gear company founded by Pat Smith in Lakewood Colorado. This was my first exposure to design and manufacturing processes. When I had my kids in 1986 and 1989, there was no technical clothing for kids. »

Polarfleece fabrics were just starting to be available, so I was making things for our family. At that time, I had a bridal and custom-wear business. We relocated to the Pacific North West, and someone said to me, you should be fixing gear!

I never looked back. I wanted to stay at home with my kids and have flexibility so that we could be together as a family for our outdoor adventures.

I handbuilt the website in 1995 when the web was just beginning. It just seemed like a good idea to get out there. I did a lot of guerilla marketing and getting customers has been all through word of mouth.

> DON'T DESPAIR IF YOU DON'T HAVE A SERGER, YOU CAN DO A LOT WITH A JUST ZIGZAG.
>
> **PENNY** SPECIALITY OUTDOORS

What are your best beginner tips for DIY activewear makes?
First, it's a lot easier than you think. Start with something simple like tights. Practice handling the materials if it's new to you, before cutting into your main fabric. Don't despair if you don't have a serger, as you can do a lot with a zigzag. Do look for good resources: lots on the web, YouTube and books like Singer Sewing Activewear.

Finding good-quality sports fabrics can be a challenge. What should we be looking for?
Think outside your local chain store for sourcing. Use the internet to your advantage, as there are lots of suppliers that sell the fabric we want for quality sportswear. Get samples and ask questions. »

151

**What activewear garments would you
rather buy than make. And why?**

For me, time is money. If I can make something
quickly that will save me a significant amount of
money, that's where I put my effort. Examples are
base layer shirts, vests, tights. Why pay $150 for a
stable-knit wool vest when I can get a yard of 60"
wide stable knit merino for $16? A vest will only take
me an hour or two of my time. I can make tights out
of powerstretch in 30 minutes. My family depends on
me whipping out neck gaiters every ski season when
they can't find last year's.

**What are your favourite things
about making your own exercise clothes?**

I get a lot of satisfaction out of turning out something
that looks ready-made on my own. That, and the
saving money part!

specialityoutdoors.com

WAISTBANDS

WAISTBANDS

Having a waistband that sit well on the body is crucial when making tight-fitting workout wear such as leggings. If you are using a commercial pattern, check the finished waistband circumference on the pattern and compare it to a well-fitting waistband that you already have.

Just make sure that the waistband on the leggings you are making sits at the same spot on your body as the one you are using for comparison. A waistband that sits higher or lower usually requires different measurements.

Drafting a separate inner waistband

You'll get a better result using a separate inner waistband pattern piece, that is slightly shorter than the outer waistband. That is because the outer waistband will fold over slightly to the inside. Think of the inner waistband being almost like a facing, in order to get a picture of how it will look.

If your pattern lacks a separate inner waistband piece, you can easily draft one by removing around 0.6 cm (around ¼") from the height.

Waistband with a separate, slightly shorter pattern piece for the inside.

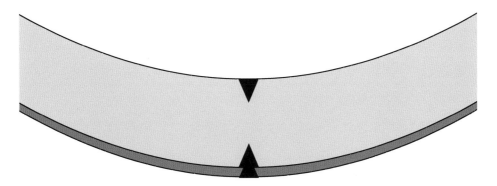

Separate outer and inner waistband. The inner waistband is slightly shorter.

ELASTICS FOR WAISTBANDS

Determining the length of the elastic

How tight you want the elastic to be is a matter of preference, and it also depends on what type of elastic you are using.

Guidelines for elastic measurements

- The elastic should always be smaller than your actual body measurement in order to stay up.

- A good rule of thumb is to measure the circumference where the waistband will sit on the body. Subtract around 15 percent, and you will have a decent fit.

- Ideally, the elastic should be as long as the size of the finished waistband piece.

- If the elastic is longer, it will result in a wobbly seam as the elastic stretches out the fabric (but it won't be noticeable when you wear your pants, as everything stretches out).

- An elastic that is shorter than the waistband causes gathers on the waistband but again those might not be visible when worn.

Picking the right elastic type

For best results, pick either clear elastic or knitted elastic. These are comfortable to wear and are easier to sew than more sturdy elastics, such as the woven ones. The width of the elastic should ideally be around 1 cm (⅖") to 1.5 cm (⅝").

Attach the elastic on the outer seam allowance.

Attaching the elastic

You attach the elastic on the outer seam allowance, but it will not be visible from the outside, especially if you use an elastic that is not overly thick. Attach the elastic to the seam allowance using a wide zigzag stitch. If you get skipped stitches, switch to a larger ballpoint needle.

A BASIC
WAISTBAND

Start with this method if you are new to sewing waistbands on tight-fitting activewear. It's an easy method that can be done entirely on a regular sewing machine.

>> **SUPPLIES**

- Stretchy fabric. You can use a different fabric for the inner waistband. In this tutorial, sports mesh is used for the inner waistband

- Knitted elastic

- Regular ballpoint stretch needle, size 90

- Twin ballpoint stretch needle (optional)

- A serger (optional)

- A coverstitch machine (optional)

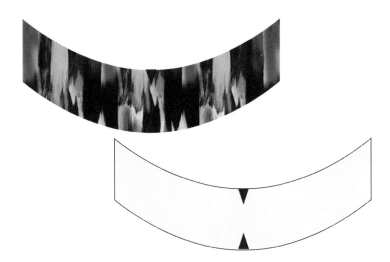

1 **Add notches.** Place the notches at the mid-back and mid-front on all pattern pieces. The notches are needed when you are sewing the inner and outer waistband together later on.

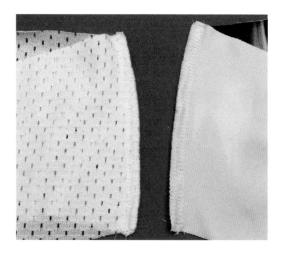

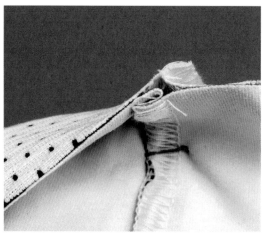

2 Sew together the side seams. Stitch the outer front waistband to the outer back waistband right sides facing. Repeat for the inner waistband.

3 Prepare for stitching the waistbands together. Place the inner waistband over the outer waistband right sides facing, matching mid-front and mid-back notches. Fold the seam allowances in opposite directions.

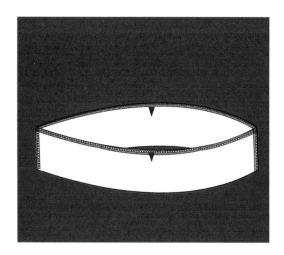

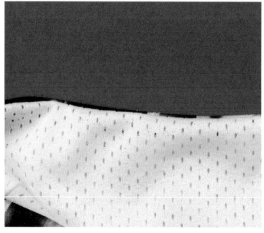

4 Stitch the waistband. Sew together the inner and outer waistband top seam, matching mid-front and mid-back. Use a machine stretch stitch or a 3-thread serger overlock seam.

5 Fold over the inner waistband. The next step is to attach the elastic. See Elastics for waistbands (page 155) for instructions on how to pick the right elastic and size for your project.

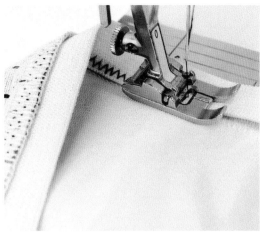

6 **Close the elastic loop.** Overlap the ends of the elastic around 1 cm (⅖"). Stitch together using two rows of zigzag stitches.

7 **Attach the elastic.** Place the elastic over the outer seam allowance. The edge of the elastic should align with the inner edge of the seam allowance. Stitch on top of the elastic close to the edge using a wide zigzag stitch.

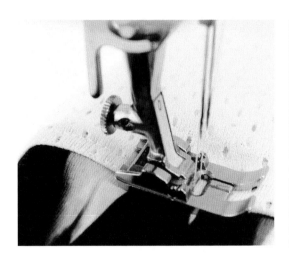

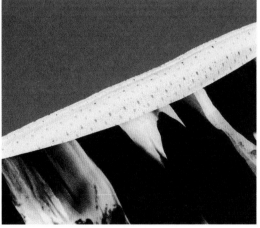

8 **Topstitch the inner waistband.** Turn seam allowances towards the inner waistband. Stitch over the inner waistband seam, close to the edge, using a twin-needle or a coverstitch.

9 **The finished waistband.** Turn the lining to the inside. Now you can attach the waistband to your leggings using a serger or sewing machine stretch seam.

BODY-SHAPING WAISTBAND

Sometimes you want a waistband that has more stability and body-shaping properties, especially if your chosen fabric is soft and supple and has very little compression. This is easily achieved by using power net as a lining.

>> SUPPLIES

- Stretchy fabric
- Power net
- Clear elastic (optional, not needed when using power net)
- Regular ballpoint stretch needle, size 90
- Twin ballpoint stretch needle (optional)
- A sewing machine or a serger
- A coverstitch machine (optional)

1 **Cut all three layers for the waistband.** You'll need to cut the outer waistband pieces, the inner waistband pieces, and then a layer of power net using the inner waistband pattern pieces.

2 **Attach the power net.** Place the power net lining on the wrong sides of the inner waistband pieces.

3 **Sew together the side seams.** Stitch the outer front waistband to the outer back waistband, right sides facing. Repeat for the inner waistband with the power net lining.

4 **Stitch the waistband.** Sew together the inner and outer waistband matching mid-front and mid-back. Use a machine stretch stitch or a 3-thread serger overlock seam.

5 **Fold over the inner waistband.** As you can see, the power net works as an underlining as it is sewn together with the inner waistband pieces.

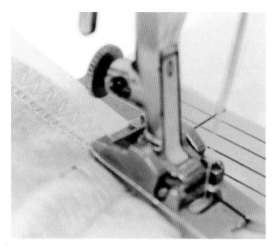

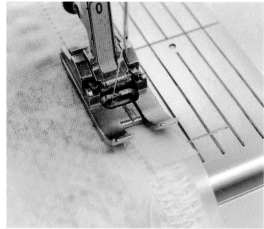

6 **Stitch the elastic.** (Optional) Power net adds bulk, so a thinner clear elastic is a better option than knit elastic. Instead of a loop, you can stitch the elastic on the flat. Stitch on top of the elastic, close to the edge using a wide zigzag stitch.

7 **Close the elastic loop.** Overlap the elastic 1–2 cm (⅖–¾") and stitch so that the seams meet.

8 **Secure the elastic.** Lift the presser foot, turn the waistband 90 degrees and sew two rows of zigzag stitches at the edges of the elastic.

9 **The finished waistband.** As a final step, you can also stitch the inner waistband using a twin-needle.

WAISTBAND WITH A POCKET

A hidden pocket in the waistband adds more functionality to your leggings. This method is based on how waistband pockets are made in the garment industry. It can a be a little tricky to figure out at first, so practice on some scraps to get the hang of it.

>> SUPPLIES

- Stretchy fabric
- Knitted elastic
- Clear elastic
- Regular ballpoint stretch needle, size 90
- Twin ballpoint stretch needle (optional)
- A sewing machine
- A serger and a coverstitch machine (optional)

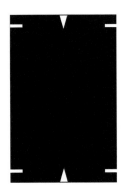

1 **Cut the pocket piece and add notches.** The pocket should be the height of the back waistband x2 and your preferred width, plus seam allowance. On the pocket, add notches 1 cm (⅖") from the edges on each side. Mark midpoint notches on the pocket, and on the inner and outer waistband pieces.

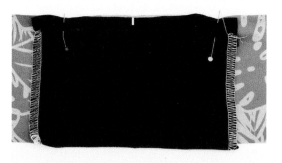

2 **Sew the side seams of the pocket.** Fold the pocket, and start sewing at the fold and stop at the notches.

3 **Pin one side of the pocket to the outer waistband.** Place the pocket towards the right side of the outer back waistband. Fold back the inner seam allowance. Match the mid-notch of the waistband with the pocket mid-notch.

4 **The folded seam allowance.** You will only sew the outer layer of the pocket. The inner pocket seam allowance will later be attached to the inner waistband.

5 **Attach the outer pocket.** Stitch the outer pocket to the waistband piece, making sure the seam only catches the outer layer of the pocket.

6 **Cut notches on the outer waistband.**
The notches should be just outside the pocket, on the outer waistband only and be as long as the seam allowance.

7 **Attach clear elastic to the seam.**
This reinforces the pocket opening and keeps it from gaping. Sew the elastic with a regular zigzag stitch.
TIP: You can also attach the clear elastic while sewing the pocket (see step 5).

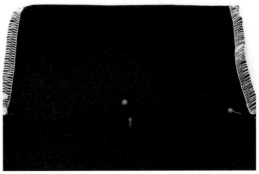

8 **Stitch down the outer waist pocket.** Fold the seam allowance towards the pocket and topstitch close to the edge using a zigzag or a 3-step security stitch.

9 **Attach the inner pocket.** Place the pocket and inner waistband right sides facing. Match the notch on the waistband to the pocket mid-notch. Sew the inner pocket top seam.

10 **Stitch the inner pocket.** Use a stretch seam or a narrow zigzag stitch.
TIP: You can skip this step and sew the entire waist seam and back pocket in one go (see step 11).

11 **Sew the side seams.** Right sides facing, stitch the outer front waistband piece to the outer back waistband piece. Do the same for the inner waistband.

12 **Join the waistband pieces.** Inner waistband to the outer waistband, right sides together, matching mid-front and mid-back. Fold the seam allowances in opposite directions for a smoother seam.

13 **Stitch the together the waistband.** Start and stop just outside the pocket.
TIP: You can also sew the back pocket and waist seam in one seam and skip step 10.

14 **Stitch the elastic.** Place the elastic over the outer seam allowance. Let it run over the inner pocket piece. See Attach the elastic on a basic waistband (page 159) for instructions on how to attach the elastic.

15 **Close the pocket sides.** Sew a stitch that is 2–3 cm (around 1") long on each side of the pocket. The seam should start outside the pocket and end after the pocket side seam. Stitch slightly below the waist seam.

16 **Topstitch the inner waistband.** Turn seam allowances towards the inner waistband. Using a sewing machine twin-needle or a coverstitch machine, stitch over the inner waistband seam.

17 **The advanced option.** You can also attach the elastic to the seam allowance and topstitch at the same time, skipping step 13. This is how it is done in the garment industry.

18 **The finished waistband.** This pocket method is more complicated than a simple waistband but you will be rewarded with a professional-looking and highly practical waistband.

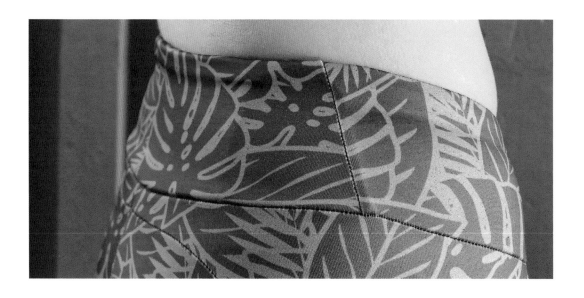

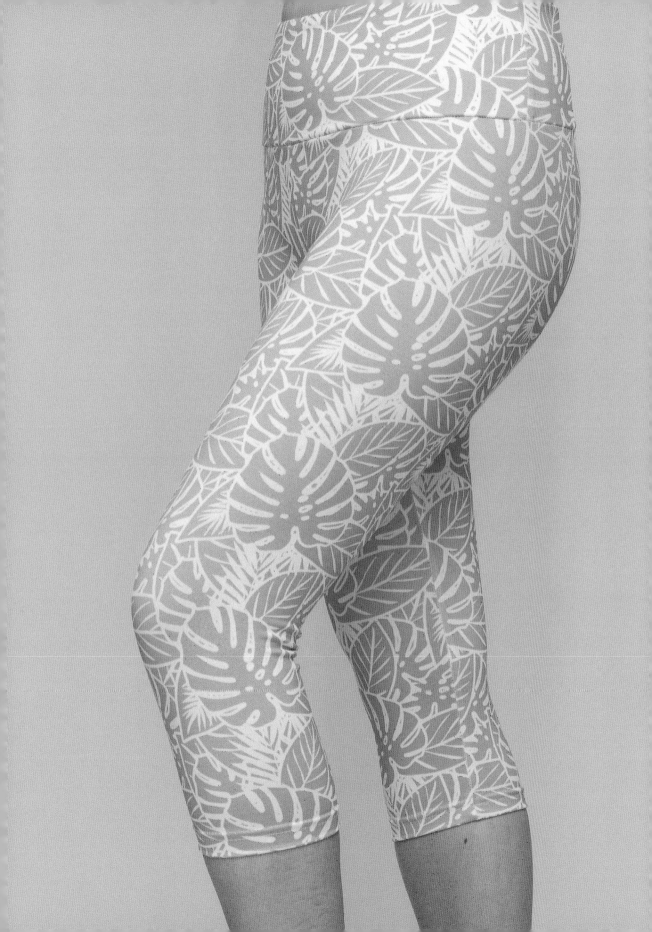

JOHANNA LUNDSTRÖM

WHO: Works in communication by day and makes clothes and creates content around sewing in her free time.

FAVOURITE EXERCISES: Weight training and running currently. But it changes depending on her mood and injury status.

FIND: thelaststitch.com

JOHANNA LUNDSTRÖM

THE AUTHOR OF THIS BOOK

Johanna began sewing activewear in the '80s when she wanted downhill skiing clothes that looked like those in the '50s and '60s. Graduated to sewing moisture-wicking Lycra garments in the early 2000s and has not looked back since. Loves trying out new sports and has activities like roller derby, triathlons, and tennis on her resume, albeit with varying success! »

Why do you make your own activewear?

I'm a DIY person at heart. I even built my own step platform back in the '90s so I could do aerobic workouts at home! Hence why sewing activewear felt like a natural progression as I was already making most of my own clothes, plus I have a very specific taste and only want clothes that fit those requirements. Once you learn how to make clothes that look and fit exactly as you had envisioned, there is no turning back!

What is your best tip for sewing activewear?

Some activewear fabrics can be tricky to sew, but don't be discouraged. Sew samples and test out the proper stitches and settings. Then move onto the real thing. I once spent eight hours, spread over three days, learning how to use the binder attachment so that I could get a professional-looking binding on my workout tops. Yes it was a huge time investment and a bit extreme, but those hours really paid off—I ended up with some beautiful neckline binding. When you have found your perfect set-up, write the settings down for future reference. »

What is your advice to a beginner who wants to start sewing workout clothes?

Don't set the bar too high on your first projects. You might be tempted by some intricate design that looks super cool on the pattern envelope. However, I would recommend that you start with something easy like a pair of leggings with only an inseam, a simple top with sleeves, or a perhaps a pair of pull-on pants. If that sounds boring, why not let the fabric do the talking? There are more and more cool and colourful activewear fabrics available, so why not pick a statement fabric if you want to add some pizazz to your beginner makes?

thelaststitch.com

BE PATIENT AND PRACTICE. DO SAMPLES BEFORE MOVING ONTO THE REAL THING

JOHANNA SEWING BOOK AUTHOR

ZIPPER POCKETS

PROFESSIONAL ZIPPER **POCKET**

This method is used in most ready-to-wear activewear and is excellent for pockets on leggings and other tight-fitting garments. The zipper tape acts as welts, so there is no need for bulky facings. To create a pocket, you can add a second layer of fabric after you attached the zipper and then insert both layers to the garment, perhaps using an oval shape for the pocket .

Another option is to use lining and attach the lining on the zipper tape, just as you would when making a welt pocket. You can also use this method for inserting zippers at necklines and leg openings, leaving one end open.

>> **SUPPLIES**

- A zipper with plastic coils that can be sewn over, preferably one that is sold by the yard. But a closed end or a separating zipper can also work, just use one that is longer than your intended opening

- A sewing machine

- An hobby knife or a pair of sharp scissors

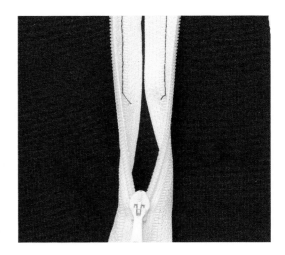

1 **Attach the zipper.** Place the zipper on the right side of the garment with the right side of the tape facing down, coils pointing outwards. Stitch rows on each tape; the stitches should be placed in the middle of the tape. Sew for a distance as long as the opening of the pocket. Notice how the slider sits; it needs to be twisted like this when the tape is placed on the fabric.

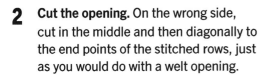

2 **Cut the opening.** On the wrong side, cut in the middle and then diagonally to the end points of the stitched rows, just as you would do with a welt opening.

3 **Turn the zipper.** Fold the zipper tape back so that the coils are facing each other. This is how it should look from the right side once you have turned the zipper.

4 **Close the ends of the opening.** Secure the triangle ends to the zipper tape with a straight stitch. Sew as close to the base of the triangle as possible. This will close the short sides of the opening.

5 **Stitch the zipper.** Edgestitch from the right side, pivot in the corners to create square corners. Use a zipper foot if a regular presser foot comes in contact with the zipper teeth.

6 **The finished zipper.** To create a pocket add a second identical layer of fabric underneath and then attach the piece to the garment, using either a stretch seam or a flatlock seam (shown).

ZIPPER POCKET
WITH LINING

If you want to make a regular zip-up pocket with a lined pocket bag, this simple method is a great choice. No separate facing is required and this pocket can be done both on woven and knit fabrics. Just make sure you interface the opening properly to prevent the fabric from stretching out, especially when sewing knits.

> ## » SUPPLIES
>
> - Pocket lining. Use either self-fabric or lining fabric that preferably has the same colour as the garment.
> - Fusible interfacing (use 1-way stretch fusible for knit fabrics)
> - A closed zipper
> - A sewing machine
> - A serger (optional)

PREPARATION

Draft the pocket piece. The width should be the length of the zipper opening + 2 cm (¾") seam allowance. The length should be the pocket depth + the width of the finished zipper opening.

Round the edges; this prevents lint getting stuck in the corner. If you are using knit fabric, cut the piece on the fabric direction that has the least amount of stretch. As knits generally have less stretch lengthwise, this will help keep the pocket opening stable. On woven fabrics cut the pocket cross-grain instead. Mark the midpoint of the pocket lining by cutting notches or use a marking pen.

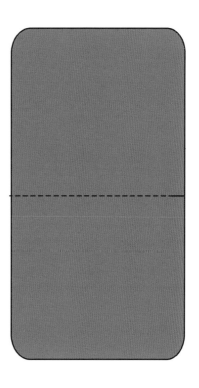

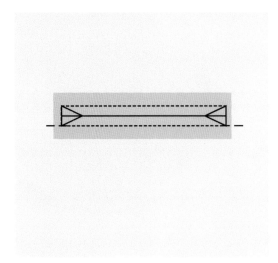

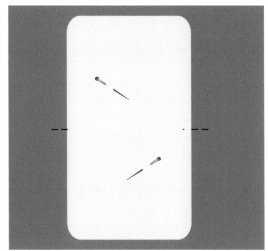

1 **Interface and mark the opening.**
Press interfacing on the wrong side.
Mark the opening equal to the length
of the zipper. Add a cutting line in
the middle and diagonal slash lines
starting 1.25 cm (½ ") from the ends.
Mark lower edge of the opening.

2 **Pin the pocket.** Right sides facing,
place the pocket so that the midpoint
of the pocket aligns with the lower
edge of the planned pocket opening.

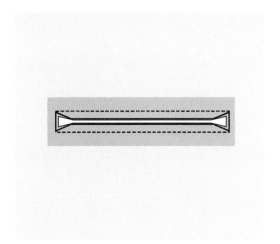

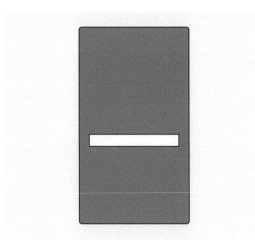

3 **Sew around the opening.** Then cut
through the middle and then diagonally
to the corners. Make sure you cut
the diagonal very close to the corner
to create a rectangular opening.

4 **Pull the pocket to the inside.**
Make sure all corners are sharp;
if not cut, the diagonal lines a
little closer to the corners.

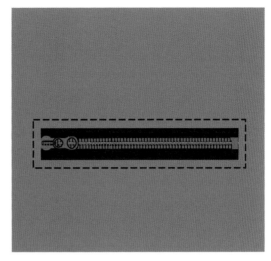

5 **Place zipper in the opening.**
TIP: Hand-baste the zipper to keep it in place when you edge stitch the zipper.

6 **Stitch the zipper.** Sew from the right side; pivot in the corners to create square corners. Switch to a zipper foot if the regular presser foot comes in contact with the zipper teeth.

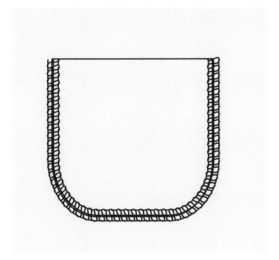

7 **Sew the pocket.** Fold the pocket edges together and stitch the pocket. If the pocket is made of knit fabric, a stretch seam that also overcasts the edges is recommended.

8 **The finished pocket.** This method can be used on both woven and knit fabrics.

Index

ACKNOWLEDGEMENTS

First of all, I want to thank the wonderful online sewing community. Without your input, encouragement, and knowledge this book would never have seen the light of day.

And speaking of the sewing internet, it also brought me a magic fairy in the form of Kylie Walker, a journalist, sewist and ultra athlete, that helped me improve my English and making sure the content was comprehensible. Thank you for reaching out to me, I will forever be grateful for your help!

I also want to say a big thank you to the wonderful sporty makers that agreed to be interviewed for this book and share their knowledge. Your skills and creativity are very inspiring.

Getting support from those who are closest to me has also been crucial in this process. I'm fortunate to have a life partner with a trained eye that shares my tendency to obsess over seemingly small details such as the placing of heading or how to crop a photo. We don't always agree, but our discussions always lead to a better end product. Plus you are the best cheerleader one could hope for, so thank you Fredrik!

My two daughters Anja and Stella have also been an integral part of this projects, both as models and Anja also happens to be my primary outfit photographer. I have a very talented family.

Making this book all by myself has been an enormous challenge, there is no way around it, especially since I did this while also juggling my full-time job. When I wrote my previous (non-sewing) books, I only had to focus on the writing and let the publishing company and their team handle the rest. This time I decided to do the writing, photography, graphic design and publishing on my own. It has been a learning curve for sure!

But I'm also grateful that I have worked in media and communication for the last 20 years, and that experience has given me skills that made this project possible. I also want to acknowledge all the helpful colleagues that have shared their knowledge and helped me improve my skills, especially when it comes to using InDesign and Photoshop.

So, even though I did the bulk of this book on my own, it still took a village to make it happen!

MORE BY **THE LAST STITCH & JOHANNA LUNDSTRÖM**

MASTER THE COVERSTICH MACHINE: The complete coverstitch sewing guide

Get ready to take your coverstitch machine skills to the next level! Learn all the necessary techniques you need in order to create professional-looking garments that will rival ready-to-wear.

The ebook Master the Coverstitch Machine will guide you through the best practices needed for successful coverstitching, with easy to understand, illustrated, step-by-step instructions.
PRINT & EBOOK

AILA WORKOUT LEGGINGS: Sewing pattern

Aila Leggings is a stylish, versatile sewing pattern designed for optimal fit and flexibility, and suitable for any type of activity. The pattern comes in 7 different views with lots of style options so that you truly make the Aila leggings your own.
PDF-PATTERN
SIZES: 34—52 (US 2—20)

Available at thelaststitch.com

Printed in Great Britain
by Amazon